THE POCKET 2005

World Advertising Research Center

ACNielsen

a VNU company

ACNIELSEN HOUSE • HEADINGTON • OXFORD OX3 9RX
Telephone: 01865 742742 • Fax: 01865 742222

THE RETAIL
POCKET BOOK

2005 Edition

© 2004 World Advertising Research Center Ltd.   ACNielsen data © 2004 ACNielsen.

ISBN   1 84116 163 2

ISSN   0966 3711

Produced and published as part of the WARC Pocket Book series by:

World Advertising Research Center Ltd.
Farm Road   Henley-on-Thames
Oxfordshire RG9 1EJ   United Kingdom
Tel: (01491) 411 000   Fax: (01491) 418 600
Email: info@warc.com

World Advertising Research Center Ltd. is an Information Sciences Group Company.

Comments and suggestions for future editions of this pocket book are welcomed. Please contact: The Editor, The Retail Pocket Book, WARC at the above address.

Whilst every effort has been made in the preparation of this book to ensure accuracy of the statistical and other contents, the publishers and data suppliers cannot accept any liability in respect of errors or omissions or for any losses or consequential losses arising from such errors or omissions. Readers will appreciate that the data contents are only as up-to-date as their availability and compilation and printing schedules will allow, and are subject to change during the natural course of events.

Printed and bound in Great Britain by Biddles Ltd, King's Lynn.

NOTES

(i) Symbols used:
  .. Nil or less than the final digit shown.
  – Data not available or not available on a comparable basis.

(ii) Constituent figures in the tables may not add up to the total, due to rounding.

(iii) For full definitions readers are referred to the sources given at the foot of the tables.

(iv) Some topics are mentioned in more than one table but the information is not necessarily from the same source. Any differences are likely to be due to difference in definition, method of calculation or periods covered.

ACKNOWLEDGEMENTS

The Publisher would like to thank all those who have contributed to this compilation of retail trade statistics, in particular ACNielsen – co-producers of the book – whose contribution and support has been invaluable.

Other contributors, including Government departments, whose help is gratefully acknowledged, are listed below:

The Association of the British Pharmaceutical Industry   (www.abpi.org.uk)
The Advertising Association   (www.adassoc.org.uk)
The Bank of England   (www.bankofengland.co.uk)
BMRB International   (www.bmrb.co.uk)
British Retail Consortium
Broadcasters' Audience Research Board Ltd. (BARB)   (www.barb.co.uk)
CACI Information Solutions   (www.caci.co.uk)
Co-operative Union Ltd.   (www.co-op.co.uk)
Department for Education and Employment   (www.dfee.gov.uk)
Department of the Environment, Transport & the Regions   (www.detr.gov.uk)
General Register Office for Scotland   (www.gro-scotland.gov.uk)
GfK Marketing Services   (www.gfk.co.uk)
Government Actuary's Department   (www.gad.gov.uk)
The Incorporated Society of British Advertisers Ltd. (ISBA) (www.isba.org.uk)
Leatherhead Food RA   (www.lfra.co.uk)
National Readership Survey   (www.nrs.co.uk)
NCH Marketing Services Ltd.   (www.nuworld.com)
Nielsen//Net Ratings   (www.netratings.com)
Northern Ireland Statistics and Research Agency   (www.nisra.gov.uk)
Office for National Statistics   (www.statistics.gov.uk)
Ofcom   (www.ofcom.org.uk)
Taylor Nelson Sofres   (www.tnsofres.com)
Verdict Research Ltd.   (www.verdict.co.uk)
World Bank Group   (www.worldbank.org)   *and many more...*

FOREWORD

This year has seen some major changes in the UK retail environment, with a blurring of the traditional boundaries between traditional grocery and convenience shopping. The top four grocery multiples (previously five) continue to dominate, and shoppers continue to spend more in retailers with a differentiated offer. Non food sales continue to put the squeeze on shelf space traditionally assigned to food, meaning that manufacturers need to continually arm themselves with powerful sales stories when entering into discussions with the retailers.

The UK food and drink industry continues to make the headlines – and in 2004 rarely a week went by without another reference to the industry's responsibilities regarding the fight against the flab. There is one thing which is not in doubt – confusion reigns within consumers' minds. One week we read about the dangers of GM foods and the next we read that organic derivatives have high fat/sugar/salt, when compared to their standard counterparts. Is the chocolate industry solely responsible for childhood obesity? An industry that has existed for well over 100 years is defending itself and arguing that personal responsibility for calorie intake and output is the real reason for the problem.

Attitudes to organic foods and how we eat throughout the day – grazing as opposed to eating three square meals a day, are having a huge impact on spend patterns and as a consequence, what retailers sell.

This year's pocket book contains a taster of these interesting insights into consumer attitudes to health and diet as well as the usual invaluable insights into the UK retail landscape.

Understanding the consumer is a consistent theme amongst both our manufacturer and retailer clients and ACNielsen continues to improve the services and insight we offer.

I am delighted that this year's **Retail Pocket Book** brings insight into both the retailer and consumer environment and am confident that you will find this invaluable information. We continually look to develop the content of the **Retail Pocket Book** using the most comprehensive sources of data. I hope this book provides you with a real opportunity to understand these industry-wide changes and gives you some insight on what the future retail landscape may hold!

*Eleni
Nicholas*

Eleni Nicholas
Area Vice President – UK and Ireland

CONTENTS

THE PRINCIPAL RETAIL ENTERPRISES

HOME SHOPPING

RETAIL CRIME AND PREVENTION

RETAIL ADVERTISING

INTERNATIONAL RETAILING

RETAILING IN IRELAND

SOME USEFUL ADDRESSES

THE ECONOMY & CONSUMER SPENDING

UK MAIN ECONOMIC INDICATORS, 1997–2003

		1997	1998	1999	2000	2001	2002	2003
Gross domestic product[1]								
at current prices	£ billion	810.9	859.4	903.9	951.3	994.0	1,043.3	1,099.4
	% change	6.2	6.0	5.2	5.2	4.5	5.0	5.4
at 2000 prices	£ billion	864.7	891.7	916.6	951.3	971.6	987.5	1,009.4
	% change	3.3	3.1	2.8	3.8	2.1	1.6	2.2
Gross domestic product per capita[1]								
at current prices	£	13,743	14,509	15,191	15,919	16,908	17,621	18,460
	% change	5.9	5.6	4.7	4.8	6.2	4.2	4.8
at 2000 prices	£	14,654	15,053	15,405	15,919	16,526	16,678	16,949
	% change	2.9	2.7	2.3	3.3	3.8	0.9	1.6
Household final consumption expenditure								
at current prices	£ billion	503.8	536.9	570.4	603.3	635.6	665.6	693.6
	% change	6.2	6.6	6.2	5.8	5.3	4.7	4.2
at 2000 prices	£ billion	531.9	552.9	577.7	603.3	622.1	643.1	659.1
	% change	3.7	3.9	4.5	4.4	3.1	3.4	2.5
Retail sales value	Index	89.9	93.4	96.5	100.0	105.9	111.1	113.8
	% change	6.3	3.9	3.3	3.6	5.9	4.9	2.4
Consumer prices	Index	96.4	97.9	99.2	100.0	101.2	102.5	103.9
	% change	1.8	1.6	1.3	0.8	1.2	1.3	1.4
Population (mid-year est.)	Million	59.0	59.2	59.5	59.8	58.8	59.2	59.6
Average earnings	Index	86.8	91.3	95.7	100.0	104.4	108.2	111.8
	% change	4.2	5.2	4.8	4.5	4.4	3.6	3.3
Industrial production	Index	96.0	97.0	98.1	100.0	98.4	95.7	95.2
	% change	1.4	1.0	1.1	1.9	−1.6	−2.7	−0.5
Unemployment rate[2]	%	5.3	4.6	4.2	3.6	3.2	3.1	3.1
Vacancies at job centres[3]	'000s	283.3	295.9	314.3	358.3	394.1	–	–
	% change	26.0	4.4	6.2	14.0	10.0	–	–
Interest rate (bank rate)[4]	%	6.56	7.24	5.34	5.97	5.13	4.00	3.69
Gross fixed capital formation								
at 2000 prices	£ billion	135.9	153.1	155.6	161.2	167.0	170.1	174.9
	% change	6.8	12.7	1.6	3.6	3.6	1.8	2.9
Gross trading profits[5]								
North Sea oil companies								
at current prices	£ billion	14.0	11.7	13.9	21.3	19.8	18.7	18.4
	% change	−11.0	−16.3	18.5	53.9	−7.1	−5.4	−1.6
Other companies								
at current prices	£ billion	145.7	151.0	154.0	153.1	153.4	160.2	172.1
	% change	9.1	3.6	2.0	−0.5	0.2	4.4	7.4
at 2000 prices	£ billion	151.2	154.2	155.2	153.1	151.6	156.3	165.6
	% change	7.2	2.0	0.6	−1.3	−1.0	3.1	6.0
Balance of payments								
at current prices	£ billion	−0.9	−4.0	−24.4	−24.1	−23.5	−17.8	−18.8

Note(s): All indices 2000 = 100. [1] Gross domestic product at market prices. [2] Unemployment rate is the total number of unemployed (excl. school leavers) expressed as a percentage of workforce jobs plus the claimant count. Workforce jobs comprise employee jobs, self-employed jobs, HM forces and participants in work-related government supported training. [3] Vacancies notified to job centres and remaining unfulfilled. [4] Selected retail banks' base rate. [5] Private non-financial corporations.

Source(s): 'Economic Trends', 'Monthly Digest of Statistics', 'Financial Statistics' and 'Consumer Trends' National Statistics © Crown Copyright 2004.

THE INTERNAL AND EXTERNAL VALUE OF THE POUND

	RPI/CPI[1] (2000 = 100)		Purchasing power of the pound, pence[2]	At end of each period £1		
	Index	% change		US$	Yen	Euro[3]
1963	8.1	2.1	1,241	2.80	1,008	–
1964	8.3	3.4	1,200	2.80	1,008	–
1965	8.7	4.7	1,146	2.80	1,008	–
1966	9.1	3.8	1,104	2.80	1,008	–
1967	9.3	2.5	1,078	2.76	994	–
1968	9.7	4.8	1,029	2.40	864	–
1969	10.2	5.1	978	2.40	864	–
1970	10.9	6.5	918	2.40	864	–
1971	11.9	9.2	841	2.43	853	–
1972	12.8	7.5	783	2.50	757	–
1973	13.9	9.1	717	2.45	666	–
1974	16.2	15.9	619	2.34	683	–
1975	20.1	24.1	499	2.21	657	–
1976	23.4	16.7	427	1.80	533	–
1977	27.1	15.9	369	1.74	468	–
1978	29.3	8.3	341	1.92	404	–
1979	33.3	13.4	300	2.12	464	–
1980	39.3	18.0	255	2.32	527	1.67
1981	43.9	11.9	228	2.01	443	1.81
1982	47.7	8.6	210	1.75	435	1.78
1983	49.9	4.6	200	1.52	360	1.70
1984	52.4	5.0	191	1.33	316	1.69
1985	55.6	6.1	180	1.28	306	1.70
1986	57.5	3.4	174	1.47	247	1.49
1987	59.8	4.1	167	1.63	236	1.42
1988	62.8	4.9	159	1.78	228	1.51
1988	68.2	–	147	1.78	228	1.51
1989	71.8	5.2	139	1.64	226	1.49
1990	76.8	7.0	130	1.78	257	1.40
1991	82.6	7.5	121	1.76	238	1.43
1992	86.1	4.2	116	1.76	222	1.36
1993	88.3	2.5	113	1.50	167	1.28
1994	90.0	2.0	111	1.53	156	1.29
1995	92.4	2.6	108	1.58	148	1.21
1996	94.7	2.5	106	1.56	170	1.23
1997	96.4	1.8	104	1.64	198	1.44
1998	97.9	1.6	102	1.66	217	1.48
1999	99.2	1.3	101	1.62	184	1.52
2000	100.0	0.8	100	1.51	163	1.65
2001	101.2	1.2	99	1.44	175	1.61
2002	102.5	1.3	98	1.50	188	1.60
2003	103.9	1.4	96	1.63	189	1.45

Note(s): Please refer to sources for full definitions. Constant price figures above the dotted line are adjusted by the Retail Prices Index; below the dotted line by the Consumer Prices Index. [1] The Consumer Prices Index measures the change in the average level of prices of the commodities and services purchased by households in the UK. [2] Movements in the purchasing power of the pound are based on movements in the RPI/CPI. [3] Prior to January 1999, a synthetic Euro has been calculated by geometrically averaging the bilateral exchange rates of the 12 Euro-area countries using 'internal weights' based on each country's share of the extra Euro-trade area.

Source(s): 'Economic Trends', 'Financial Statistics', National Statistics © Crown Copyright 2004; IMF; World Bank; IFS; OECD.

INTERNAL PURCHASING POWER OF THE POUND
(BASED ON RPI)

Year in which purchasing power was 100p

	1992	1993	1994	1995	1996	1997	1998	1999	2000	2001	2002	2003
1992	**100**	102	104	108	110	114	118	119	123	125	127	131
1993	98	**100**	102	106	109	112	116	118	121	123	125	129
1994	96	98	**100**	103	106	109	113	115	118	120	122	126
1995	93	94	97	**100**	102	106	109	111	114	116	118	122
1996	91	92	94	98	**100**	103	108	112	113	115	119
1997	88	89	92	95	97	**100**	103	105	108	110	112	115
1998	85	86	88	92	94	97	**100**	102	105	106	108	111
1999	84	85	87	90	92	95	98	**100**	103	105	107	110
2000	81	83	85	88	90	92	96	97	**100**	102	103	106
2001	80	81	83	86	88	91	94	95	98	**100**	102	105
2002	79	80	82	85	87	89	92	94	97	98	**100**	103
2003	76	78	79	82	84	87	90	91	94	96	97	**100**

Note(s):   To find the purchasing power of the pound in 2003, given that it was 100 pence in 1995, select the column headed 1995 and look at the 2003 row. The result is 82 pence.

Source(s):   'Monthly Digest of Statistics', National Statistics © Crown Copyright 2003.

HOUSEHOLD FINAL CONSUMPTION EXPENDITURE: COMPONENT CATEGORIES, 1983–2003

£ bn

	Total	Durable Goods	Non-Durable Goods					Other Services	
			Food & Drink	Alcoholic Drink & Tobacco[1]	Clothing & Footwear	Energy Products[1]	Other Goods	Rent, Rates & Water	Other Services
Current Prices									
1983	176.9	18.3	28.1	19.5	12.1	16.2	18.8	19.0	44.9
1984	189.2	18.6	29.3	20.9	13.2	17.0	20.6	20.0	49.7
1985	206.6	20.2	30.7	22.7	14.9	18.6	23.1	21.6	55.0
1986	228.8	22.9	32.6	23.9	16.6	18.2	25.9	23.4	65.4
1987	251.1	26.3	34.4	25.1	17.8	18.6	28.9	25.4	74.6
1988	283.4	32.3	36.5	26.6	19.0	19.3	32.6	28.0	89.2
1989	310.5	35.3	39.1	27.8	19.8	20.5	36.3	31.3	100.4
1990	336.5	34.5	41.8	30.0	21.2	22.4	39.7	36.5	110.3
1991	357.8	32.9	44.0	32.7	22.2	25.0	42.2	42.4	116.4
1992	379.8	74.2	45.7	17.0	23.6	14.4	44.4	55.5	105.0
1993	402.0	78.5	47.2	17.7	24.9	14.6	46.9	59.3	112.9
1994	422.4	82.5	47.9	18.4	26.9	14.9	50.9	62.5	118.5
1995	443.4	87.0	49.8	18.8	28.0	15.2	56.3	66.2	122.1
1996	473.8	94.6	53.0	20.4	29.5	16.1	60.5	69.8	129.9
1997	503.4	103.6	53.8	21.4	30.9	15.3	64.2	74.9	139.1
1998	536.2	110.2	55.2	22.4	32.2	14.3	68.9	81.8	151.1
1999	569.5	116.0	56.6	24.3	33.3	13.8	72.5	87.9	165.1
2000	603.3	124.1	58.6	24.6	35.5	14.5	75.2	91.1	179.7
2001	635.6	129.5	60.0	25.2	37.0	14.6	79.9	98.8	190.5
2002	665.9	133.5	61.2	26.0	39.3	14.5	87.9	104.3	199.2
2003	693.6	134.9	63.1	27.3	41.2	15.0	92.4	110.4	209.2
Constant 2003 Prices[2]									
1983	377.5	39.0	59.9	41.6	25.9	34.6	40.0	40.7	95.9
1984	384.8	37.9	59.5	42.6	26.8	34.5	42.0	40.6	101.0
1985	396.0	38.7	58.8	43.4	28.6	35.6	44.2	41.4	105.3
1986	424.2	42.4	60.4	44.3	30.9	33.8	48.0	43.3	121.2
1987	447.0	46.8	61.2	44.7	31.8	33.2	51.4	45.1	132.7
1988	431.7	49.2	55.6	40.5	29.0	29.4	49.6	42.6	135.9
1989	449.5	51.1	56.7	40.2	28.7	29.6	52.6	45.3	145.3
1990	455.2	46.7	56.6	40.6	28.7	30.3	53.6	49.4	149.2
1991	450.1	41.3	55.4	41.1	27.9	31.4	53.1	53.4	146.5
1992	458.3	89.6	55.1	20.5	28.5	17.4	53.6	67.0	126.7
1993	473.2	92.4	55.5	20.8	29.3	17.2	55.2	69.8	132.9
1994	487.6	95.3	55.2	21.2	31.0	17.2	58.8	72.1	136.8
1995	498.6	97.8	56.0	21.1	31.5	17.1	63.3	74.4	137.3
1996	520.0	103.8	58.2	22.4	32.4	17.7	66.4	76.6	142.6
1997	542.6	111.7	58.0	23.1	33.3	16.5	69.2	80.8	150.0
1998	569.2	117.0	58.6	23.8	34.2	15.2	73.1	86.9	160.4
1999	596.4	121.5	59.3	25.4	34.8	14.4	75.9	92.1	172.9
2000	626.9	128.9	60.9	25.6	36.9	15.1	78.2	94.7	186.7
2001	652.4	133.0	61.6	25.8	38.0	15.0	82.0	101.5	195.6
2002	675.0	135.3	62.0	26.3	39.8	14.7	89.1	105.8	201.9
2003	693.6	134.9	63.1	27.3	41.2	15.0	92.4	110.4	209.2

Note(s): [1] Due to changes in data collection methodology, data from 1992 onwards are not comparable to those recorded for 1983–1991. [2] Constant Price figures above the dotted line are adjusted by the Retail Prices Index; below the dotted line by the Consumer Prices Index.

Source(s): 'Consumer Trends', National Statistics © Crown Copyright 2004.

TRENDS IN CONSUMER SPENDING BY CATEGORY

£ million

† Constant 2003 Prices	1999	2000	2001	2002	2003
Alcoholic & tobacco					
Alcoholic drink (revised to include on & off trade)					
Beer	18,082	17,728	17,802	18,354	18,850
Spirits	7,086	7,060	7,156	7,528	7,865
Wine, cider & perry	10,229	11,203	12,000	12,944	12,428
Total alcoholic drink	35,397	35,992	36,957	38,826	39,143
Tobacco	14,968	14,777	14,841	14,821	15,291
Total alcohol & tobacco	**50,365**	**50,769**	**51,798**	**53,647**	**54,434**
Clothing & footwear					
Clothing					
Clothing materials	495	494	416	383	481
Garments	28,290	30,116	30,418	31,051	31,973
Other clothing & accessories	851	958	1,116	1,237	1,194
Clothing services	664	693	713	706	683
Footwear					
Shoes & other footwear	4,465	4,549	4,650	4,808	5,052
Footwear services	84	55	52	45	69
Total clothing & footwear	**34,849**	**36,865**	**37,366**	**38,230**	**39,452**
Energy products & utilities					
Water & misc. services					
Water supply	2,642	2,507	2,496	2,519	2,589
Refuse collection	53	55	55	65	81
Sewerage collection	2,751	2,667	2,643	2,724	2,823
Total water & misc. services	5,447	5,230	5,195	5,307	5,493
Fuel & power					
Electricity	7,771	7,745	7,608	7,466	7,587
Gas	5,641	6,162	6,210	6,164	6,399
Liquid fuels	425	693	603	577	670
Solid fuels	588	500	619	492	382
Total fuel & power	14,425	15,100	15,040	14,699	15,038
Total energy products & utilities	**19,872**	**20,329**	**20,235**	**20,006**	**20,531**
Financial services					
Insurance					
Life insurance	17,023	17,674	20,121	19,086	17,093
Dwelling insurance	3,694	4,082	3,768	3,784	3,967
Health insurance	977	1,287	961	1,000	917
Transport insurance	806	1,321	1,441	2,117	2,098
Other insurance	319	372	330	378	385
Total insurance	22,820	24,737	26,621	26,365	24,460
Other financial services[1]	10,322	12,281	11,809	11,945	12,214
Total financial services	**33,142**	**37,017**	**38,430**	**38,310**	**36,674**
Food					
Bread & cereals	8,447	8,672	8,975	9,169	9,149
Meat & bacon	12,445	12,744	12,726	12,706	13,917
Fish	2,161	2,236	2,345	2,407	2,395
Milk, cheese & eggs	7,607	7,701	7,699	7,490	7,736
Oils & fats	1,281	1,267	1,251	1,194	1,188
Fruit	4,148	4,227	4,306	4,546	4,762
Vegetables	8,617	8,657	8,559	8,361	8,580
Sugar & sweet products	6,859	6,903	6,906	6,992	7,068
Tea coffee & cocoa	1,749	1,828	1,892	1,810	1,683
Soft drinks	4,907	5,158	5,415	5,620	6,142
Other food	1,503	1,457	1,454	1,419	1,414
Total food	**59,723**	**60,850**	**61,526**	**61,714**	**64,034**

TRENDS IN CONSUMER SPENDING BY CATEGORY (Cont.)

£ million

† Constant 2003 Prices	1999	2000	2001	2002	2003
Household goods					
Soft furnishings &					
floor coverings[2]	12,981	14,245	15,275	18,078	17,796
Household textiles	4,160	4,639	4,801	5,379	5,029
Household appliances					
Major household appliances[3]	3,998	3,880	4,905	4,608	4,519
Small electric					
household appliances	682	637	677	786	614
Repair of household appliances	597	624	632	560	533
Total household appliances	5,276	5,474	6,214	5,953	5,666
Household utensils	3,898	4,604	4,780	5,282	5,279
Tools & equipment	2,708	2,828	3,038	3,195	3,578
Routine maintenance of					
non-durable household goods	2,783	2,895	3,019	3,198	3,343
Total household goods	**31,807**	**34,686**	**37,129**	**41,085**	**46,357**
Housing					
Actual rentals for housing[4]	23,653	24,516	25,954	26,159	26,328
Imputed rentals for housing	53,416	55,830	60,495	62,620	64,967
Maintenance & repair	9,059	9,104	9,964	11,035	11,411
Total housing	**86,128**	**89,451**	**96,413**	**99,813**	**102,706**
Medical goods					
Pharmaceutical products	2,786	2,912	3,215	3,137	3,228
Other medical products	472	483	490	524	488
Therapeutic appliances & equip.	1,970	2,075	2,220	2,447	3,445
Total medical goods	**5,228**	**5,471**	**5,925**	**6,108**	**7,161**
Personal care					
Hairdressing/grooming					
establishments	3,621	3,893	4,073	4,098	4,211
Electric personal appliances	682	699	753	1,023	1,202
Other appliances	9,553	9,833	10,111	10,212	10,961
Total personal care	**13,855**	**14,425**	**14,938**	**15,333**	**16,374**
Personal effects					
Jewellery, clocks & watches	3,559	3,536	3,618	3,616	3,820
Other personal effects	1,335	1,398	1,494	1,595	1,671
Total personal effects	**4,894**	**4,933**	**5,112**	**5,211**	**5,491**
Publications & stationery					
Books	2,439	2,641	2,776	2,926	3,058
Newspapers & periodicals	4,455	4,502	4,562	4,592	4,671
Stationery & drawing materials	3,637	3,526	3,356	3,595	3,418
Total publications	**10,532**	**10,669**	**10,693**	**11,113**	**11,147**
Recreation & culture					
Audio-visual					
Audio-visual equipment[5]	4,044	4,020	4,404	4,086	3,952
Photographic &					
optical equipment	2,394	2,470	2,571	2,545	2,439
Information processing equip.	4,786	4,810	5,247	5,145	4,841
Recording media[6]	5,645	6,097	5,926	5,358	5,060
Repairs of audio-visual equip.	215	198	196	152	139
Total audio-visual	17,084	17,595	18,345	17,286	16,431
Major outdoor					
recreation durables	3,501	3,859	4,144	4,454	5,009
Major indoor recreation	212	196	219	172	161
durables					

TRENDS IN CONSUMER SPENDING BY CATEGORY (Cont.)

£ million

† Constant 2003 Prices	1999	2000	2001	2002	2003
Maintenance of other recreation durables	39	43	62	65	76
Games, toys & hobbies[7]	9,370	10,035	10,469	10,607	10,745
Sport, camping & outdoor	2,496	2,428	2,428	2,436	2,573
Garden products	2,854	3,102	3,171	3,529	3,526
Pets & pet services[8]	3,770	3,799	3,819	3,968	3,957
Total recreation & culture	**39,326**	**41,057**	**42,655**	**42,517**	**42,478**
Restaurants & hotels					
Catering services					
Restaurants, cafés etc	52,437	55,249	57,773	60,748	62,155
Canteens	5,364	5,937	6,218	6,843	7,013
Total catering services	57,801	61,186	63,991	67,591	69,168
Accommodation services	9,659	9,910	9,514	9,972	10,207
Total restaurants & hotels	**67,461**	**71,096**	**73,505**	**77,563**	**79,375**
Transport					
Purchase of vehicles					
Motor cars	31,509	32,623	35,602	37,051	38,469
Motor cycles	951	893	849	811	755
Bicycles	902	951	972	987	1,043
Total purchase of vehicles	33,361	34,466	37,423	38,849	40,267
Motor vehicle spares	3,161	2,880	2,822	3,195	3,569
Motor vehicle maintenance & repair	10,722	11,441	12,571	14,030	14,617
Other vehicle services	3,125	3,417	3,543	3,577	3,638
Vehicle fuels & lubricants	15,919	17,364	16,091	14,655	14,117
Transport services					
Railways	4,076	4,282	4,314	4,365	4,403
Road	6,299	6,654	6,935	7,169	7,348
Air	9,199	10,291	10,366	10,424	10,590
Seas & inland waterways	1,517	1,493	1,633	2,045	2,146
Other	798	869	935	1,034	982
Total transport services	21,888	23,589	24,183	25,037	25,469
Total transport	**88,177**	**93,157**	**96,634**	**99,343**	**101,677**
Other items & services					
Household & domestic services	2,549	2,657	2,716	2,714	2,698
Social protection	8,846	8,981	9,175	9,675	10,014
Communication	12,573	13,878	14,522	15,101	15,513
Recreational & cultural services	23,174	23,311	24,047	26,847	28,652
Out-patient services	2,191	2,263	2,258	2,692	2,694
Hospital services	1,513	1,604	1,571	1,724	1,783
Education	9,366	10,010	9,484	8,747	9,649
Other miscellaneous services[9]	10,933	11,694	12,484	13,546	14,068
Total	**596,427**	**626,912**	**652,426**	**674,967**	**693,551**

Note(s): **Due to changes in data collection methodology, data are no longer comparable with that of previous years. Please refer to source for full definitions. † Deflated by the Consumer Prices Index (2003=100).** [1] Includes fees, charges and commissions paid to banks, etc. [2] Includes all household furniture, lights, lamps, pictures, but excludes works of art and antiques. [3] Includes cookers, washing machines, refrigerators, heaters, vacuum cleaners, sewing machines, power tools, lawnmowers, etc. [4] Includes the imputed value of rent for the owner-occupied sector. [5] Includes all audio-visual goods, computers, calculators, musical instruments, etc. [6] Includes records and pre-recorded tapes and CDs, pre-recorded video tapes, floppy disks, blank tapes, video tapes, CDRs, unexposed film. [7] Includes all toys, games, collectable stamps and coins. [8] Includes pet accessories and veterinary costs. [9] Includes window cleaners, gardeners, child minders, home helps, cleaners etc.

Source(s): 'Consumer Trends', National Statistics © Crown Copyright 2004; WARC.

AVERAGE WEEKLY HOUSEHOLD EXPENDITURE, 2001/02–2002/03

As a percentage of total regional household expenditure, unless otherwise indicated

	North East	North West	Yorks./ Humber.	East Midlands	West Midlands	Eastern	London	South East	South West	England	Wales	Scotland	Northern Ireland	United Kingdom
Food & non-alcoholic drinks	**11.41**	**10.73**	**10.64**	**10.99**	**11.28**	**10.67**	**9.16**	**9.46**	**11.08**	**10.34**	**11.79**	**11.55**	**12.06**	**10.54**
Food	10.38	9.81	9.79	10.08	10.32	9.77	8.34	8.64	10.19	9.46	10.83	10.45	10.97	9.64
Bread, rice & cereals	1.05	1.01	0.99	1.00	1.04	0.89	0.81	0.80	0.95	0.92	1.04	1.10	1.24	0.95
Pasta products	0.09	0.08	0.07	0.08	0.07	0.09	0.09	0.07	0.08	0.08	0.09	0.12	0.08	0.08
Buns, cakes, biscuits etc.	0.79	0.71	0.71	0.70	0.73	0.71	0.51	0.59	0.75	0.66	0.75	0.73	0.90	0.68
Pastry (savoury)	0.20	0.17	0.16	0.17	0.15	0.16	0.12	0.15	0.16	0.15	0.14	0.17	0.15	0.16
Beef (fresh/chilled/frozen)	0.33	0.33	0.38	0.36	0.38	0.32	0.24	0.27	0.34	0.32	0.34	0.45	0.67	0.34
Pork (fresh/chilled/frozen)	0.15	0.15	0.18	0.14	0.18	0.13	0.11	0.12	0.17	0.14	0.16	0.13	0.16	0.14
Lamb (fresh/chilled/frozen)	0.11	0.16	0.13	0.13	0.17	0.15	0.17	0.14	0.15	0.15	0.19	0.08	0.08	0.14
Poultry (fresh/chilled/frozen)	0.38	0.37	0.36	0.38	0.40	0.39	0.36	0.34	0.37	0.37	0.39	0.40	0.46	0.37
Bacon & ham	0.26	0.26	0.25	0.22	0.25	0.20	0.14	0.17	0.24	0.21	0.28	0.26	0.31	0.22
Other meat & meat prep.	1.42	1.30	1.21	1.23	1.26	1.17	0.89	1.03	1.11	1.13	1.44	1.43	1.32	1.17
Fish & fish products	0.43	0.42	0.44	0.45	0.42	0.48	0.50	0.41	0.47	0.45	0.50	0.44	0.35	0.45
Milk	0.61	0.60	0.59	0.58	0.61	0.50	0.40	0.42	0.57	0.52	0.61	0.58	0.75	0.53
Cheese & curd	0.32	0.31	0.30	0.37	0.37	0.37	0.30	0.34	0.39	0.34	0.34	0.36	0.27	0.34
Eggs	0.11	0.09	0.10	0.10	0.11	0.09	0.10	0.09	0.11	0.10	0.11	0.11	0.12	0.10
Other milk products	0.37	0.33	0.32	0.38	0.34	0.36	0.29	0.34	0.38	0.34	0.37	0.35	0.33	0.34
Butter	0.08	0.07	0.07	0.07	0.06	0.06	0.05	0.06	0.07	0.06	0.09	0.08	0.10	0.07
Margarine/vegetable fats	0.11	0.11	0.10	0.12	0.13	0.11	0.07	0.09	0.11	0.10	0.13	0.10	0.12	0.10
Peanut butter	0.01					0.01	0.01	0.01	0.01	0.01	–	0.01		0.01
Cooking oils & fats	0.04	0.05	0.05	0.05	0.05	0.05	0.06	0.04	0.05	0.05	0.05	0.04	0.04	0.05
Fresh fruit	0.51	0.53	0.54	0.59	0.57	0.64	0.60	0.57	0.70	0.59	0.60	0.56	0.51	0.58
Other fresh/chilled/ frozen fruits	0.04	0.05	0.05	0.04	0.04	0.05	0.06	0.06	0.05	0.05	0.05	0.06	0.04	0.05
Dried fruit & nuts	0.08	0.07	0.08	0.08	0.07	0.09	0.09	0.09	0.12	0.09	0.09	0.06	0.06	0.08
Preserved fruit & fruit based products	0.03	0.03	0.03	0.04	0.03	0.04	0.03	0.03	0.04	0.03	0.05	0.04	0.04	0.04
Fresh vegetables	0.65	0.67	0.73	0.77	0.79	0.82	0.81	0.75	0.82	0.76	0.78	0.64	0.58	0.75

	North East	North West	Yorks./Humber.	East Midlands	West Midlands	Eastern	London	South East	South West	England	Wales	Scotland	Northern Ireland	United Kingdom
Dried/preserved/process. veg.	0.28	0.25	0.25	0.27	0.27	0.24	0.23	0.23	0.26	0.25	0.27	0.27	0.27	0.25
Potatoes	0.22	0.20	0.19	0.21	0.22	0.19	0.17	0.17	0.20	0.19	0.26	0.20	0.33	0.20
Other tubers/tuber products	0.39	0.31	0.29	0.32	0.36	0.27	0.19	0.23	0.29	0.28	0.38	0.39	0.37	0.29
Sugar & sugar products	0.07	0.06	0.07	0.07	0.08	0.07	0.05	0.06	0.07	0.06	0.08	0.07	0.05	0.06
Jams, marmalades	0.05	0.05	0.05	0.06	0.05	0.05	0.04	0.05	0.06	0.05	0.06	0.05	0.07	0.05
Chocolate	0.40	0.35	0.34	0.37	0.37	0.32	0.23	0.28	0.35	0.32	0.37	0.37	0.36	0.33
Confectionery products	0.20	0.16	0.17	0.15	0.16	0.14	0.10	0.11	0.13	0.14	0.18	0.17	0.20	0.14
Edible ices & ice cream	0.14	0.12	0.11	0.13	0.13	0.14	0.11	0.12	0.13	0.12	0.14	0.13	0.13	0.12
Other food products	0.47	0.45	0.47	0.48	0.45	0.46	0.40	0.42	0.48	0.45	0.48	0.50	0.49	0.45
Non-alcoholic drinks	**1.03**	**0.93**	**0.85**	**0.91**	**0.96**	**0.91**	**0.82**	**0.81**	**0.89**	**0.88**	**0.95**	**1.10**	**1.09**	**0.91**
Coffee	0.14	0.13	0.14	0.14	0.15	0.12	0.08	0.12	0.16	0.12	0.15	0.13	0.11	0.13
Tea	0.13	0.13	0.12	0.13	0.14	0.12	0.09	0.10	0.14	0.12	0.14	0.10	0.13	0.12
Cocoa & powdered chocolate	0.02	0.03	0.02	0.03	0.03	0.03	0.02	0.02	0.03	0.02	0.02	0.01	0.01	0.02
Fruit & veg. juices, mineral waters	0.27	0.27	0.23	0.28	0.26	0.31	0.33	0.28	0.29	0.28	0.25	0.30	0.29	0.28
Soft drinks	0.47	0.37	0.34	0.34	0.38	0.33	0.30	0.29	0.27	0.33	0.39	0.56	0.55	0.36
Alcoholic drinks	**1.64**	**1.70**	**1.51**	**1.55**	**1.55**	**1.34**	**1.18**	**1.27**	**1.55**	**1.43**	**1.72**	**1.72**	**1.32**	**1.46**
Spirits & liqueurs (home)	0.28	0.38	0.24	0.28	0.35	0.25	0.21	0.22	0.34	0.28	0.36	0.56	0.34	0.30
Wines, fortified wines (home)	0.66	0.74	0.67	0.78	0.68	0.65	0.69	0.69	0.80	0.71	0.72	0.68	0.55	0.70
Beer, lager, ciders & perry (home)	0.66	0.54	0.57	0.46	0.48	0.40	0.26	0.31	0.38	0.41	0.60	0.43	0.38	0.42
Alcopops (brought home)	0.03	0.04	0.03	0.03	0.04	0.04	0.02	0.04	0.03	0.03	0.04	0.04	0.05	0.04
Tobacco & narcotics	**1.55**	**1.51**	**1.63**	**1.46**	**1.64**	**1.01**	**0.94**	**1.06**	**1.28**	**1.27**	**1.61**	**1.94**	**2.22**	**1.36**
Cigarettes	1.40	1.33	1.48	1.31	1.46	0.92	0.82	0.91	1.10	1.12	1.39	1.75	2.08	1.21
Cigars, other tobacco products & narcotics	0.14	0.18	0.15	0.16	0.18	0.09	0.13	0.14	0.18	0.15	0.22	0.19	0.13	0.15
Clothing & footwear	**6.01**	**6.17**	**5.35**	**5.00**	**6.06**	**5.35**	**5.66**	**5.34**	**4.73**	**5.51**	**5.31**	**6.32**	**7.89**	**5.62**
Clothing	**4.89**	**4.96**	**4.36**	**4.08**	**4.99**	**4.49**	**4.61**	**4.43**	**3.95**	**4.52**	**4.23**	**5.18**	**6.21**	**4.60**
Men's outer garments	1.26	1.22	1.21	0.90	1.24	1.14	1.17	1.04	0.99	1.12	0.90	1.24	1.65	1.14
Men's under garments	0.10	0.11	0.09	0.13	0.10	0.13	0.09	0.10	0.09	0.11	0.07	0.11	0.14	0.10

	North East	North West	Yorks./ Humber.	East Midlands	West Midlands	Eastern	London	South East	South West	England	Wales	Scotland	Northern Ireland	United Kingdom
Women's outer garments	1.92	2.08	1.76	1.77	2.12	1.90	1.97	2.09	1.76	1.95	2.06	2.19	2.51	1.99
Women's under garments	0.32	0.36	0.31	0.32	0.41	0.36	0.25	0.29	0.32	0.32	0.26	0.35	0.36	0.32
Boys' outer garments (5–15)	0.36	0.22	0.26	0.18	0.25	0.17	0.19	0.18	0.13	0.20	0.19	0.27	0.41	0.21
Girls' outer garments (5–15)	0.40	0.33	0.21	0.30	0.32	0.29	0.29	0.24	0.24	0.28	0.26	0.40	0.44	0.29
Infants' outer garments (0–5)	0.20	0.20	0.17	0.13	0.13	0.15	0.16	0.11	0.09	0.14	0.17	0.18	0.24	0.15
Children's under garments (under 16)	0.12	0.13	0.10	0.09	0.12	0.09	0.08	0.08	0.08	0.10	0.10	0.12	0.14	0.10
Accessories	0.15	0.17	0.13	0.17	0.17	0.17	0.19	0.16	0.13	0.16	0.13	0.20	0.19	0.17
Haberdashery & clothing hire	0.06	0.06	0.05	0.02	0.06	0.05	0.11	0.06	0.05	0.06	0.04	0.06	0.06	0.06
Dry cleaners, laundry & dyeing	–	0.09	0.06	0.06	0.06	0.06	0.11	0.08	0.07	0.07	0.04	0.07	0.07	0.07
Footwear	1.12	1.21	0.99	0.92	1.07	0.86	1.06	0.91	0.78	0.98	1.08	1.14	1.67	1.02
Housing, fuel & power	8.58	8.55	8.95	8.10	8.61	8.84	11.42	8.46	9.49	9.14	9.49	8.88	7.92	9.11
Actual rentals for housing	5.67	5.27	5.24	3.40	5.03	4.75	9.39	4.31	4.45	5.47	4.88	5.39	3.88	5.40
Gross rent	5.66	5.18	5.24	3.39	5.01	4.74	9.39	4.30	4.44	5.45	4.88	5.38	3.88	5.38
Less housing benefit, rebates & allowances received	3.35	3.03	2.51	1.60	2.62	1.60	2.90	1.42	1.72	2.22	2.53	2.76	2.28	2.28
Net rent	2.32	2.15	2.73	1.80	2.38	3.14	6.49	2.88	2.72	3.23	2.34	2.62	1.60	3.10
Second dwelling rent	–	–	–	–	–	–	–	–	–	0.02	–	–	–	0.02
Maintenance & repair of dwelling	1.53	1.81	1.72	1.99	1.72	1.61	1.55	1.87	2.04	1.77	1.89	1.46	1.72	1.75
Water supply & miscellaneous services relating to the dwelling	1.29	1.42	1.37	1.22	1.35	1.32	1.21	1.24	1.55	1.32	1.71	1.41	0.08	1.31
Electricity, gas & other fuels	3.44	3.08	3.13	3.09	3.14	2.76	2.16	2.46	3.17	2.81	3.54	3.38	4.53	2.93
Electricity	1.64	1.45	1.50	1.42	1.51	1.34	1.06	1.24	1.67	1.37	1.72	1.91	2.07	1.44
Gas	1.58	1.54	1.45	1.48	1.49	1.10	1.09	1.10	1.20	1.28	1.60	1.28	0.14	1.27
Other fuels	0.22	0.09	0.17	0.19	0.14	0.32	0.01	0.12	0.30	0.15	0.23	0.19	2.31	0.21
Household goods & services	6.92	7.76	7.66	7.85	7.49	7.19	6.95	7.45	8.04	7.47	7.82	7.29	8.18	7.49

	North East	North West	Yorks./ Humber.	East Midlands	West Midlands	Eastern	London	South East	South West	England	Wales	Scotland	Northern Ireland	United Kingdom
Furniture, furnishings, carpets & other floor coverings	**3.42**	**4.31**	**3.88**	**3.90**	**4.03**	**3.67**	**3.80**	**3.75**	**4.11**	**3.89**	**3.80**	**3.38**	**4.38**	**3.86**
Furniture & furnishings	2.43	3.29	2.89	2.77	2.98	2.89	3.08	2.79	3.07	2.95	2.94	2.69	3.32	2.94
Floor coverings	0.99	1.01	0.98	1.10	1.05	0.77	0.72	0.96	1.04	0.94	0.85	0.69	1.06	0.91
Household textiles	**0.56**	**0.49**	**0.52**	**0.55**	**0.53**	**0.53**	**0.43**	**0.50**	**0.49**	**0.50**	**0.59**	**0.66**	**0.50**	**0.52**
Household appliances	**0.92**	**0.81**	**0.96**	**1.20**	**0.80**	**0.77**	**0.79**	**0.89**	**0.93**	**0.88**	**1.18**	**1.24**	**0.80**	**0.92**
Glassware, tableware & household utensils	0.37	0.36	0.45	0.37	0.32	0.41	0.30	0.51	0.58	0.41	0.37	0.35	0.38	0.40
Tools & equipment for house & garden	**0.56**	**0.58**	**0.63**	**0.68**	**0.63**	**0.66**	**0.57**	**0.69**	**0.68**	**0.64**	**0.75**	**0.63**	**1.03**	**0.65**
Goods & services for household maintenance	**1.10**	**1.20**	**1.23**	**1.14**	**1.18**	**1.16**	**1.07**	**1.10**	**1.26**	**1.15**	**1.11**	**1.03**	**1.08**	**1.14**
Cleaning materials	0.55	0.52	0.54	0.53	0.56	0.53	0.40	0.46	0.51	0.50	0.59	0.50	0.55	0.50
Household goods & hardware	0.30	0.25	0.26	0.30	0.26	0.29	0.23	0.26	0.30	0.27	0.27	0.27	0.26	0.27
Dom. services/carpet cleaning	0.25	0.43	0.43	0.32	0.36	0.33	0.43	0.38	0.45	0.39	0.25	0.26	0.27	0.37
Health	**0.94**	**0.89**	**1.09**	**1.00**	**0.98**	**1.61**	**1.33**	**1.32**	**1.40**	**1.21**	**0.85**	**0.98**	**0.74**	**1.17**
Medical products, appliance & equipment	**0.71**	**0.65**	**0.83**	**0.66**	**0.60**	**0.88**	**0.56**	**0.80**	**0.87**	**0.73**	**0.56**	**0.69**	**0.51**	**0.71**
Medicines, prescriptions etc.	0.33	0.37	0.46	0.35	0.35	0.42	0.33	0.41	0.38	0.38	0.37	0.30	0.31	0.37
Spectacles, lenses, access.	0.38	0.27	0.37	0.27	0.24	0.43	0.21	0.38	0.43	0.33	0.19	0.37	0.20	0.32
Non-optical appliances and equipment (e.g. wheelchairs, batteries for hearing aids, etc.)	–	–	–	–	–	–	–	–	–	0.02	–	–	–	0.02
Hospital services	**0.23**	**0.24**	**0.26**	**0.33**	**0.37**	**0.72**	**0.76**	**0.52**	**0.53**	**0.48**	**0.29**	**0.29**	**0.22**	**0.45**
Transport	**14.57**	**14.28**	**14.87**	**15.26**	**14.66**	**16.42**	**12.80**	**15.38**	**14.59**	**14.69**	**13.39**	**13.81**	**13.75**	**14.55**
Purchase of vehicles	**6.54**	**6.68**	**7.54**	**7.42**	**6.54**	**7.82**	**4.81**	**7.07**	**6.36**	**6.66**	**5.39**	**5.88**	**5.64**	**6.52**
Purchase of new cars & vans	2.80	2.67	3.37	2.60	2.44	3.55	2.22	3.21	2.63	2.83	1.72	2.23	2.99	2.74
Purchase of second hand cars or vans	3.61	3.85	4.08	4.56	3.97	4.09	2.38	3.61	3.45	3.62	3.51	3.54	2.49	3.58
Purchase of motorcycles & other vehicles	–	0.16	–	0.27	–	0.19	0.21	0.26	0.29	0.20	–	–	–	0.19

	North East	North West	Yorks./ Humber.	East Midlands	West Midlands	Eastern	London	South East	South West	England	Wales	Scotland	Northern Ireland	United Kingdom
Operation of personal transport	**5.71**	**5.64**	**5.60**	**6.45**	**6.49**	**6.59**	**4.31**	**6.30**	**6.88**	**5.92**	**6.36**	**5.67**	**6.12**	**5.92**
Spares & accessories	0.43	0.42	0.36	0.50	0.51	0.59	0.40	0.63	0.62	0.51	0.46	0.50	0.42	0.50
Petrol, diesel/other motor oils	3.87	3.68	3.52	4.12	4.29	4.08	2.26	3.72	4.18	3.63	4.19	3.69	4.43	3.68
Repairs & servicing	1.02	1.09	1.25	1.38	1.25	1.35	1.24	1.46	1.48	1.30	1.24	1.08	0.95	1.27
Other motoring costs	0.39	0.44	0.47	0.44	0.44	0.57	0.41	0.49	0.59	0.48	0.46	0.40	0.33	0.47
Transport services	**2.31**	**1.96**	**1.73**	**1.38**	**1.63**	**2.00**	**3.69**	**2.01**	**1.35**	**2.12**	**1.64**	**2.26**	**1.98**	**2.11**
Rail & tube fares	0.32	0.25	0.22	0.23	0.24	0.86	0.83	0.61	0.29	0.49	0.20	0.37	0.08	0.46
Bus & coach fares	0.47	0.42	0.51	0.32	0.36	0.21	0.45	0.21	0.27	0.34	0.34	0.57	0.29	0.36
Combined fares	–	–	–	–	–	0.14	1.26	0.11	–	0.26	–	–	–	0.22
Other travel & transport	1.45	1.26	0.95	0.83	1.02	0.79	1.15	1.08	0.79	1.03	1.09	1.28	1.61	1.07
Communication	**2.88**	**2.46**	**2.57**	**2.47**	**2.69**	**2.59**	**2.98**	**2.45**	**2.47**	**2.61**	**2.52**	**2.65**	**2.66**	**2.61**
Postal services	0.15	0.10	0.13	0.10	0.11	0.12	0.12	0.13	0.16	0.12	0.09	0.12	0.09	0.12
Telephone & telefax equip.	0.34	0.14	0.13	0.18	0.18	0.16	0.21	0.13	0.10	0.16	0.09	0.15	0.10	0.16
Telephone & telefax services	2.39	2.22	2.30	2.19	2.39	2.31	2.65	2.19	2.21	2.32	2.34	2.38	2.47	2.33
Recreation & culture	**14.74**	**14.72**	**14.64**	**14.59**	**14.24**	**13.55**	**11.67**	**14.01**	**13.08**	**13.72**	**15.25**	**13.53**	**12.54**	**13.74**
Audio-visual, photographic & info. processing equipment	**1.92**	**1.99**	**2.12**	**1.97**	**2.36**	**1.77**	**1.93**	**2.12**	**1.54**	**1.98**	**3.01**	**1.78**	**1.46**	**1.99**
Audio equipment & access.	0.64	0.69	0.76	0.58	0.54	0.67	0.58	0.75	0.55	0.65	0.53	0.63	0.40	0.64
TV, video & computers	1.20	1.12	1.21	1.10	1.66	0.92	1.17	1.17	0.81	1.14	2.27	1.00	1.00	1.18
Photographic/cinemat. equip.	0.07	0.18	0.16	0.29	0.17	0.18	0.18	0.21	0.18	0.19	0.21	0.16	0.05	0.18
Other major durables for recreation & culture	–	–	–	–	**0.28**	**0.38**	–	**0.49**	–	**0.44**	–	**0.24**	**0.63**	**0.42**
Other rec. items & equipment, gardens & pets	**2.61**	**2.39**	**2.26**	**2.64**	**2.45**	**2.59**	**1.74**	**2.78**	**2.82**	**2.45**	**2.80**	**2.10**	**2.06**	**2.43**
Games, toys & hobbies	0.72	0.56	0.45	0.59	0.56	0.58	0.50	0.50	0.57	0.54	0.62	0.51	0.56	0.54
Computer software & games	0.29	0.29	0.35	0.18	0.34	0.23	0.15	0.25	0.21	0.24	0.40	0.32	0.26	0.26
Equipment for sport, camping & open-air recreation	–	–	0.13	0.37	0.22	0.16	0.13	0.30	0.27	0.23	0.30	0.24	0.18	0.23
Horticult. goods/equip./plants	0.60	0.62	0.63	0.79	0.64	0.78	0.57	0.90	0.84	0.72	0.66	0.51	0.60	0.70

	North East	North West	Yorks./Humber.	East Midlands	West Midlands	Eastern	London	South East	South West	England	Wales	Scotland	Northern Ireland	United Kingdom
Pets & pet food	0.50	0.74	0.71	0.70	0.70	0.84	0.43	0.82	0.94	0.71	0.81	0.51	0.47	0.69
Recreational & cultural serv.	**5.30**	**4.49**	**4.25**	**4.28**	**4.17**	**4.09**	**3.98**	**3.72**	**4.00**	**4.13**	**4.27**	**4.60**	**4.06**	**4.17**
Sports admiss'ns. subscrip.	1.23	1.26	1.08	1.29	1.14	1.32	1.62	1.29	1.32	1.31	1.04	1.37	1.26	1.30
Cinema, theatre & museums	0.40	0.38	0.32	0.41	0.42	0.35	0.49	0.43	0.40	0.41	0.28	0.52	0.40	0.41
TV, video, satellite rental, cable subscriptions, TV licences & the internet	1.46	1.38	1.21	1.28	1.21	1.16	0.99	1.02	1.12	1.16	1.52	1.33	1.08	1.19
Misc. entertainments	0.32	0.28	0.24	0.19	0.23	0.30	0.20	0.25	0.25	0.25	0.22	0.21	0.31	0.24
Development of photos	0.11	0.15	0.09	0.09	0.13	0.13	0.08	0.10	0.11	0.11	0.10	0.09	0.08	0.11
Gambling payments	1.78	1.05	1.33	1.01	1.05	0.82	0.30	0.62	0.80	0.90	1.10	1.08	0.92	0.92
Newsp./books/stationery	**1.74**	**1.64**	**1.51**	**1.68**	**1.52**	**1.57**	**1.51**	**1.48**	**1.75**	**1.57**	**1.68**	**1.78**	**1.55**	**1.59**
Books, diaries, cards etc.	0.88	0.86	0.74	0.89	0.78	0.87	0.90	0.87	0.94	0.86	0.87	0.87	0.67	0.86
Newspapers	0.57	0.50	0.49	0.51	0.48	0.42	0.37	0.37	0.50	0.45	0.55	0.65	0.62	0.47
Magazines & periodicals	0.28	0.28	0.28	0.28	0.26	0.28	0.24	0.24	0.31	0.26	0.27	0.26	0.27	0.26
Package holidays	**3.02**	**3.56**	**3.74**	**2.91**	**3.45**	**3.15**	**2.36**	**3.43**	**2.83**	**3.15**	**3.26**	**3.03**	**2.78**	**3.14**
Package holidays – UK	–	0.22	0.37	0.29	0.22	0.23	0.20	0.16	0.19	0.22	–	–	0.19	0.21
Package holidays – abroad	2.92	3.34	3.36	2.63	3.23	2.92	2.16	3.27	2.64	2.93	3.03	2.94	2.59	2.93
Education	**1.01**	**1.38**	**1.06**	**0.99**	**0.77**	**1.25**	**2.12**	**1.64**	**1.21**	**1.39**	**0.87**	**1.15**	**1.08**	**1.34**
Education fees	0.97	1.29	0.98	0.91	0.73	1.19	2.01	1.58	1.15	1.32	0.84	1.12	0.96	1.27
Ad-hoc expenditure (e.g. school trips)	–	0.09	0.08	0.08	0.03	0.06	0.11	0.06	0.06	0.07	–	–	0.12	0.07
Restaurants & hotels	**9.39**	**8.60**	**9.64**	**8.89**	**8.67**	**7.95**	**9.02**	**7.74**	**7.72**	**8.50**	**8.68**	**8.52**	**9.15**	**8.52**
Catering services	**8.59**	**7.66**	**8.57**	**7.66**	**7.53**	**6.70**	**7.78**	**6.46**	**6.51**	**7.33**	**7.67**	**7.59**	**8.65**	**7.40**
Restaurant & café meals	2.65	2.59	2.69	2.86	2.53	2.84	3.14	2.64	2.81	2.77	2.57	2.58	2.99	2.75
Alcoholic drinks (from home)	3.08	2.50	2.61	2.40	2.33	1.67	1.98	1.85	1.93	2.15	2.61	2.17	2.29	2.17
Take away meals (eaten at home)	1.12	0.88	1.04	0.87	1.06	0.78	0.87	C.74	0.64	0.86	0.96	1.02	1.38	0.89
Other take-away & snack food	1.18	1.12	1.09	0.93	0.97	0.90	1.31	0.84	0.73	1.00	1.05	1.22	1.31	1.03
Contract catering (food)	–	–	–	–	–	–	–	–	–	0.12	–	–	–	0.10

	North East	North West	Yorks./ Humber.	East Midlands	West Midlands	Eastern	London	South East	South West	England	Wales	Scotland	Northern Ireland	United Kingdom
Canteens	0.54	0.45	0.46	0.51	0.49	0.45	0.46	0.35	0.36	0.44	0.47	0.53	0.65	0.45
Accommodation services	**0.80**	**0.94**	**1.08**	**1.23**	**1.15**	**1.25**	**1.24**	**1.28**	**1.21**	**1.17**	**1.01**	**0.93**	**0.51**	**1.12**
Holiday in the UK	0.52	0.57	0.64	0.67	0.78	0.62	0.44	0.56	0.60	0.59	0.57	0.47	0.17	0.57
Holiday abroad	0.27	0.36	0.43	0.55	0.36	0.63	0.80	0.66	0.59	0.56	0.43	0.45	0.34	0.54
Misc. goods & services	**7.21**	**8.37**	**7.27**	**7.80**	**7.77**	**8.11**	**8.12**	**8.15**	**8.40**	**8.01**	**7.53**	**7.47**	**8.21**	**7.95**
Personal care	**2.19**	**2.30**	**2.08**	**2.31**	**2.11**	**2.16**	**1.96**	**2.08**	**2.23**	**2.14**	**2.13**	**2.25**	**2.49**	**2.16**
Hairdressing, beauty treatm'nt	0.51	0.73	0.66	0.65	0.60	0.64	0.58	0.71	0.75	0.66	0.51	0.61	0.75	0.65
Toilet paper	0.18	0.17	0.17	0.17	0.19	0.17	0.14	0.15	0.18	0.16	0.21	0.19	0.20	0.17
Toiletries & soap	0.49	0.46	0.45	0.53	0.48	0.47	0.47	0.44	0.49	0.47	0.51	0.53	0.52	0.48
Baby toiletries & accessories	0.17	0.13	0.13	0.15	0.13	0.14	0.14	0.10	0.13	0.13	0.13	0.15	0.21	0.13
Hair products, cosmetics & electrical personal appl.	0.82	0.80	0.68	0.81	0.73	0.73	0.64	0.67	0.68	0.71	0.78	0.78	0.81	0.72
Personal effects	**0.65**	**0.83**	**0.63**	**0.49**	**0.64**	**0.65**	**0.84**	**0.87**	**0.64**	**0.73**	**0.67**	**0.72**	**0.54**	**0.72**
Social protection	0.55	0.64	0.51	0.50	0.44	0.99	0.95	0.45	0.57	0.64	0.70	0.65	0.69	0.65
Insurance	**3.05**	**3.60**	**3.14**	**3.53**	**3.58**	**3.27**	**3.25**	**3.54**	**3.73**	**3.43**	**3.19**	**2.87**	**3.72**	**3.38**
Household insurances	1.13	1.18	1.06	1.20	1.10	1.05	1.09	1.09	1.14	1.11	1.11	1.06	0.93	1.10
Medical insurance premiums	0.12	0.27	0.21	0.25	0.30	0.36	0.46	0.51	0.44	0.36	0.26	0.12	0.18	0.34
Vehicle insurance including boat insurance	1.80	2.12	1.82	2.02	2.12	1.84	1.67	1.90	2.10	1.92	1.81	1.62	2.54	1.91
Non-package holiday, other travel insurance	–	–	–	–	–	–	–	–	–	0.04	–	–	–	0.04
Other services	**0.77**	**1.01**	**0.91**	**0.97**	**0.99**	**1.03**	**1.11**	**1.22**	**1.23**	**1.07**	**0.84**	**0.97**	**0.77**	**1.04**
Moving house	0.31	0.43	0.42	0.58	0.45	0.71	0.69	0.79	0.75	0.61	0.40	0.42	0.20	0.58
Bank, building society, post office, credit card charges	0.05	0.08	0.08	0.08	0.09	0.08	0.09	0.09	0.11	0.09	0.09	0.12	0.14	0.09
Other services & professional fees	0.41	0.49	0.41	0.31	0.45	0.24	0.33	0.35	0.36	0.37	0.34	0.44	0.43	0.37
All expenditure groups	**86.87**	**87.12**	**86.89**	**85.95**	**86.39**	**85.87**	**83.37**	**83.71**	**85.03**	**85.30**	**86.83**	**85.82**	**87.72**	**85.47**
Other expenditure items	**13.13**	**12.88**	**13.11**	**14.05**	**13.61**	**14.13**	**16.63**	**16.29**	**14.97**	**14.70**	**13.17**	**14.18**	**12.28**	**14.53**

	North East	North West	Yorks./ Humber.	East Midlands	West Midlands	Eastern	London	South East	South West	England	Wales	Scotland	Northern Ireland	United Kingdom
Housing: mortgage interest payments, water, council tax etc.	9.61	9.14	8.37	9.79	9.65	10.13	10.09	10.84	10.28	9.90	8.25	9.63	6.77	9.73
Licences, fines & transfers	0.57	0.65	0.63	0.81	0.74	0.77	–	0.69	0.81	0.88	0.68	0.60	0.66	0.84
Holiday spending	–	1.13	1.40	1.66	1.17	1.39	2.38	1.55	1.74	1.58	1.48	1.51	1.90	1.57
Money transfers & credit	**1.89**	**1.96**	**2.71**	**1.79**	**2.06**	**1.83**	**2.46**	**3.21**	**2.14**	**2.35**	**2.76**	**2.44**	**2.95**	**2.39**
Money, cash gifts given to children	0.03	0.03	0.07	0.05	0.04	0.03	0.03	0.01	0.02	0.03	–	0.06	0.08	0.05
Cash gifts & donations	1.54	1.52	2.28	1.38	1.72	1.38	2.01	2.71	1.75	1.91	2.18	2.03	2.67	1.95
Other items recorded														
Club instalment payments (child) & interest on credit cards	0.32	0.41	0.35	0.36	0.30	0.42	0.42	0.48	0.37	0.40	0.31	0.36	0.21	0.39
Life assurance/pension funds	4.84	4.92	7.53	6.67	5.36	5.81	5.45	5.83	5.15	5.64	4.99	5.68	4.71	5.59
Other insurance inc. Friendly Societies	0.15	0.22	0.35	0.35	0.26	0.25	0.22	0.36	0.33	0.29	0.30	0.19	0.14	0.27
Income tax, payments less refunds	15.67	15.11	15.96	18.41	16.84	19.98	24.33	20.68	17.14	18.99	15.30	17.03	12.49	18.52
National insurance contrib.	4.96	4.48	4.45	5.03	5.18	5.22	5.20	4.73	4.33	4.84	4.64	4.92	4.12	4.82
Purchase or alteration of dwellings, mortgages	7.82	6.41	6.18	9.11	6.34	–	–	15.27	19.52	20.26	5.35	4.87	4.80	18.03
Savings & investments	1.48	1.53	1.27	2.49	1.67	2.36	1.45	1.75	2.54	1.82	1.16	1.20	1.26	1.72
Pay off loan to clear other debt	0.84	0.65	0.92	0.78	0.65	0.65	0.51	0.67	0.57	0.66	0.52	0.50	0.14	0.63
Windfall receipts from gambling etc.	–	0.47	0.92	–	0.26	0.33	0.23	0.34	0.35	0.60	0.41	0.41	0.42	0.57
Total expenditure	**340.80**	**376.00**	**351.00**	**387.50**	**362.20**	**422.60**	**485.60**	**475.00**	**380.50**	**408.50**	**335.70**	**365.10**	**382.80**	**400.30**
Average weekly expenditure per person	**140.96**	**157.92**	**152.61**	**161.55**	**147.62**	**177.48**	**193.98**	**205.30**	**170.25**	**172.08**	**146.13**	**156.79**	**142.65**	**168.63**

Note(s): **Please refer to source for full definitions.**
Source(s): 'Family Spending: A Report on the 2001/02–2002/03 Expenditure and Food Survey', National Statistics © Crown Copyright 2003; WARC.

PERCENTAGE OF CONSUMERS' EXPENDITURE PASSING THROUGH RETAIL OUTLETS, 1994–2003

Percentage

	All Retailers[1]	Predominantly Food Stores	Total	Non-Specialised	Textile, Clothing & Footwear	H'hold Goods	Other
			Predominantly Non-Food Stores				
1994	43.1	18.3	22.4	3.7	6.3	5.4	6.8
1995	42.6	18.5	22.0	3.7	6.2	5.3	6.6
1996	42.0	18.2	21.7	3.7	6.1	5.4	6.4
1997	42.0	18.0	21.9	3.7	6.1	5.6	6.4
1998	41.0	17.8	21.2	3.5	5.8	5.5	6.3
1999	39.9	17.3	20.6	3.4	5.6	5.4	6.1
2000	39.1	16.9	20.2	3.4	5.5	5.4	6.0
2001	39.3	17.1	20.3	3.4	5.5	5.5	5.9
2002	39.3	16.9	20.6	3.3	5.6	5.6	6.1
2003	38.7	16.9	20.2	3.2	5.6	5.4	5.9

Note(s):   [1] 'All retailers' also includes the extra category 'Non-store retailing and repair'.
Source(s):   'Business Monitor SDM28 – Retail Sales', National Statistics © Crown Copyright 2004; WARC.

RETAIL SALES INDICES, 1994–2003

	All Retailers[1]	Predominantly Food Stores	Total	Non-Specialised	Textile, Clothing & Footwear	H'hold Goods	Other
			Predominantly Non-Food Stores				
Sales in 2003, £m							
	268,158	117,365	139,906	22,351	39,095	37,667	40,848
Value of retail sales at current prices (Index: 2003 = 100)							
1994	67.9	66.0	67.5	70.0	68.2	61.1	69.9
1995	70.5	69.9	69.6	72.6	70.5	63.0	71.9
1996	74.3	73.7	73.6	78.6	73.5	67.9	74.8
1997	79.0	77.4	79.0	83.9	78.9	74.4	79.0
1998	82.1	81.4	81.3	84.9	79.2	78.6	82.4
1999	84.8	84.1	84.0	87.3	81.1	82.1	85.7
2000	87.9	87.1	87.2	91.7	84.5	85.8	88.5
2001	93.1	92.4	92.4	96.2	89.4	93.1	92.5
2002	97.6	96.2	97.8	98.8	94.8	99.5	98.8
2003	100.0	100.0	100.0	100.0	100.0	100.0	100.0
Volume of retail sales (Index: 2003 = 100)							
1994	70.3	76.9	63.8	71.5	59.9	52.9	75.1
1995	71.1	78.4	64.9	72.2	61.4	54.3	75.1
1996	73.4	79.8	67.7	76.5	64.1	58.0	76.0
1997	77.2	83.0	72.1	80.5	68.2	63.6	79.4
1998	79.5	85.3	74.2	80.5	68.8	68.0	81.9
1999	82.2	86.9	77.8	82.7	72.0	73.4	85.0
2000	85.9	89.4	82.5	88.0	77.5	79.2	87.5
2001	91.2	93.0	88.9	93.2	84.7	87.9	91.5
2002	96.8	96.6	96.1	97.5	93.6	95.7	98.1
2003	100.0	100.0	100.0	100.0	100.0	100.0	100.0

Note(s):   [1] 'All retailers' also includes the extra category 'Non-store retailing and repair'.
Source(s):   'Business Monitor SDM28 – Retail Sales', National Statistics © Crown Copyright 2004; WARC.

CONSUMER CREDIT, 1994–2003

£million

	Total	Credit cards[1]	%	Retailers[2]	%	Other[3]	%
Amount outstanding							
1994	58,051	11,914	20.5	2,644	4.6	43,493	74.9
1995	68,205	13,836	20.3	2,509	3.7	51,860	76.0
1996	77,494	16,161	20.9	2,586	3.3	58,747	75.8
1997	88,100	18,997	21.6	2,750	3.1	66,353	75.3
1998	102,222	23,252	22.7	2,757	2.7	76,213	74.6
1999	116,155	33,117	28.5	2,860	2.5	83,038	71.5
2000	128,041	38,702	30.2	2,575	2.0	89,339	69.8
2001	141,718	42,802	30.2	2,548	1.8	98,917	69.8
2002	157,844	48,248	30.6	2,607	1.7	109,596	69.4
2003	170,546	53,539	31.4	2,211	1.3	117,006	68.6
Net transactions							
1994	5,743	1,483	25.8	83	1.4	4,177	72.7
1995	8,234	2,103	25.5	–33	–1.6	6,264	76.1
1996	11,215	3,029	27.0	75	0.7	8,111	72.3
1997	12,013	3,507	29.2	208	1.7	8,298	69.1
1998	14,489	4,858	33.5	7	..	9,624	66.4
1999	14,858	5,676	38.2	103	0.7	9,182	61.8
2000	14,235	6,686	47.0	–285	–2.0	7,550	53.0
2001	17,719	6,229	35.2	–27	–0.2	11,492	64.9
2002	21,154	7,579	35.8	59	0.3	13,577	64.2
2003	18,739	8,206	43.8	–396	–2.1	10,533	56.2

Note(s): [1] Lending on all bank credit cards and charge cards, including MasterCard and Visa. [2] Consumer credit financed directly by retailers. [3] Non-credit card lending by banks, building societies, other specialist lenders and insurance companies.
Source(s): 'Financial Statistics', National Statistics © Crown Copyright 2004; WARC.

HOUSEHOLD PENETRATION OF CONSUMER DURABLES, GB

	1985 %	1990 %	1999 %	2000 %	2001 %	2002 %	2003 %
Refrigerator	98	99	100	99	99	96	100
Telephone	80	90	95	95	95	96	98
Washing machine	85	89	93	93	93	91	95
Colour television	89	94	98	99	99	–	95
Central heating system	69	80	90	91	91	91	94
Microwave oven	18	52	79	82	85	86	86
Double glazing	29	45	70	72	75	76	85
Mobile phone	–	–	–	63	66	75	78
Loft insulation	70	75	72	71	71	71	75
Clothes dryer	44	44	39	41	40	43	43
Car, one only	45	46	41	41	40	39	39
Car, two or more	19	25	35	31	35	36	36
Gas cooker	–	–	38	36	37	33	31
Electric cooker	–	32	32	33	31	31	31
Dishwasher	6	13	23	24	25	24	26

Source(s): GfK Marketing Services Ltd; Target Group Index, © BMRB 2004 (April 2003 – March 2004).

DEMOGRAPHICS

POPULATION OF THE UK BY NATION, MID-2003

			Thousands
	Total	Males	Females
England	49,855.7	24,415.0	25,440.7
Wales	2,938.0	1,425.6	1,512.4
Scotland	5,057.4	2,434.6	2,622.8
Great Britain	**57,851.1**	**28,275.2**	**29,575.9**
Northern Ireland	1,702.6	832.8	869.8
United Kingdom	**59,553.8**	**29,108.0**	**30,445.7**

Source(s): 'Mid-2003 Population Estimates' National Statistics © Crown Copyright 2004; General Register Office for Scotland; Northern Ireland Statistics and Research Agency.

POPULATION OF THE UK BY SEX AND AGE, MID-2003

	Total		Males		Females	
	'000s	%	'000s	%	'000s	%
0–4	3,382.7	5.7	1,733.1	2.9	1,649.6	2.8
5–9	3,650.1	6.1	1,869.3	3.1	1,780.9	3.0
10–14	3,891.4	6.5	1,995.2	3.4	1,896.2	3.2
15–19	3,855.3	6.5	1,982.6	3.3	1,872.7	3.1
20–24	3,719.3	6.2	1,867.0	3.1	1,852.3	3.1
25–29	3,659.4	6.1	1,830.3	3.1	1,829.2	3.1
30–34	4,410.8	7.4	2,187.8	3.7	2,223.0	3.7
35–39	4,710.7	7.9	2,335.5	3.9	2,375.2	4.0
40–44	4,397.2	7.4	2,178.0	3.7	2,219.2	3.7
45–49	3,870.8	6.5	1,916.7	3.2	1,954.1	3.3
50–54	3,743.2	6.3	1,853.1	3.1	1,890.1	3.2
55–59	3,810.2	6.4	1,883.2	3.2	1,927.1	3.2
60–64	2,942.7	4.9	1,438.6	2.4	1,504.0	2.5
65–69	2,657.2	4.5	1,278.8	2.1	1,378.4	2.3
70–74	2,347.7	3.9	1,075.2	1.8	1,272.5	2.1
75–79	1,932.5	3.2	820.2	1.4	1,112.3	1.9
80–84	1,468.3	2.5	550.5	0.9	917.8	1.5
85+	1,104.2	1.9	313.1	0.5	791.2	1.3
Total	**59,553.8**	**100.0**	**29,108.0**	**48.9**	**30,445.7**	**51.1**

Source(s): 'Mid-2003 Population Estimates' National Statistics © Crown Copyright 2004; General Register Office for Scotland; Northern Ireland Statistics and Research Agency.

WORKFORCE JOBS, UK

Seasonally adjusted

	June 1971		March 2003		March 2004	
	'000s	%	'000s	%	'000s	%
Employee jobs						
Male	13,735	54.4	13,153	42.5	13,161	42.2
Female	8,396	33.3	12,831	41.5	12,977	41.6
All employee jobs	22,131	87.7	25,984	84.0	26,138	83.8
Self-employed jobs	2,026	8.0	3,717	12.0	3,868	12.4
HM forces	368	1.5	206	0.7	207	0.7
Government supported trainees	–	–	99	0.3	113	0.4
Workforce jobs	24,525	97.2	30,006	97.0	30,325	97.2
Claimant unemployment	710	2.8	942	3.0	882	2.8
Total	**25,235**	**100.0**	**30,948**	**100.0**	**31,207**	**100.0**
Index (June 1971 = 100)	100		123		124	

Note(s):   Employer surveys now measure 'jobs' rather than 'people'. Therefore, figures for the 'total working population' are no longer published. (Please refer to the source below for full definitions and notes).
Source(s):   'Labour Market Trends', National Statistics © Crown Copyright 2004.

POPULATION PROJECTIONS, UK

Thousands

	2002 (base)	2006	2011	2016	2021
0–4	3,435	3,360	3,417	3,480	3,541
5–15	8,352	7,139	7,262	7,394	7,525
16–44	23,870	21,658	22,029	22,430	22,829
45–64	12,735	15,719	15,988	16,279	16,569
65–74	6,456	6,299	6,407	6,524	6,640
75+	4,442	5,820	5,919	6,027	6,134
All ages	**59,232**	**59,995**	**61,022**	**62,134**	**63,239**
of which					
England	49,562	50,310	51,315	52,396	53,478
Wales	2,919	2,942	2,971	3,006	3,038
Scotland	5,055	5,022	4,984	4,949	4,911
N Ireland	1,697	1,720	1,751	1,782	1,811

Source(s):   'Mid-2003 Population Estimates', National Statistics © Crown Copyright 2004.

RESIDENT POPULATION OF UNITARY AUTHORITIES & LOCAL GOVERNMENT DISTRICTS, MID-2003

	'000s		'000s
ENGLAND		Blackpool	142.4
Outer London	4,483.3	Blackburn with Darwen	139.8
Inner London	2,904.6	Redcar and Cleveland	139.1
Bristol, City of	391.5	Middlesbrough	139.0
East Riding of Yorkshire	321.3	Poole	137.5
Leicester	283.9	Isle of Wight	136.3
Nottingham	273.9	Windsor and Maidenhead	135.3
Brighton and Hove	251.5	Torbay	131.3
Medway	251.1	Slough	118.8
Kingston upon Hull, City of	247.9	Halton	118.4
South Gloucestershire	246.8	Bracknell Forest	110.1
Plymouth	241.5	Darlington	98.2
Stoke-on-Trent	238.0	Hartlepool	90.2
Derby	233.2	Rutland	35.7
Southampton	221.1		
Milton Keynes	215.7	**WALES**	
Warrington	193.2	Cardiff	315.1
North Somerset	191.4	Rhondda, Cynon, Taff	231.6
Portsmouth	188.7	Swansea	224.6
Stockton-on-Tees	186.3	Carmarthenshire	176.0
Luton	185.2	Caerphilly	170.2
York	183.1	Flintshire	149.4
Swindon	181.2	Newport	139.3
Herefordshire, County of	176.9	Neath Port Talbot	135.3
Bath and North East Somerset	170.9	Bridgend	129.9
Bournemouth	163.7	Wrexham	129.7
Southend-on-Sea	160.3	Powys	129.3
Telford and Wrekin	160.3	The Vale of Glamorgan	121.2
Peterborough	158.8	Gwynedd	117.5
North East Lincolnshire	157.4	Pembrokeshire	116.3
North Lincolnshire	155.0	Conwy	110.9
Wokingham	151.2	Denbighshire	94.9
Thurrock	145.3	Torfaen	90.7
West Berkshire	144.2	Monmouthshire	86.2
Reading	144.1	Ceredigion	77.2

RESIDENT POPULATION OF UNITARY AUTHORITIES & LOCAL GOVERNMENT DISTRICTS, MID-2003 (Cont.)

	'000s		'000s
Blaenau Gwent	68.9	Clackmannanshire	47.7
Isle of Anglesey	68.4	Eilean Siar	26.1
Merthyr Tydfil	55.4	Shetland Islands	21.9
		Orkney Islands	19.3
SCOTLAND			
Glasgow City	577.1	**NORTHERN IRELAND**	
Edinburgh, City of	448.4	Belfast	271.6
Fife	352.0	Lisburn	109.6
North Lanarkshire	321.8	Derry	106.5
South Lanarkshire	303.0	Newry & Mourne	89.6
Aberdeenshire	229.3	Craigavon	82.2
Highland	209.1	Newtownabbey	80.3
Aberdeen City	206.6	North Down	77.1
Renfrewshire	171.0	Ards	74.4
West Lothian	161.0	Castlereagh	66.1
Dumfries & Galloway	147.2	Down	65.2
Falkirk	145.9	Ballymena	59.5
Dundee City	143.1	Fermanagh	58.7
North Ayrshire	136.0	Coleraine	56.0
Perth & Kinross	136.0	Armagh	55.4
East Ayrshire	119.5	Omagh	49.6
South Ayrshire	111.6	Antrim	49.3
Scottish Borders	108.3	Dungannon	48.7
Angus	107.5	Banbridge	43.1
East Dunbartonshire	107.0	Magherafelt	40.8
West Dunbartonshire	92.3	Strabane	38.6
Argyll & Bute	91.3	Carrickfergus	38.5
East Lothian	91.1	Limavady	33.6
East Renfrewshire	89.7	Cookstown	33.4
Moray	87.5	Larne	30.9
Stirling	86.4	Ballymoney	27.8
Inverclyde	83.1	Moyle	16.3
Midlothian	79.7		

Source(s): 'Mid-2003 Population Estimates' National Statistics © Crown Copyright 2004; General Register Office for Scotland; Northern Ireland Statistics and Research Agency.

ETHNIC MINORITY POPULATION, GB

Population by Ethnic Group

	1995 '000s	2000 '000s	2002–2002/2003[1] '000s	2002–2002/2003[1] %
Black–Caribbean	486	529	584	1.0
Black–African	292	440	541	0.9
Black–Other	232	307	59	0.1
Indian	866	985	1,016	1.7
Pakistani	548	675	718	1.2
Bangladeshi	184	257	273	0.5
Chinese	123	151	199	0.3
Other–Asian	173	242	302	0.5
White & Black–Caribbean	–	–	234	0.4
White & Black–African	–	–	72	0.1
White & Asian	–	–	129	0.2
Other mixed	–	–	74	0.1
Other	333	459	458	0.8
All ethnic minorities	3,237	4,045	4,659	7.9
White–British	–	–	51,010	86.0
White–Other	–	–	1,946	3.3
White–Total	52,894	54,670	52,956	89.3
Total population[1]	**56,144**	**58,731**	**59,330**	**100.0**

Estimated Size of Ethnic Minority Population

	1951	1961	1971	1981	2002–2002/2003[1]
Population ('000s)	200	500	1,200	2,100	4,659
of total GB population (%)	0.4	1.0	2.3	3.9	7.9

Ethnic Minority Population of Government Office Regions, 2001/2002[2]

	'000s	%		'000s	%
North East	50	2.0	London	2,087	28.3
North West	335	4.9	South East	323	4.0
Yorkshire/Humberside	303	6.1	South West	106	2.2
East Midlands	233	5.6	England	4,225	8.5
West Midlands	566	10.8	Wales	58	2.0
East	221	4.1	Scotland	84	1.7

Composition of the Ethnic Minority Population

	1995	2000	2001–2001/02[2]	2002–2002/03[1]
Black–Caribbean	15.0	13.1	14.2	12.5
Black–African	9.0	10.9	11.6	11.6
Black–Other	7.2	7.6	1.6	1.3
Indian	26.8	24.4	21.9	21.8
Pakistani	16.9	16.7	16.7	15.4
Bangladeshi	5.7	6.4	6.0	5.9
Chinese	3.8	3.7	4.1	4.3
Other–Asian	5.3	6.0	5.7	6.5
White & Black–Caribbean	–	–	6.2	5.0
White & Black–African	–	–	1.5	1.5
White & Asian	–	–	3.3	2.8
Other mixed	–	–	0.7	1.6
Other	10.3	6.4	6.5	9.8
All ethnic minority groups[3]	**100.0**	**100.0**	**100.0**	**100.0**

Note(s): Covers population in private households, students in halls of residence and those in NHS accommodation only. [1] Spring 2002 to Winter 2002/2003. [2] Spring 2001 to Winter 2001/2003. [3] Includes ethnic group not stated.

Source(s): 'Labour Force Survey'; National Statistics © Crown Copyright 2004.

DISTRIBUTION OF UK POPULATION & HOUSEHOLDS BY GOVERNMENT OFFICE REGION, 2002–2003

	Number of households '000s	%	Population '000s	%	Persons per household
North East	1,020	4.0	2,539	4.3	2.5
North West	2,780	11.0	6,805	11.4	2.4
Yorkshire/Humberside	2,130	9.0	5,009	8.4	2.4
East Midlands	1,720	7.0	4,252	7.1	2.5
West Midlands	2,120	9.0	5,320	8.9	2.5
East	2,230	9.0	5,463	9.2	2.4
London	2,850	12.0	7,388	12.4	2.6
South East	3,390	14.0	8,080	13.6	2.4
South West	2,160	9.0	4,999	8.4	2.3
Wales	1,250	5.0	2,938	4.9	2.4
Scotland	2,140	9.0	5,057	8.5	2.4
Northern Ireland	620	3.0	1,703	2.9	2.7
Total	**24,400**	**3.0**	**59,554**	**100.0**	**2.4**

Source(s): 'Family Spending', National Statistics © Crown Copyright 2004; 'Mid-2003 Population Estimates', National Statistics © Crown Copyright 2004; General Register Offices for Scotland and Northern Ireland; WARC.

DISTRIBUTION OF UK HOUSEHOLDS BY SIZE, 2002–2003

	Grossed Number of Households '000s	Percentage of All Households[1]
One person	6,590	27.0
Two persons	8,850	36.0
Three persons	4,090	17.0
Four persons	3,250	13.0
Five persons	1,090	4.0
Six persons	340	1.0
Seven persons	90	. .
Eight persons	20	. .
Nine or more persons	. .	. .
Total	**24,320**	**100.0**

Note(s): [1] Based on grossed number of households.
Source(s): 'Family Spending', National Statistics © Crown Copyright 2004; WARC.

NRS POPULATION BY SOCIAL GRADE
OF CHIEF INCOME EARNER

Social grade	All adults 15+		Men		Women		Main shoppers (female)	
	'000s	%	'000s	%	'000s	%	'000s	%
A	1,492	3.2	848	3.7	644	2.6	559	2.7
B	10,108	21.5	5,216	23.0	4,892	20.1	4,251	20.4
C1	13,696	29.1	6,212	27.4	7,484	30.8	6,336	30.5
C2	9,817	20.9	5,255	23.2	4,563	18.8	3,862	18.6
D	7,638	16.2	3,624	16.0	4,014	16.5	3,414	16.4
E	4,276	9.1	1,539	6.8	2,737	11.2	2,374	11.4
Total	**47,028**	**100.0**	**22,694**	**100.0**	**24,334**	**100.0**	**20,796**	**100.0**

Note(s):   Figures are based on the social grade of the Chief Income Earner.
Source(s):   National Readership Survey (NRS Ltd.), July 2003 – June 2004.

Main Shoppers

Main shoppers are identified as those who personally select half or more of the items bought for their household from supermarkets and food shops. This household member may be male or female.

	'000s	%
Female main shopper	20,796	67.7
Male main shopper	9,928	32.3
Total	**30,723**	**100.0**

Source(s):   National Readership Survey (NRS Ltd.), July 2003 – June 2004.

NRS SOCIAL GRADE DEFINITIONS

Social Grade[1]	% of Adult Pop.[2]	Social Status	Occupation
A	3.5	Upper middle class	Higher managerial, administrative or professional
B	21.5	Middle class	Intermediate managerial, admin. or professional
C1	29.1	Lower middle class	Supervisory/clerical and junior managerial, administrative or professional
C2	20.9	Skilled working class	Skilled manual workers
D	6.2	Working class	Semi and unskilled manual workers
E	9.1	Those at lowest levels of subsistence	State pensioners or widows (no other earner), casual or lowest-grade workers

Note(s):   [1] These are the standard social grade classifications using definitions agreed between IPSOS-RSL and NRS Ltd. [2] Adults aged 15+
Source(s):   National Readership Survey (NRS Ltd.), July 2003 – June 2004.

NRS POPULATION PROFILES OF GB

	All adults 15+		Men		Women		Main shoppers[1]	
	'000s	%	'000s	%	'000s	%	'000s	%
ISBA Area								
London	9,503	20.2	4,611	20.3	4,892	20.1	4,163	20.0
Midlands	7,507	16.0	3,685	16.0	3,822	15.7	3,207	15.4
Lancashire	5,485	11.7	2,620	11.5	2,865	11.8	2,503	12.0
Yorkshire	4,666	9.9	2,254	9.9	2,412	9.9	2,027	9.7
Southern	4,432	9.4	2,135	9.4	2,297	9.4	1,986	9.5
East of England	3,460	7.4	1,689	7.4	1,771	7.3	1,516	7.3
Wales & the West	3,806	8.1	1,824	8.0	1,982	8.1	1,691	8.1
Central Scotland	2,917	6.2	1,372	6.0	1,545	6.3	1,355	6.5
North East	2,313	4.9	1,111	4.9	1,201	4.9	1,011	4.9
South West	1,460	3.1	681	3.0	779	3.2	665	3.2
Northern Scotland	996	2.1	488	2.2	508	2.1	445	2.1
Border	483	1.0	224	1.0	259	1.1	228	1.1
Total	**47,028**	**100.0**	**22,694**	**100.0**	**24,334**	**99.9**	**20,796**	**100.0**
ITV Area								
London	12,067	25.7	5,835	25.7	6,232	25.6	5,290	25.4
East & West Midlands	9,463	20.1	4,640	20.4	4,824	19.8	4,084	19.6
North West	6,050	12.9	2,877	12.7	3,173	13.0	2,756	13.3
Yorkshire	5,853	12.4	2,804	12.4	3,049	12.5	2,601	12.5
South & South East	5,562	11.8	2,685	11.8	2,876	11.8	2,476	11.9
East of England	4,873	10.4	2,384	10.5	2,489	10.2	2,113	10.2
Wales/West of England	5,248	11.2	2,530	11.1	2,719	11.2	2,330	11.2
Central Scotland	3,185	6.8	1,504	6.6	1,681	6.9	1,474	7.1
North East	2,626	5.6	1,278	5.6	1,348	5.5	1,129	5.4
South West	1,854	3.9	866	3.8	989	4.1	855	4.1
North Scotland	1,100	2.3	535	2.4	565	2.3	495	2.4
Border	526	1.1	246	1.1	281	1.2	249	1.2
Total	**58,407**	**123.4**	**28,184**	**124.1**	**30,226**	**124.1**	**25,852**	**124.3**

NRS POPULATION PROFILES OF GB (Cont.)

	All adults 15+		Men		Women		Main shoppers[1]	
	'000s	%	'000s	%	'000s	%	'000s	%
Occupation (Group)								
Corporate managers	2,568	5.5	1,729	7.6	839	3.4	748	3.6
Managers (agric/serv)	961	2.0	593	2.6	368	1.5	340	1.6
Science/tech profs	853	1.8	726	3.2	127	0.5	115	0.6
Health profs	182	0.4	99	0.4	83	0.3	73	0.4
Teach/research profs	1,300	2.8	506	2.2	794	3.3	714	3.4
Bus/pub serv prof	955	2.0	603	2.7	352	1.4	327	1.6
Sci/tech ass prof	415	0.9	334	1.5	81	0.3	74	0.4
Health ass prof	874	1.9	135	0.6	739	3.0	705	3.4
Protective serv	377	0.8	320	1.4	56	0.2	52	0.3
Cult/media/sports	561	1.2	385	1.7	176	0.7	153	0.7
Bus/ pub ass profs	855	1.8	522	2.3	334	1.4	297	1.4
Administrative	3,198	6.8	1,001	4.4	2,197	9.0	1,930	9.3
Secretarial	650	1.4	27	0.1	623	2.6	547	2.6
Skilled agric	357	0.8	303	1.3	54	0.2	53	0.3
Skilled metal/elec	1,428	3.0	1,377	6.1	51	0.2	42	0.2
Skilled construct	1,297	2.8	1,267	5.6	30	0.1	22	0.1
Textiles/print/other	461	1.0	345	1.5	116	0.5	111	0.5
Caring services	1,249	2.7	152	0.7	1,097	4.5	995	4.8
Leisure services	465	1.0	128	0.6	337	1.4	279	1.3
Sales occupations	1,214	2.6	310	1.4	903	3.7	763	3.7
Customer services	50	0.1	7	–	42	0.2	40	0.2
Ind plnt/mach ops	892	1.9	664	2.9	229	0.9	200	1.0
Drivers/mob mch ops	1,035	2.2	982	4.3	52	0.2	46	0.2
Element/plnt occs	835	1.8	665	2.9	169	0.7	143	0.7
Elemnt/admin occs	1,873	4.0	732	3.2	1,142	4.7	1,007	4.8
Insuff info/not asked	22,124	47.0	8,780	38.7	13,344	54.8	11,020	53.0
Total	**47,028**	**100.0**	**22,694**	**100.0**	**24,334**	**100.0**	**20,796**	**100.0**
Industry (SIC Division)								
Agric/hunt/fish	548	1.2	410	1.8	138	0.6	128	0.6
Fishing	31	0.1	19	0.1	11	–	11	0.1
Mining/quarrying	15	–	15	0.1	..	..	..	..
Manufacturing	3,881	8.3	2,978	13.1	903	3.7	784	3.8
Elec/gas/water supp	173	0.4	140	0.6	33	0.1	30	0.1
Construction	2,141	4.6	1,955	8.6	186	0.8	156	0.7
Wholesale/retail	3,127	6.6	1,574	6.9	1,553	6.4	1,343	6.5
Hotels/restaurants	1,256	2.7	459	2.0	797	3.3	686	3.3
Trans/storage/comms	2,053	4.4	1,607	7.1	446	1.8	370	1.8
Financial	862	1.8	436	1.9	426	1.7	378	1.8
Real estate/rent	2,768	5.9	1,538	6.8	1,230	5.1	1,088	5.2
Pub admin/defence	1,712	3.6	896	3.9	816	3.4	723	3.5
Education	2,008	4.3	666	2.9	1,342	5.5	1,230	5.9
Health/social work	3,057	6.5	594	2.6	2,463	10.1	2,295	11.0
Oth comm/soc act	1,190	2.5	595	2.6	595	2.4	513	2.5
Private h'holds/ emp person	35	0.1	1	–	34	0.1	29	0.1
Ext territorial org	–	..	..	..	..	..	..	..
Insuff info/not asked	22,171	47.1	8,811	38.8	13,360	54.9	11,033	53.1
Total	**47,028**	**100.0**	**22,694**	**100.0**	**24,333**	**100.0**	**20,797**	**100.0**

Note(s): [1] Only 33.1% of 'Main shoppers' are male. [2] Due to overlap of ITV areas, figures will add to more than 100%.

Source(s): National Readership Survey (NRS Ltd.), July 2003 – June 2004.

CACI ACORN PROFILE OF THE UNITED KINGDOM

This table shows the ACORN profile of CACI's 2004 population projections for the UK. The table shows the 17 ACORN groups and 56 ACORN Types (plus 1 'unclassified') in the ACORN classification which is derived from the Government's 2001 Census of Great Britain.

ACORN Categories	ACORN Groups		ACORN Types	CACI's 2004 Population Projections Number	% of total
1 Wealthy achievers	A	Wealthy executives	1 Wealthy mature professionals, large houses	910,634	1.5
			2 Wealthy working families with mortgages	787,387	1.3
			3 Villages with wealthy commuters	1,673,380	2.8
			4 Well-off managers, larger houses	1,606,739	2.7
	B	Affluent greys	5 Older affluent professionals	959,555	1.6
			6 Farming communities	1,142,988	1.9
			7 Old people, detached homes	1,119,361	1.9
	C	Flourishing families	8 Mature couples, smaller detached homes	1,193,842	2.0
			9 Older families, prosperous suburbs	1,316,014	2.2
			10 Well-off working families with mortgages	1,382,413	2.3
			11 Well-off managers, detached houses	2,408,494	4.0
			12 Large families and houses in rural areas	365,121	0.6
2 Urban prosperity	D	Prosperous professionals	13 Well-off professionals, larger houses and converted flats	466,419	0.8
			14 Older professionals in suburban houses and apartments	843,525	1.4
	E	Educated urbanites	15 Affluent urban professionals, flats	652,963	1.1
			16 Prosperous young professionals, flats	494,234	0.8
			17 Young educated workers, flats	329,891	0.6
			18 Multi-ethnic young, converted flats	667,067	1.1
			19 Suburban privately renting professionals	561,259	0.9
	F	Aspiring singles	20 Student flats and cosmopolitan sharers	392,463	0.7
			21 Singles and sharers, multi-ethnic areas	1,014,727	1.7
			22 Low income singles, small rented flats	736,861	1.2
			23 Student terraces	239,451	0.4
3 Comfortably off	G	Starting out	24 Young couples, flats and terraces	552,549	0.9
			25 White-collar singles/sharers, terraces	835,095	1.4
	H	Secure families	26 Younger white-collar couples with mortgages	1,122,479	1.9
			27 Middle income, home owning areas	2,045,238	3.4
			28 Working families with mortgages	1,530,952	2.6

H Secure families (cont.)	29	Mature families in suburban semis	1,987,871	3.3
	30	Established home owning workers	2,284,331	3.8
	31	Home owning Asian family areas	653,036	1.1
3 Comfortably off (cont.) **I Settled suburbia**	32	Retired home owners	512,288	0.9
	33	Middle income, older couples	1,765,633	3.0
	34	Lower incomes, older people, semis	1,262,693	2.1
J Prudent pensioners	35	Elderly singles, purpose built flats	358,854	0.6
	36	Older people, flats	1,215,048	2.0
K Asian communities	37	Crowded Asian terraces	269,216	0.5
	38	Low income Asian families	624,518	1.0
4 Moderate means **L Post industrial families**	39	Skilled older families, terraces	1,677,613	2.8
	40	Young working families	1,170,142	2.0
M Blue-collar roots	41	Skilled workers, semis and terraces	2,289,256	3.8
	42	Home owning families, terraces	1,570,320	2.6
	43	Older people, rented terraces	1,041,137	1.7
N Struggling families	44	Low incomes larger families, semis	2,023,627	3.4
	45	Low income, older people, smaller semis	1,853,694	3.1
	46	Low income, routine jobs, terraces and flats	792,960	1.3
	47	Low income families, terraced estates	1,572,871	2.6
	48	Families and single parents, semis and terraces	1,278,089	2.1
	49	Large families and single parents, many children	904,576	1.5
5 Hard-pressed **O Burdened singles**	50	Single elderly people, council flats	951,337	1.6
	51	Single parents and pensioners, council terraces	1,061,787	1.8
	52	Families and single parents, council flats	509,718	0.9
P High-Rise hardship	53	Old people, many high-rise flats	385,342	0.6
	54	Singles and single parents, high-rise estates	492,156	0.8
Q Inner city adversity	55	Multi-ethnic purpose built estates	626,469	1.1
	56	Multi-ethnic crowded flats	628,975	1.1
UNCLASSIFIED			490,427	0.8
TOTAL			59,605,085	100.0

FINANCIAL ACORN PROFILE OF THE UNITED KINGDOM

This table shows the Financial*ACORN profile of CACI's 2004 population projections for the UK. The table shows the 11 Financial*ACORN groups and 49 Financial*ACORN Types (plus 1 'unclassified') in the Financial*ACORN classification which is derived from the Government's 2001 Census of Great Britain and data from NOP's Financial Research Survey (FRS).

Financial ACORN groups		Financial ACORN types	CACI's 2004 population projections	
			Number	% of total
A	**Wealthy investors**	1 Wealthiest middle-aged couples, many investments	1,648,531	2.8
		2 Wealthy older couples, substantial savings	1,782,875	3.0
		3 Semi rural empty nesters, high value investments	1,010,496	1.7
		4 Retired wealthy suburban investors, many shares	349,636	0.6
B	**Prospering families**	5 Wealthy suburbanites, large houses and mortgages	454,932	0.8
		6 Older professional families, spending and investing	1,569,112	2.6
		7 Affluent families, spending and planning their future	834,886	1.4
		8 Prosperous communities, building assets	1,417,860	2.4
C	**Traditional money**	9 High spending pensioners, many investments	566,683	1.0
		10 Farming communities, long term savings	919,411	1.5
		11 Middle aged and pensioner couples, asset rich	2,030,527	3.4
		12 Better-off pensioners, varied investments	1,370,967	2.3
D	**Young urbanites**	13 Affluent young professionals, dealing direct	632,749	1.1
		14 Young well-off private renters, less financially active	1,210,617	2.0
		15 Well-off urban professionals, many investments	967,150	1.6
		16 Students and young people, banking direct	254,692	0.4
E	**Middle aged comfort**	17 Middle-aged families, financially secure	870,456	1.5
		18 Careful families, managing their money	1,609,967	2.7
		19 Multi-ethnic families, credit and investments	975,178	1.6
		20 Older couples, mortgage paid off, financially inactive	1,247,845	2.1
		21 Mature homeowners, savings and investments	2,819,181	4.7
F	**Contented pensioners**	22 Well-off seniors, some assets	267,722	0.4
		23 Elderly couples, little financial activity	1,358,261	2.3

F	**Contented pensioners (Cont.)**			
	24	Comfortable pensioners, safe investments	547,393	0.9
	25	Single pensioners, modest investments	457,475	0.8
G	**Settling down**			
	26	New families, heavy borrowing	861,501	1.4
	27	Well off young professionals, financially active	486,078	0.8
	28	Couples starting families, first time mortgages	188,935	0.3
	29	Young cosmopolitans, basic finances	1,321,582	2.2
	30	Mortgaged families, living on credit	771,976	1.3
H	**Moderate living**			
	31	Established homeowners, saving and borrowing	710,674	1.2
	32	Families and empty nesters, moving money around	1,812,395	3.0
	33	Younger people, buying and renting	1,291,465	2.2
	34	Suburban families, moderate investments	1,719,043	2.9
	35	Settled couples, average savings	2,743,758	4.6
I	**Meagre means**			
	36	Older families, uncomplicated finances	808,765	1.4
	37	Young people, first step on housing ladder	957,280	1.6
	38	Crowded Asian communities, low income	1,002,418	1.7
	39	Working families, buying their terrace	1,202,181	2.0
	40	Low income council tenants, sometimes in debt	1,026,520	1.7
	41	Low income workers, struggling to buy	2,059,029	3.5
J	**Inner city existence**			
	42	Low income singles and couples, little financial activity	573,075	1.0
	43	Multi ethnic young singles renting flats	1,622,751	2.7
	44	High rise poverty, banking on welfare	1,483,203	2.5
	45	Poor young multi ethnic, financially inactive	714,880	1.2
K	**Impoverished pensioners**			
	46	Elderly council tenants, making ends meet	2,511,535	4.2
	47	Poor families, borrowing to live	3,174,094	5.3
	48	Poor unemployed without current accounts	2,430,384	4.1
	49	Poor pensioners, queuing for cash	466,534	0.8
U	**UNCLASSIFIED**		**490,427**	**0.8**
	TOTAL		**59,605,085**	**100.0**

Source(s): ONS © Crown Copyright, 2001.

THE OVERALL RETAIL PICTURE

VOLUME OF RETAIL SALES, 1998–2003

Index numbers of sales per week (average 2000 prices), 2000 = 100

		Predominantly non-food stores						
	Predominantly			Non-	Textile			Non-store
	All	food		specialised	clothing	Household	Other	retailers/
	retailers	stores	Total	stores	& footwear	goods	stores	repair
	(3,984)	**(1,712)**	**(2,045)**	**(361)**	**(536)**	**(533)**	**(615)**	**(226)**
1998	93	96	90	92	89	86	94	93
1999	96	97	94	94	93	93	97	96
2000	100	100	100	100	100	100	100	100
2001	106	104	108	106	109	111	105	106
2002	113	108	117	111	121	121	112	113
2003	116	112	121	114	129	126	115	108

Note(s):   Figures in brackets refer to average weekly sales in 2000 (£ million).
Source(s): 'Business Monitor SDM28 – Retail Sales', National Statistics © Crown Copyright 2004.

THE NORMAL SEASONALITY OF THE VOLUME OF RETAIL SALES, 2003

Normal monthly variations in the volume of retail sales occur each year – for example, sales in February by textile, clothing and footwear retailers are on average less than half those in December. The Office for National Statistics has observed the monthly pattern of sales over a number of years and developed seven series which describe them. These series are also combined into a series for all retailers.

2003 = 100

		Predominantly non-food stores						
		Predominantly		Non-	Textile			Non-store
	All	food		specialised	clothing	Household	Other	retailers/
	retailers	stores	Total	stores	& footwear	goods	stores	repair
January	90	93	88	88	84	97	84	94
February	90	95	86	81	79	93	88	96
March	92	97	88	83	84	91	91	97
April	96	101	93	87	91	99	94	96
May	94	98	92	85	92	95	94	89
June	96	100	93	87	96	89	97	93
July	99	100	99	96	106	94	97	96
August	96	99	93	89	94	95	94	89
September	96	97	94	88	96	96	95	99
October	101	99	102	101	105	104	98	111
November	112	104	116	131	114	112	114	129
December	133	115	150	175	153	133	148	111

Source(s): 'Business Monitor SDM28 – Retail Sales', National Statistics © Crown Copyright 2004.

RETAIL SALES BY TYPE OF BUSINESS, GB

Current Prices, £ billion

	1996	1997	1998	1999	2000	2001	2002
All retailers	**175.68**	**186.68**	**194.02**	**200.52**	**207.85**	**221.02**	**230.19**
Predominantly food stores	**78.88**	**82.93**	**87.12**	**90.12**	**93.19**	**99.56**	**103.68**
Fruit & vegetables	1.28	1.31	1.44	1.33	1.39	1.63	1.42
Meat & meat products	2.44	2.31	2.24	2.29	2.41	2.54	2.54
Fish	0.25	0.24	0.21	0.16	0.16	0.18	0.17
Bread, cakes & confectionery	1.80	1.85	1.96	1.94	1.99	2.05	2.16
Alcohol & other beverages	3.24	3.34	3.37	3.53	3.21	3.27	3.08
Tobacco products	3.94	4.06	4.18	4.38	4.65	5.05	5.09
Other specialised food stores	1.26	1.30	1.32	1.44	1.52	1.52	1.52
Non-specialised food stores	64.84	68.48	72.12	75.15	77.57	83.02	87.87
Predominantly non-food stores	**88.01**	**94.50**	**97.16**	**100.40**	**104.81**	**111.55**	**116.12**
Textiles, clothing, footwear & leather	**27.20**	**29.18**	**29.34**	**29.99**	**30.90**	**32.94**	**34.77**
Textiles	0.69	0.73	0.74	0.75	0.79	0.78	0.75
Clothing	22.83	24.33	24.77	25.41	26.27	27.78	29.72
Footwear & leather goods	3.75	4.06	3.79	3.83	3.90	4.25	4.37
Household goods	**21.33**	**23.39**	**24.67**	**25.76**	**27.36**	**29.26**	**30.19**
Furniture, lighting, etc.	6.91	7.81	8.19	8.13	8.51	9.09	9.34
Electrical household appliances	8.35	9.20	9.58	10.20	10.90	11.59	11.82
Hardware, paint & glass	6.04	6.43	6.88	7.39	7.96	8.58	8.97
Other specialised non-food stores	**23.19**	**24.51**	**25.58**	**26.58**	**27.49**	**29.32**	**30.46**
Books, newspapers & periodicals	4.24	4.45	4.77	4.81	4.81	5.02	5.26
Pharmaceutical, medical, cosmetic & toilet goods	3.23	3.45	3.58	3.67	3.80	3.96	4.18
Floor coverings	1.12	1.21	1.03	0.94	0.98	0.99	1.01
Photographic & optical equip., office supplies	2.78	2.76	2.78	3.08	3.32	3.64	3.83
Second hand goods	1.05	1.16	1.13	1.08	1.30	1.55	1.35
Others	10.71	11.43	12.24	13.06	13.26	14.18	14.79
Non-specialised non-food stores	**16.27**	**17.37**	**17.58**	**18.07**	**19.03**	**20.04**	**20.75**
Non-store retailing & repair	**8.82**	**9.24**	**9.78**	**9.95**	**9.78**	**9.98**	**10.29**
Mail order houses	6.83	7.23	7.76	8.15	8.02	7.95	8.35
Non-store retail, excl. mail order	1.54	1.57	1.56	1.34	1.36	1.47	1.36
Repair of personal & h'hold goods	0.42	0.45	0.45	0.43	0.43	0.53	0.55

Note(s): See 'Note(s)' and 'Source(s)' on the following page.

RETAIL SALES BY TYPE OF BUSINESS, GB (Cont.)

Constant 1995 Prices, £ billion

	1996	1997	1998	1999	2000	2001	2002
All retailers	**179.98**	**197.24**	**212.06**	**222.51**	**237.37**	**257.05**	**272.07**
Predominantly food stores	**80.82**	**87.62**	**95.23**	**100.01**	**106.43**	**115.79**	**122.55**
Fruit & vegetables	1.31	1.38	1.57	1.48	1.58	1.90	1.68
Meat & meat products	2.50	2.44	2.45	2.54	2.76	2.95	3.00
Fish	0.26	0.26	0.23	0.18	0.19	0.20	0.20
Bread, cakes & confectionery	1.84	1.95	2.14	2.15	2.28	2.38	2.55
Alcohol & other beverages	3.32	3.53	3.68	3.92	3.66	3.81	3.64
Tobacco products	4.04	4.29	4.57	4.86	5.31	5.87	6.01
Other specialised food stores	1.29	1.37	1.44	1.60	1.73	1.76	1.79
Non-specialised food stores	66.43	72.35	78.82	83.39	88.59	96.56	103.86
Predominantly non-food stores	**90.16**	**99.84**	**106.19**	**111.42**	**119.70**	**129.73**	**137.26**
Textiles, clothing, footwear & leather	**27.86**	**30.83**	**32.06**	**33.28**	**35.29**	**38.31**	**41.09**
Textiles	0.71	0.78	0.81	0.84	0.90	0.91	0.88
Clothing	23.39	25.71	27.07	28.20	30.00	32.31	35.13
Footwear & leather goods	3.84	4.29	4.14	4.24	4.46	4.94	5.16
Household goods	**21.85**	**24.71**	**26.97**	**28.59**	**31.25**	**34.03**	**35.68**
Furniture, lighting, etc.	7.08	8.25	8.95	9.02	9.72	10.57	11.04
Electrical household appliances	8.55	9.72	10.47	11.32	12.44	13.48	13.97
Hardware, paint & glass	6.18	6.80	7.52	8.20	9.08	9.97	10.60
Other specialised non-food stores	**23.76**	**25.89**	**27.96**	**29.50**	**31.40**	**34.10**	**36.00**
Books, newspapers & periodicals	4.34	4.70	5.21	5.34	5.50	5.83	6.22
Pharmaceutical, medical, cosmetic & toilet goods	3.31	3.65	3.91	4.07	4.34	4.60	4.94
Floor coverings	1.15	1.28	1.13	1.04	1.12	1.15	1.20
Photographic & optical equip., office supplies	2.85	2.91	3.04	3.41	3.79	4.23	4.52
Second hand goods	1.07	1.22	1.24	1.20	1.49	1.80	1.59
Others	10.97	12.07	13.38	14.49	15.14	16.49	17.48
Non-specialised non-food stores	**16.67**	**18.35**	**19.21**	**20.05**	**21.74**	**23.31**	**24.52**
Non-store retailing & repair	**9.04**	**9.77**	**10.69**	**11.04**	**11.17**	**11.61**	**12.16**
Mail order houses	7.00	7.63	8.48	9.05	9.16	9.25	9.87
Non-store retail, excl. mail order	1.58	1.66	1.70	1.49	1.55	1.71	1.61
Repair of personal & household goods	0.43	0.47	0.49	0.48	0.49	0.62	0.66

Note(s):   Deflated by the Retail Prices Index (1995 = 100).
Source(s):   'Business Monitor SDM28 – Retail Sales', National Statistics © Crown Copyright 2003; WARC.

MONTHLY VARIATION IN VALUE OF TURNOVER BY TYPE OF RETAILER

Percentage variation from trend

Type of business	Jan	Feb	Mar	Apr	May	Jun	Jul	Aug	Sep	Oct	Nov	Dec
All retailers	–8	–8	–5	–3	–3	–2	–2	–4	–5	0	9	32
Predominantly food stores	–8	–4	–2	0	0	0	–2	–3	–5	–3	1	11
Fruit & vegetables	–4	1	4	8	15	16	12	3	–7	–8	–9	1
Meat & meat products	0	0	–2	1	–1	–2	–1	0	–2	1	2	25
Fish	–10	–4	–4	–1	–3	–2	–2	–2	–7	–3	–4	–1
Bread, cakes & confectionery	–13	–4	–1	–1	–5	–4	–2	–1	–5	–2	6	7
Alcohol & other beverages	–22	–15	–14	–9	–7	–6	–5	–6	–11	–10	–7	22
Tobacco products	–2	3	3	5	4	2	4	4	1	–5	5	4
Other specialised food stores	–2	1	1	3	3	1	3	2	–1	2	3	5
Non-specialised food stores	–8	–5	–2	0	0	–3	–3	–3	–5	–3	1	11
Predominantly non–food stores	–9	–12	–9	–5	–5	–4	–3	–6	–5	1	16	51
Textiles, clothing, footwear & leather	–17	–23	–16	–8	–6	–6	–2	–8	–6	0	13	57
Textiles	5	–3	–4	–3	–8	–7	3	1	1	9	12	17
Clothing	–17	–22	–15	–8	–6	–9	–3	–10	–7	1	17	65
Footwear & leather goods	–18	–30	–23	–8	–3	–6	1	1	–3	–6	–8	23
Household goods	8	1	1	3	0	–2	–1	–1	1	8	18	34
Furniture, lighting, etc.	18	10	7	4	–1	–1	4	1	4	15	19	22
Electrical household appliances	10	–5	–9	–10	–16	–15	–11	–8	–4	5	25	74
Hardware, paint & glass	–5	0	10	22	23	7	8	8	3	7	7	–4
Other specialised non–food stores	–14	–10	–7	–4	–3	–3	–3	–5	–6	–2	11	46
Books, newspapers & periodicals	–8	–5	–6	–10	–12	–13	–10	–9	–4	2	13	46
Pharmaceutical, medical, cosmetic	–11	–11	–11	–8	–5	–5	–1	–4	–8	–6	1	31
Floor coverings	–5	–8	–7	–7	–15	–14	–12	–11	–9	1	9	–10
Photographic & optical equip., office supp.	0	2	3	2	2	2	9	7	3	6	11	24
Second-hand goods	–18	–10	–10	–12	–9	–6	–14	–18	–12	–2	4	–7
Others	–24	–15	–7	–1	3	–1	–1	–3	–7	–5	14	70
Non-specialised non–food stores	–12	–16	–12	–9	–12	–9	–5	–10	–9	–2	–9	72
Non-store retailing & repair	–7	5	0	–3	–5	–4	–4	–6	–1	9	19	10
Mail order houses	–9	7	0	–5	–7	–8	–8	–9	–1	11	23	8
Non-store retail, excl. mail order	–9	–7	–7	–5	–5	–5	–4	–7	–6	–2	4	7
Repair of personal & household goods	1	0	–2	0	–4	–5	–2	0	1	5	10	18

Note(s): The variation is calculated as the average variation for each month from the trend of the retail sales value series over the period January 1989 to May 2003.

Source(s): 'Business Monitor SDM28 – Retail Sales', National Statistics © Crown Copyright 2003; WARC.

TRADE SECTOR SHARES BY VALUE OF CONSUMER PURCHASES IN VARIOUS PRODUCT AREAS

(as measured by TNS, GfK Marketing Services Ltd & ACNielsen)

Packaged Groceries, 2003	%
Multiples	90.8
Co-ops	5.6
Independents/Symbols	3.6
	100.0

Source(s): TNS Superpanel.

Toiletries & healthcare, 2003	%
Multiples	48.2
Chemists/Drugstores (incl. Boots)	39.6
Co-op grocers	1.2
Independents/Symbols	0.5
All others	10.5
	100.0

Source(s): TNS Superpanel.

Chocolate confectionery, 2003	%
Grocers	65.0
CTNs	13.3
All others	21.7
	100.0

Source(s): TNS Superpanel.

Fruit & vegetables, 2003	%
Grocers	88.5
Greengrocers/Fruiterers	4.7
Market stalls/Farm shops	2.6
All others	4.2
	100.0

Source(s): TNS Superpanel.

Meat, bacon & poultry, 2003	%
Grocers	83.4
Butchers	10.9
Freezer centres	0.7
All others	5.0
	100.0

Source(s): TNS Superpanel.

Take Home alcoholic Drink (off-trade), 2003	%
Grocers	78.2
Specialists	21.8
	100.0

Source(s): ACNielsen.

Adult clothing	%
Multiple clothing retailers	30.0
General stores	18.1
Independent clothing retailers	10.4
Mail order/direct mail	7.0
Department stores	9.2
Sports shops/clubs	6.2
Value[1]	15.5
Other outlets	3.6
	100.0

Note(s): [1] Discount/cash & carry/supermarkets.
Source(s): TNS Fashion Trak.

Adult footwear	%
Total shoe shops	33.9
Sports shops	24.6
Mail order/direct mail	7.6
Total clothing shops	13.0
General stores	8.1
Other outlets	14.7
	100.0

Source(s): TNS Fashion Trak.

Small electrical appliances, January–December 2003	%
Electrical chains	14.0
Mail order	7.0
Electrical independents	2.0
Other mass merchandisers	76.0
	100.0

Source(s): GfK Marketing Services Ltd ©.

Major electrical appliances, January–December 2003	%
Electrical chains	42.0
Electrical independents	23.0
Hypermarkets/dept./variety stores	18.0
Kitchen/DIY/furniture	10.0
Mail order	7.0
	100.0

Source(s): GfK Marketing Services Ltd ©.

TV/Video (bought), January–December 2003	%
Electrical chains	37.0
Electrical independents	31.0
Mail order	6.0
Other mass merchandisers	26.0
	100.0

Source(s): GfK Marketing Services Ltd ©.

THE RETAIL LANDSCAPE

TOTAL COVERAGE, GB

	No. of stores	Turnover £m
Total grocery multiples	4,907	65,503
Total impulse	77,876	33,218
Co-op grocers	2,298	4,641
Convenience multiples	2,807	2,481
Multiple forecourts	4,065	2,058
Multiple off-licences	3,995	2,370
Symbol groups	6,360	4,331
Independents	54,933	12,615
Other impulse	3,418	4,724
Total coverage GB	**82,783**	**98,721**

Source(s): ACNielsen, January 2003.

Number of stores (%)

Independents 66%

Symbol groups 8%
Multiple off-licences 5%
Multiple forecourts 5%
Convenience multiples 3%
Co-op grocers 3%
Grocery multiples 6%
Other impulse 4%

Source(s): ACNielsen, January 2003.

TOTAL COVERAGE, GB (Cont.)

Turnover (£ million)

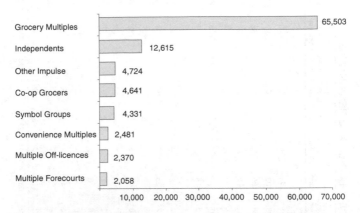

Source(s): ACNielsen, January 2003.

DEFINITIONS

Grocer A retail outlet with 20% or more of its turnover in groceries and/or provisions, and not having a larger proportion of turnover in any other commodity unless it is one, or a combination, of the following; off-licence trade, bakery goods, tobacco (if less than 70% of total sales).

Multiple A grocer belonging to a group of ten or more retail shops operated under common ownership.

Co-operative A grocer owned and operated by a co-operative society.

Independent Single enterprise of up to nine stores under common ownership.

Symbol groups An organisation of independent retailers who buy supplies through a specific wholesaler which are then delivered direct to the store. This enables them to get large quantity discounts which otherwise might only be possible for multiple retailers. In return the independent retailer gives a percentage of its takings and a fixed amount to the symbol group.

Source(s): ACNielsen, January 2003.

RETAILER SHOP NUMBERS BY TRADE CHANNEL AND REGION, 2003

	London	South & South East	East of England	Central	South West	Wales & West	Lancs.	Yorks.	North East	English Border	Scottish Border	Central Scotland	North East Scotland	Total
Grocery multiples														
Asda	29	21	10	33	5	21	48	26	21	2	–	26	8	250
Iceland	162	69	46	99	19	68	103	45	37	4	3	57	7	719
Kwik Save	29	12	11	161	3	98	185	91	64	5	3	48	8	718
Morrisons	2	–	7	16	–	1	25	44	13	2	–	–	–	110
NETTO	9	5	11	12	–	–	23	49	15	1	–	–	–	125
Safeway	68	42	21	57	15	31	27	38	43	4	10	75	29	460
Safeway/BP	17	8	2	10	2	3	4	1	2	–	–	4	–	53
Sainsbury Central	8	–	–	1	1	1	1	1	–	–	–	2	–	15
Sainsbury Local	22	2	–	2	–	2	2	–	–	–	–	2	–	30
Sainsbury Stores	130	53	35	65	11	27	35	22	6	1	–	13	3	401
Savacentre	4	2	–	2	–	–	2	1	2	–	–	1	–	14
Somerfield	86	71	37	93	49	88	41	35	14	–	4	32	19	570
Somerfield/Elf	10	2	–	2	–	–	5	–	–	–	–	1	–	19
Tesco Express	50	15	2	7	2	1	2	2	2	–	–	1	–	84
Tesco Extra	13	6	6	3	–	6	8	2	4	–	–	3	2	53
Tesco Metro	14	2	4	4	2	6	4	–	1	–	–	2	3	42
Tesco Superstores	101	62	45	72	25	54	41	48	8	4	3	41	20	524
Waitrose	64	34	14	16	4	5	–	1	–	–	–	–	–	138
Other grocery multiples	54	33	29	83	17	82	111	53	49	9	3	45	14	582
Total	**872**	**439**	**280**	**738**	**155**	**492**	**667**	**459**	**281**	**33**	**26**	**352**	**113**	**4,907**

RETAILER SHOP NUMBERS BY TRADE CHANNEL AND REGION, 2003 (Cont.)

	London	South & South East	East of England	Central	South West	Wales & West	Lancs.	Yorks.	North East	English Border	Scottish Border	Central Scotland	North East Scotland	Total
Co-ops														
The Co-operative shop	153	108	72	101	46	125	51	92	111	21	5	106	44	1,035
United Co-op	–	–	–	39	–	–	294	3	–	4	–	–	–	340
Other Co-ops	12	73	152	260	51	25	2	201	22	8	20	77	20	923
Total	**165**	**181**	**224**	**400**	**97**	**150**	**347**	**296**	**133**	**33**	**25**	**183**	**64**	**2,298**
Convenience multiples														
Budgens	96	20	28	16	–	5	–	3	–	–	–	–	–	168
Jacksons	–	–	–	16	–	–	–	76	6	–	–	–	–	98
McColls	18	15	14	13	7	10	13	5	3	–	–	13	6	117
Right Choice	–	–	–	5	–	2	35	4	20	1	–	–	–	67
R.S McColls	–	–	–	–	–	–	–	–	–	–	1	137	38	176
T&S Convenience	110	202	128	147	21	91	83	70	18	–	–	–	–	870
Other conv. multiples	246	200	85	278	38	109	23	44	102	14	7	73	92	1,311
Total	**470**	**437**	**255**	**475**	**66**	**217**	**154**	**202**	**149**	**15**	**8**	**223**	**136**	**2,807**
Multiple forecourts														
BP	106	45	45	63	4	12	35	25	13	–	–	22	11	381
BP Connect	39	3	15	4	–	–	2	–	–	–	–	3	–	66
Esso	174	78	35	93	24	57	66	60	19	8	1	60	16	691
Q8	5	5	11	2	–	1	–	2	1	–	–	2	–	29
Total Fina Elf	125	43	35	77	–	19	44	59	25	–	–	–	–	427
Remaining forecourts	537	236	176	402	65	190	290	264	126	15	7	123	40	2,471
Total	**986**	**410**	**317**	**641**	**93**	**279**	**437**	**410**	**184**	**23**	**8**	**210**	**67**	**4,065**

RETAILER SHOP NUMBERS BY TRADE CHANNEL AND REGION, 2003 (Cont.)

	London	South & South East	East of England	Central	South West	Wales & West	Lancs.	Yorks.	North East	English Border	Scottish Border	Central Scotland	North East Scotland	Total
Multiple off-licences														
Cellar 5 Booze Buster	–	–	2	40	–	7	140	38	83	18	–	–	–	328
Cellar 5 Wine Cellar	5	3	–	9	–	3	14	8	9	2	–	–	–	53
First Quench	583	269	100	311	57	168	382	142	69	9	16	263	69	2,438
Oddbins	106	20	8	17	3	9	18	7	5	1	–	29	7	230
Other multiple off-licences	321	127	69	102	1	15	223	41	4	2	–	40	1	946
Total	**1,015**	**419**	**179**	**479**	**61**	**202**	**777**	**236**	**170**	**32**	**16**	**332**	**77**	**3,995**
Independents														
Independents licenced	4,729	1,902	1,670	4,451	949	2,538	3,377	3,283	1,701	263	200	2,112	745	27,920
Independents specialist	1,614	560	388	1,144	263	588	1,096	875	402	69	581	–	146	7,726
Independents unlicenced	3,808	1,424	922	2,953	637	1,610	2,886	2,026	885	201	96	1,417	422	19,287
Total	**10,151**	**3,886**	**2,980**	**8,548**	**1,849**	**4,736**	**7,359**	**6,184**	**2,988**	**533**	**877**	**3,529**	**1,313**	**54,933**
Other impulse multiples														
Forbuoys	92	64	40	66	13	25	58	44	30	4	–	5	6	447
Martins	159	63	48	42	14	28	69	32	24	–	–	–	–	479
WH Smith	121	56	33	85	22	49	47	36	21	6	6	40	16	538
Woolworths	172	89	53	112	35	85	73	56	40	8	5	54	22	804
Other impulse multiples	172	74	76	295	9	95	112	211	75	3	–	21	7	1,150
Total	**716**	**346**	**250**	**600**	**93**	**282**	**359**	**379**	**190**	**21**	**11**	**120**	**51**	**3,418**

Source(s): ACNielsen, January 2003.

RETAIL STATISTICS BY TRADE CHANNEL, 2003

	Shop numbers		Turnover	
	No.	%	£m	%
Total coverage				
London	15,345	18.5	20,049	20.3
South & South East	6,620	8.0	10,135	10.3
East of England	4,885	5.9	7,152	7.2
Central	12,851	15.5	14,627	14.8
South West	2,683	3.2	3,194	3.2
Wales & West	7,091	8.6	8,477	8.6
Lancashire	10,898	13.2	11,389	11.5
Yorkshire	8,805	10.6	8,947	9.1
North East	4,498	5.4	4,683	4.7
English Border	690	0.8	703	0.7
Scottish Border	971	1.2	442	0.4
Central Scotland	5,417	6.5	6,511	6.6
North East Scotland	2,029	2.5	2,413	2.4
Total	**82,783**	**100.0**	**98,721**	**100.0**
Total impulse				
London	14,473	18.6	5,990	18.0
South & South East	6,181	7.9	2,984	9.0
East of England	4,605	5.9	2,337	7.0
Central	12,113	15.6	5,201	15.7
South West	2,528	3.2	1,115	3.4
Wales & West	6,599	8.5	2,850	8.6
Lancashire	10,231	13.1	3,974	12.0
Yorkshire	8,346	10.7	3,162	9.5
North East	4,217	5.4	1,703	5.1
English Border	657	0.8	243	0.7
Scottish Border	945	1.2	218	0.7
Central Scotland	5,065	6.5	2,469	7.4
North East Scotland	1,916	2.5	971	2.9
Total	**77,876**	**100.0**	**33,218**	**100.0**

Source(s): ACNielsen, January 2003.

RETAIL STATISTICS BY TRADE CHANNEL, 2003 (Cont.)

	Shop numbers		Turnover	
	No.	%	£m	%
Grocery multiples				
London	872	17.8	14,059	21.5
South & South East	439	8.9	7,151	10.9
East of England	280	5.7	4,815	7.4
Central	738	15.0	9,426	14.4
South West	155	3.2	2,079	3.2
Wales & West	492	10.0	5,627	8.6
Lancashire	667	13.6	7,415	11.3
Yorkshire	459	9.4	5,785	8.8
North East	281	5.7	2,980	4.5
English Border	33	0.7	459	0.7
Scottish Border	26	0.5	224	0.3
Central Scotland	352	7.2	4,042	6.2
North East Scotland	113	2.3	1,441	2.2
Total	**4,907**	**100.0**	**65,503**	**100.0**
Co-ops				
London	165	7.2	339	7.3
South & South East	181	7.9	398	8.6
East of England	224	9.7	464	10.0
Central	400	17.4	860	18.5
South West	97	4.2	225	4.8
Wales & West	150	6.5	421	9.1
Lancashire	347	15.1	462	9.9
Yorkshire	296	12.9	489	10.5
North East	133	5.8	249	5.4
English Border	33	1.4	50	1.1
Scottish Border	25	1.1	42	0.9
Central Scotland	183	8.0	459	9.9
North East Scotland	64	2.8	184	4.0
Total	**2,298**	**100.0**	**4,641**	**100.0**

Source(s): ACNielsen, January 2003.

RETAIL STATISTICS BY TRADE CHANNEL, 2003 (Cont.)

	Shop numbers		Turnover	
	No.	%	£m	%
Convenience multiples				
London	470	16.7	501	20.2
South & South East	437	15.6	411	16.6
East of England	255	9.1	264	10.6
Central	475	16.9	362	14.6
South West	66	2.4	50	2.0
Wales & West	217	7.7	178	7.2
Lancashire	154	5.5	112	4.5
Yorkshire	202	7.2	218	8.8
North East	149	5.3	114	4.6
English Border	15	0.5	11	0.4
Scottish Border	8	0.3	6	0.2
Central Scotland	223	7.9	154	6.2
North East Scotland	136	4.8	101	4.1
Total	**2,807**	**100.0**	**2,481**	**100.0**
Multiple forecourts				
London	986	24.3	540	26.2
South & South East	410	10.1	203	9.9
East of England	317	7.8	173	8.4
Central	641	15.8	309	15.0
South West	93	2.3	48	2.3
Wales & West	279	6.9	140	6.8
Lancashire	437	10.8	207	10.1
Yorkshire	410	10.1	184	8.9
North East	184	4.5	81	3.9
English Border	23	0.6	12	0.6
Scottish Border	8	0.2	4	0.2
Central Scotland	210	5.2	119	5.8
North East Scotland	67	1.6	39	1.9
Total	**4,065**	**100.0**	**2,058**	**100.0**

Source(s): ACNielsen, January 2003.

RETAIL STATISTICS BY TRADE CHANNEL, 2003 (Cont.)

	Shop numbers		Turnover	
	No.	%	£m	%
Multiple off-licences				
London	1,015	25.4	606	25.6
South & South East	419	10.5	228	9.6
East of England	179	4.5	95	4.0
Central	479	12.0	285	12.0
South West	61	1.5	36	1.5
Wales & West	202	5.1	110	4.6
Lancashire	777	19.4	501	21.1
Yorkshire	236	5.9	128	5.4
North East	170	4.3	80	3.4
English Border	32	0.8	18	0.7
Scottish Border	16	0.4	10	0.4
Central Scotland	332	8.3	226	9.5
North East Scotland	77	1.9	48	2.0
Total	**3,995**	**100.0**	**2,370**	**100.0**
Independents				
London	10,151	18.5	2,380	18.9
South & South East	3,886	7.1	910	7.2
East of England	2,980	5.4	726	5.8
Central	8,548	15.6	1,972	15.6
South West	1,849	3.4	432	3.4
Wales & West	4,736	8.6	1,085	8.6
Lancashire	7,359	13.4	1,657	13.1
Yorkshire	6,184	11.3	1,285	10.2
North East	2,988	5.4	684	5.4
English Border	533	1.0	119	0.9
Scottish Border	877	1.6	140	1.1
Central Scotland	3,529	6.4	899	7.1
North East Scotland	1,313	2.4	326	2.6
Total	**54,933**	**100.0**	**12,615**	**100.0**

Source(s): ACNielsen, January 2003.

RETAIL STATISTICS BY TRADE CHANNEL, 2003 (Cont.)

	Shop numbers		Turnover	
	No.	%	£m	%
Other impulse multiples				
London	716	20.9	1,011	21.4
South & South East	346	10.1	508	10.8
East of England	250	7.3	353	7.5
Central	600	17.6	767	16.2
South West	93	2.7	153	3.2
Wales & West	282	8.3	407	8.6
Lancashire	359	10.5	494	10.5
Yorkshire	379	11.1	414	8.8
North East	190	5.6	221	4.7
English Border	21	0.6	35	0.7
Scottish Border	11	0.3	16	0.3
Central Scotland	120	3.5	254	5.4
North East Scotland	51	1.5	91	1.9
Total	**3,418**	**100.0**	**4,724**	**100.0**

Source(s): ACNielsen, January 2003.

IMPORTANCE OF CATEGORIES

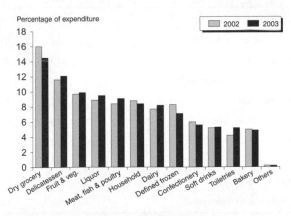

Percentage of expenditure

Legend: 2002 ■ 2003

Source(s): ACNielsen Homescan, 52 weeks ending December 2003.

TOP TEN FROZEN CATEGORIES, TOTAL COVERAGE

Top ten by market size

	2002 £ million	2003 £ million	% growth
Total frozen ready meals	581.2	559.0	−3.8
Total hand held ice cream	420.4	447.0	6.3
Pizza whole/slice	352.1	355.2	0.9
Total frozen poultry treated/pieces	337.3	335.6	−0.5
Frozen potato chips	308.5	303.4	−1.7
Frozen confectionery desserts	263.6	257.6	−2.3
Frozen ready meals – traditional	227.2	230.1	1.3
Hand held ice cream – stick lines	193.9	225.1	16.1
Ice cream <1 litre	183.8	201.4	9.6
Total frozen red/pork treated/pieces	176.8	178.9	1.2

Share of category by trade channel, 2003

	Grocery multiples (%)	Impulse (%)
Total frozen ready meals	83.7	16.3
Total hand held ice cream	60.8	39.2
Pizza whole/slice	86.0	14.0
Total frozen poultry treated/pieces	92.3	7.7
Frozen potato chips	86.0	14.0
Frozen confectionery desserts	85.9	14.1
Frozen ready meals – traditional	80.0	20.0
Hand held ice cream – stick lines	58.1	41.9
Ice cream <1 litre	80.4	19.6
Total frozen red/pork treated/pieces	89.3	10.7

Source(s): ACNielsen Scantrack, 52 weeks ending December 2003.

TOP TEN CONFECTIONERY CATEGORIES, TOTAL COVERAGE

Top ten by market size

	2002 £ million	2003 £ million	% growth
Potato chips	827.3	835.7	1.0
Chocolate countlines	853.4	828.9	−2.9
Savoury snacks	713.2	709.3	−0.5
Moulded chocolate	457.3	521.7	14.1
Fruit confectionery	416.8	414.3	−0.6
Chocolate biscuit countlines	416.8	394.8	−5.3
Chocolate assortments	338.6	332.4	−1.8
Bitesize chocolate	320.3	331.0	3.3
Chewing gum	263.8	277.3	5.1
Easter eggs	225.8	244.7	8.4

Share of category by trade channel, 2003

	Grocery multiples (%)	Impulse (%)
Potato chips	68.7	31.3
Chocolate countlines	40.5	59.5
Savoury snacks	64.7	35.3
Moulded chocolate	40.1	59.9
Fruit confectionery	39.7	60.3
Chocolate biscuit countlines	84.4	15.6
Chocolate assortments	57.7	42.3
Bitesize chocolate	38.3	61.7
Chewing gum	31.7	68.3
Easter eggs	59.6	40.4

Source(s): ACNielsen Scantrack, 52 weeks ending December 2003.

TOP TEN SOFT DRINKS CATEGORIES, TOTAL COVERAGE

Top ten by market size

	2002 £ million	2003 £ million	% growth
Colas	1,104.0	1,223.5	10.8
Fruit juice	683.6	748.6	9.5
Fruit drinks	520.9	564.8	8.4
Squashes/health drinks	441.8	464.7	5.2
Still mineral waters	300.9	380.5	26.5
Glucose/energy drinks	291.8	359.9	23.4
Lemonade	140.0	138.9	−0.8
Drinking yoghurt	79.1	118.9	50.3
Sparkling mineral waters	106.3	114.7	7.9
Mixers	104.2	107.8	3.4

Share of category by trade channel, 2003

	Grocery multiples (%)	Impulse (%)
Colas	53.0	47.0
Fruit juice	85.5	14.5
Fruit drinks	65.2	34.8
Squashes/health drinks	82.9	17.1
Still mineral water	57.7	42.3
Glucose/energy drinks	31.9	68.1
Lemonade	70.5	29.5
Drinking yoghurt	88.7	11.3
Sparkling mineral water	82.3	17.7
Mixers	76.3	23.7

Source(s): ACNielsen Scantrack, 52 weeks ending December 2003.

TOP TEN HOUSEHOLD CATEGORIES, TOTAL COVERAGE

Top ten by market size

	2002 £ million	2003 £ million	% growth
Toilet tissues	870.6	874.8	0.5
Cat food (canned/foil/chub)	508.5	518.4	2.0
Powder detergents	450.8	461.4	2.4
Dog food (canned/foil/chub)	316.3	313.5	−0.9
Kitchen towels	253.5	263.8	4.1
Detergent tablets	250.8	253.4	1.0
Fabric softeners	241.7	242.6	0.4
Liquid detergents	196.4	217.8	10.9
Facial tissues	191.3	186.1	−2.7
Washing up liquid	168.8	170.5	1.0

Share of category by trade channel, 2003

	Grocery multiples (%)	Impulse (%)
Toilet tissues	86.3	13.7
Cat food (canned/foil/chub)	82.7	17.3
Powder detergents	84.7	15.3
Dog food (canned/foil/chub)	79.4	20.6
Kitchen towels	88.3	11.7
Detergent tablets	88.7	11.3
Fabric softeners	88.6	11.4
Liquid detergents	92.3	7.7
Facial tissues	86.0	14.0
Washing up liquid	83.2	16.8

Source(s): ACNielsen Scantrack, 52 weeks ending December 2003.

TOP TEN BAKERY CATEGORIES, TOTAL COVERAGE

Top ten by market size

	2002 £ million	2003 £ million	% growth
Bread sliced/slicing (incl. instore)	1,300.5	1,368.3	5.2
Bread rolls/baps (incl. instore)	354.4	365.0	3.0
Sweet buns/scones/teacakes (incl. instore)	226.2	234.9	3.8
Baguettes/french sticks/pain (incl. instore)	112.1	112.5	0.4
Small whole cakes	205.2	214.0	4.3
Large whole cakes	133.7	138.1	3.3
Flans/tarts/pies short life	97.6	100.1	2.6
Novelty & special occasion cakes	86.5	95.8	10.7
Small fruit pieces	76.0	75.0	−1.3
Individual cake slices	54.6	59.4	8.8

Share of category by trade channel, 2003

	Grocery multiples (%)	Impulse (%)
Bread sliced/slicing (incl. instore)	72.7	27.3
Bread rolls/baps (incl. instore)	80.8	19.2
Sweet buns/scones/teacakes (incl. instore)	84.3	15.7
Baguettes/french sticks/pain (incl. instore)	82.0	18.0
Small whole cakes	72.6	27.4
Large whole cakes	79.4	20.6
Flans/tarts/pies short life	91.6	8.4
Novelty & special occasion cakes	98.9	1.1
Small fruit pieces	80.7	19.3
Individual cake slices	80.6	19.4

Source(s): ACNielsen Scantrack, 52 weeks ending December 2003.

TOP TEN DAIRY/DELI CATEGORIES, TOTAL COVERAGE

Top ten by market size

	2002 £ million	2003 £ million	% growth
Fresh milk	1,934.2	2,062.0	6.6
Prepared sliced meat	1,078.6	1,158.6	7.4
Total yoghurt	751.1	778.7	3.7
Fresh ready meals (meat/fish)	561.5	632.8	12.7
Fresh sandwiches	516.7	577.8	11.8
Packaged salad	514.2	589.0	14.5
Total yellow fats	498.0	483.3	-2.9
Hard cheese fixed weight	495.4	533.2	7.6
Total chilled desserts	431.3	451.1	4.6
Eggs	411.9	441.7	7.2

Share of category by trade channel, 2003

	Grocery multiples (%)	Impulse (%)
Fresh milk	63.2	36.8
Prepared sliced meat	87.0	13.0
Total yoghurt	88.5	11.5
Fresh ready meals (meat/fish)	94.3	5.7
Fresh sandwiches	59.1	40.9
Packaged salad	91.4	8.6
Total yellow fats	83.1	16.9
Hard cheese fixed weight	79.6	20.4
Total chilled desserts	87.9	12.1
Eggs	84.9	15.1

Source(s): ACNielsen Scantrack, 52 weeks ending December 2003.

TOP TEN DRY GROCERY CATEGORIES, TOTAL COVERAGE

Top ten by market size

	2002 £ million	2003 £ million	% growth
Sweet biscuits	1,024.4	1,058.6	3.3
Ready to eat cereals	1,023.8	1,046.0	2.2
Instant coffee	535.4	542.0	1.2
Tea bags	510.1	493.1	−3.3
Canned fish	387.8	383.3	−1.2
Ready to serve soup	326.2	339.3	4.0
Savoury biscuits	255.8	266.6	4.2
Sugar	240.2	249.3	3.8
Pasta sauces	227.5	237.6	4.4
Baked beans	190.1	195.0	2.6

Share of category by trade channel, 2003

	Grocery multiples (%)	Impulse (%)
Sweet biscuits	79.5	20.5
Ready to eat cereals	87.7	12.3
Instant coffee	83.3	16.7
Tea bags	82.3	17.7
Canned fish	89.6	10.4
Ready to serve soup	85.3	14.7
Savoury biscuits	86.4	13.6
Sugar	78.2	21.8
Pasta sauces	89.1	10.9
Baked beans	87.5	12.5

Source(s): ACNielsen Scantrack, 52 weeks ending December 2003.

CATEGORY TRENDS, TOTAL COVERAGE

To end 2003	Sales £million	Growth %	To end 2003	Sales £million	Growth %
Aerosols/pump sprays fresheners	45.7	−1.7	Fresh cream	136.2	5.6
			Fromage frais	177.9	8.2
Aluminium foil	82.6	−1.5	Ground coffee	91.5	4.3
Baked beans	195.0	2.6	Herbs/spices	87.5	2.6
Bin liners	153.4	1.9	Honey	52.6	20.8
Bleach	103.6	−2.8	Hot instant cereals	33.0	12.7
Brown/fruity sauce	41.6	..	Hot oat cereals	30.2	5.4
Butter	338.7	4.2	Instant tea	11.9	−9.1
Canned fruit	139.0	2.9	Jam	84.9	−0.4
Canned pasta	113.9	..	Laundry stain removers	51.0	16.5
Cat food (dry)	120.2	8.1	Marmalade	57.4	−1.9
Cat food (semi moist)	0.2	4.2	Milk puddings (canned)	33.7	−7.5
Chilled desserts	451.1	4.6	Milk/cream canned	36.2	0.0
Cleaning cloths	125.3	9.9	Mustard	25.5	−0.6
Cold meat (canned)	102.6	0.3	Noodles (instant)	40.5	2.4
Cooking oils	99.8	1.6	Olive oil	92.4	6.4
Cottage cheese (fixed weight)	49.1	−1.9	Packet tea excl. instant	23.0	−10.1
			Polishes floor/furniture	29.2	−1.7
Cream UHT	58.9	4.5	Processed cheese (fixed weight)	167.3	5.1
Custard	64.1	−0.2			
Desserts (longlife/RTE)	40.6	5.0	Ready meals– (ambient/m'wave)	0.7	−13.5
Dishwasher products	169.9	10.3			
Dog biscuits	23.3	−1.4	Salt	26.0	−0.9
Dog foods (semi moist)	5.5	−22.7	Savoury rice	42.4	16.5
Dog meals/mixers	144.6	10.7	Scourers (cream/pastes)	18.0	−8.6
Dried fruit	105.9	2.1	Scourers (powders)	1.0	−6.9
Dried rice	143.1	3.4	Shoe polish	14.6	−7.9
Dry casserole mixes	55.0	0.2	Slow release fresheners	166.0	8.2
Dry packet soup	80.7	−5.8	Sweet pickle	62.8	−0.3
Dry pasta	116.3	−0.3	Sweet spreads	14.0	−2.6
Dry pasta in sauce	29.9	6.7	Table jelly	21.2	1.5
Dry ready meals	3.7	−0.9	Tomato ketchup	99.2	4.6
Dry savoury mixes	30.3	−2.1	UHT/longlife milk	166.8	7.9
Fabric softeners	242.6	0.4	Vinegar malt	15.8	0.5
Flour	47.7	−0.6	White fats	15.3	−7.8
Food bags	40.1	5.4	Yellow fats	483.3	−2.9
Food wrapping rolls	24.9	2.8	Yoghurt	778.7	3.7

Note(s): Based on a selection of 70 product categories.
Source(s): ACNielsen Scantrack, 52 weeks ending December 2003.

GROCERY OWN LABEL MARKET SHARES, 2002–2003

	2002	2003	% Change
FOODS: own label market share, %			
Cottage cheese	92.4	92.7	0.4
Fresh cream including substitutes	90.3	91.1	0.8
Non flavoured nuts	90.1	90.1	0.1
Pastes/spreads/pate	79.4	86.0	8.3
Canned apricots	81.8	85.5	4.5
Milk (fresh & UHT)	83.8	85.0	1.4
Eggs	82.3	79.6	-3.4
Canned mandarin/satsumas/oranges	73.3	77.4	5.7
Cooking salt	73.6	75.5	2.7
Lard	76.5	73.8	-3.5
Tomato paste	75.7	71.8	-5.2
Apple sauce	72.3	71.3	-1.4
Chilled pure fruit/vegetable juice	71.0	71.0	0.0
Bacon sliced packaged	69.6	70.6	1.3
Canned tomatoes	76.7	70.2	-8.4
Seafood sauce	74.0	69.2	-6.5
Mint sauces & jellies	67.9	66.5	-2.1
Pepper groud black & white	62.2	61.7	-0.9
Dried rice	65.1	61.3	-5.9
Mixers	58.9	60.7	3.1
Mincemeat	65.3	60.0	-8.1
Peanut butter	54.0	59.1	9.5
Canned processed peas	58.1	57.5	-1.1
Beetroot	59.8	56.1	-6.2
Olive oil	55.2	53.9	-2.3
Hard cheese	52.9	51.5	-2.6
Sugar demerara	53.3	51.1	-4.0
Pickled onions	53.3	50.4	-5.4
Honey	51.3	49.0	-4.5
Chilled desserts	48.7	48.7	0.1
NON-FOODS: own label market share, %			
Greaseproof paper	94.4	93.1	-1.4
Bin liners	90.6	90.1	-0.5
Cotton wool	90.8	88.2	-2.9
Food bags	84.5	85.4	1.1
Aluminium foil	79.1	81.9	3.6
Sun burn products	59.7	77.5	29.7
Cotton wool sticks	75.7	73.1	-3.4
Household fresheners – oil/pot pourri	43.8	72.4	65.3
Cat litter	73.4	70.8	-3.5
Kitchen towels	59.1	64.0	8.3
Bleach	61.2	58.4	-4.6
Long life scouring pads	52.6	54.4	3.4
Household gloves	49.5	47.4	-4.3
Facial tissues	45.9	47.0	2.4
Talcum powder	47.8	45.3	-5.3
Disinfectants liquid	53.8	43.7	-18.9
Toilet tissues	41.4	41.9	1.2
Cleaning coths (incl. moist household)	35.5	33.9	-4.5
Coffee filters/papers/bags	39.6	27.8	-29.7
Moist cleansing tissues	32.3	27.8	-13.9

Source(s): ACNielsen Homescan, 52 weeks ending December 2003.

OWN LABEL MARKET SHARE BY GROCERY MARKET

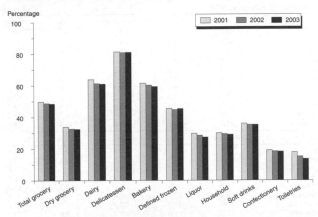

Source(s): ACNielsen Homescan, 52 weeks ending December 2003.

BUDGET BRANDS

Share of expenditure within defined product categories (%)

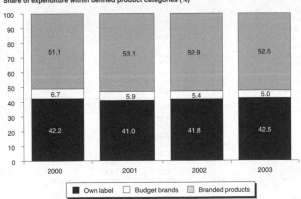

Source(s): ACNielsen Homescan, 12 weeks ending December 2003.

OWN LABEL VALUE SHARES

Value share by category, 2003

Percentage

	Dry Grocery	Dairy	Delicatessen	Frozen	Bakery
Asda	37.6	63.5	83.7	57.3	59.4
Co-op	28.9	62.6	68.9	29.4	44.7
Iceland	15.0	41.1	67.5	61.1	24.1
Kwik Save	8.4	30.2	47.0	16.0	21.8
Morrisons	25.2	56.8	80.9	23.8	71.6
Safeway	22.6	53.6	69.2	34.6	56.3
Sainsbury's	36.5	58.5	82.7	44.0	61.1
Somerfield	20.0	54.2	74.2	34.4	43.6
Tesco	33.6	57.3	85.6	49.1	63.4
Waitrose	32.2	55.0	81.4	48.0	66.5
All stores	**32.4**	**60.9**	**81.0**	**45.4**	**59.3**

	Confectionery	Liquor	Household	Toiletries	Soft drinks
Asda	22.9	32.2	38.9	22.1	42.3
Co-op	14.3	32.0	27.6	15.1	31.9
Iceland	8.5	0.0	8.4	. .	7.6
Kwik Save	2.0	9.8	9.9	1.8	16.9
Morrisons	11.4	11.3	23.6	8.8	28.1
Safeway	8.8	20.7	24.4	11.0	21.9
Sainsbury's	20.0	31.3	30.4	12.5	37.9
Somerfield	5.6	21.8	19.7	5.8	23.1
Tesco	22.5	30.6	32.1	17.6	41.5
Waitrose	19.2	25.3	28.0	7.0	28.9
All Stores	**18.2**	**27.3**	**29.0**	**13.6**	**35.2**

Value growth by category, 2003

Percentage

	Dry Grocery	Dairy	Delicatessen	Frozen	Bakery
Asda	8.6	11.1	11.9	13.0	11.0
Co-op	−4.6	5.8	3.9	−13.4	−2.0
Iceland	0.6	29.0	3.2	5.3	−15.7
Kwik Save	273.5	380.9	36.9	73.9	209.6
Morrisons	−5.1	8.0	2.6	−15.9	−2.5
Safeway	−8.7	−6.2	2.8	−4.1	−6.2
Sainsbury's	−7.7	−4.6	−0.2	−10.4	−5.3
Somerfield[1]	−4.0	1.7	3.7	−17.5	8.4
Tesco	4.6	7.9	13.1	10.1	1.0
Waitrose	3.9	13.1	10.3	−8.0	−2.5
All stores	**1.6**	**2.7**	**7.1**	**2.2**	**0.6**

	Confectionery	Liquor	Household	Toiletries	Soft drinks
Asda	0.1	21.5	8.5	3.1	17.1
Co-op	−10.6	−0.4	3.7	3.8	18.1
Iceland	−11.9	−100.0	9.7	0.0	−7.8
Kwik Save	185.5	5.5	183.2	20.1	698.0
Morrisons	6.5	−9.3	−0.8	−9.5	−0.1
Safeway	−14.2	−14.7	−3.8	−1.1	−10.0
Sainsbury's	−10.1	0.2	−10.8	−10.0	−0.9
Somerfield[1]	−33.8	−25.5	−8.3	−21.6	−1.4
Tesco	10.5	−0.2	3.4	1.1	14.0
Waitrose	2.0	22.1	10.6	3.0	−5.7
All stores	**0.9**	**2.3**	**1.5**	**−4.3**	**10.5**

Note(s): [1] Growth increase due to a change in stocking patterns of Somerfield Own Label.
Source(s): ACNielsen Homescan, 52 weeks ending December 2003.

THE OFF-LICENCE TRADE, GB 2004

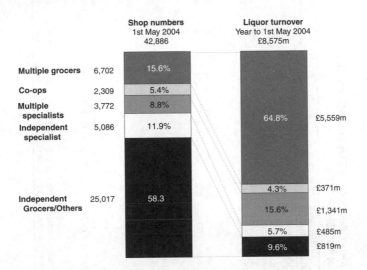

		Shop numbers 1st May 2004 42,886	Liquor turnover Year to 1st May 2004 £8,575m
Multiple grocers	6,702	15.6%	
Co-ops	2,309	5.4%	
Multiple specialists	3,772	8.8%	
Independent specialist	5,086	11.9%	64.8% £5,559m
Independent Grocers/Others	25,017	58.3	4.3% £371m
			15.6% £1,341m
			5.7% £485m
			9.6% £819m

DEFINITIONS

Off-licence — An outlet authorised to sell alcoholic drink for consumption off the premises only, excluding those limited to sales of medicinal wine and those where the major business is wholesale/cash and carry.

Specialist off-licence — An off-licence with 50% or more of its all commodity turnover in alcoholic drink. This must be 80% or more if the balance is in groceries. (Big two specialists are Thresher and Victoria Wine. Other Multiples are free trade and other brewery managed outlets).

Grocer/other off-licences — An off-licence with 20% or more of its all commodity turnover in groceries, or in any other single commodity, with no greater proportion in any other commodity unless it be alcoholic drink. (Multiple grocers normally belong to an organisation with ten or more branches of which five or more have licences).

Source(s): ACNielsen, year to May 2004.

OFF-LICENCES (GB): NUMBERS AND TURNOVER, YEAR ENDING MAY 2004 BY REGION AND SHOP TYPE

	TOTAL GB	London	Meridian	Harlech & Westward	Central	Anglia	Granada[1]	Yorkshire	Tyne Tees	Scotland
GROCERS										
Multiples										
No. of shops	6,702	1,135	838	812	988	547	762	614	356	650
Turnover £m	5,559.0	992.7	590.1	658.2	799.7	464.9	716.4	512.9	270.0	553.9
Co-ops										
No. of shops	2,309	154	187	246	381	240	382	348	105	266
Turnover £m	371.4	23.7	30.9	49.4	67.2	40.1	41.5	44.8	17.6	56.2
Independents										
No. of shops	25,017	3,209	2,041	3,625	3,175	2,163	2,875	3,070	2,063	2,796
Turnover £m	819.0	58.2	48.7	152.2	92.0	71.1	90.9	101.0	36.4	168.6
SPECIALISTS										
Multiple specialists										
No. of shops	3,772	955	441	263	421	209	621	257	200	405
Turnover £m	1,341.1	387.7	154.4	87.6	132.9	69.9	202.2	85.0	52.7	168.7
Independent specialists										
No. of shops	5,086	1,427	298	308	805	177	890	587	173	421
Turnover £m	484.8	169.5	36.1	17.0	55.0	16.3	64.7	34.1	9.4	82.7

Note(s): [1] Includes part Border TV in England.
Source(s): ACNielsen.

TURNOVER AND AVERAGE WEEKLY SALES PER SHOP

	Turnover £ million	Ave. weekly sales per shop, £
Total GB	**8,575**	**3,845**
2004 by ACNielsen Liquor Region		
London	1,632	4,561
TUS	860	4,348
Harwest & Westwood	964	3,530
Central	1,147	3,822
Anglia	662	3,818
Granada	1,116	3,880
Yorkshire	778	3,068
Tyne Tees	386	2,563
Scotland	1,030	4,365
2004 by type of off-licence		
Grocers		
Multiples	5,559	15,951
Co-ops	371	3,093
Independents	819	630
Specialists		
Multiples	1,341	6,837
Independents	485	1,833

Source(s): ACNielsen Statistics, year ending May 2004.

TOP TEN OFF LICENCE MARKETS, 2002–2003

	2002 £ million	2003 £ million	% growth 2002–03
Top ten by Market Size			
Light wine	3,383.1	3,560.1	5.2
Lager	2,372.2	2,502.4	5.5
Scotch whisky	807.1	786.1	–2.6
Vodka	513.2	543.5	5.9
Ale	453.0	446.9	–1.3
Fabs	353.6	339.1	–4.1
Cider	340.4	329.9	–3.1
Gin	240.2	250.0	4.4
Champagne	234.0	247.4	5.8
Sparkling wine	164.3	178.0	8.3
Top ten by market growth			
Non-french grape brandy	8.6	10.7	24.6
Golden rum	9.9	11.5	16.5
Imported whisky	80.9	89.9	11.1
Speciality drinks	95.8	104.1	8.6
Sparkling wine	164.3	178.0	8.3
Vodka	513.2	543.5	5.9
Champagne	234.0	247.4	5.8
Lager	2,372.2	2,502.4	5.5
Cream liqueurs	126.7	133.5	5.4
Light wine	3,383.1	3,560.1	5.2

Note(s): [1] FAB = Flavoured Alcoholic Beverage.
Source(s): ACNielsen Scantrack.

OTHER TRADE STATISTICS

SIZE OF THE CLOTHING MARKET, 2000–2004

Expenditure, £m

	2000	2001	2002	2003	2004
Women's clothing[1]	12,008	12,360	13,237	13,454	13,660
Men's clothing[1]	6,644	6,770	7,172	7,189	7,334
Children's clothing[1]	3,232	3,269	3,531	3,583	3,677
Women's footwear	2,109	2,188	2,373	2,391	2,446
Men's footwear	1,600	1,612	1,750	1,795	1,831
Children's footwear	723	702	776	800	814
Total	**26,316**	**26,901**	**28,839**	**29,212**	**29,762**

Note(s): [1] Includes accessories.
Source(s): 'FashionTrak', Taylor Nelson Sofres, 52 weeks ending July.

SHARE OF CLOTHING EXPENDITURE BY OUTLET TYPE

Percentage

	2000	2001	2002	2003	2004
Clothing multiples	24.4	24.7	23.8	24.7	25.8
Clothing independents	10.0	9.7	9.2	8.1	8.8
Footwear multiples	4.6	4.6	4.8	4.9	4.5
Footwear independents	1.8	1.7	1.7	1.6	1.7
General stores	17.1	15.3	15.6	15.7	15.1
Department stores	8.9	9.0	8.4	8.3	8.2
Mail order	8.5	8.6	8.1	7.3	6.5
Discounters/cash & carry	7.4	9.0	9.4	10.1	9.8
Sports shops	9.2	9.5	10.5	10.4	10.4
Supermarkets	3.6	3.7	4.1	4.7	5.5
Other outlets	4.7	4.3	4.5	4.3	3.7
Total market	**100.0**	**100.0**	**100.0**	**100.0**	**100.0**

Source(s): 'FashionTrak', Taylor Nelson Sofres, 52 weeks ending July.

SIZE OF THE CLOTHING MARKET BY AGE, 2000–2004

Expenditure, £m

	2000	2001	2002	2003	2004
Under 25	4,451	4,432	4,521	4,683	4,859
25–34	5,157	5,296	5,772	5,451	5,313
35–44	5,610	5,802	6,563	6,833	7,025
45–54	4,846	5,057	5,532	5,496	5,704
55–64	3,462	3,421	3,439	3,609	3,805
65–74	2,789	2,892	3,013	3,139	3,057
Total	**26,316**	**26,901**	**28,839**	**29,212**	**29,762**

Source(s): 'FashionTrak', Taylor Nelson Sofres, 52 weeks ending July.

CLOTHING SPEND[1] BY DRESS SIZE[2], 2000–2004

Percentage

	2000	2001	2002	2003	2004
10 or under	16.5	18.8	19.2	18.4	19.7
12	25.3	26.2	24.6	24.8	25.6
14	23.2	20.8	22.3	22.5	21.2
16	17.1	16.3	15.3	16.3	15.8
18	9.9	9.7	9.9	9.6	9.1
20	4.7	4.9	5.2	4.7	4.7
22+	3.3	3.4	3.5	3.7	3.9
TOTAL	**100.0**	**100.0**	**100.0**	**100.0**	**100.0**

Note(s):   [1] Women's clothing and accessories bought for self.   [2] Dress size of purchaser.
Source(s):   'FashionTrak', Taylor Nelson Sofres, 52 weeks ending July.

SPEND DISTRIBUTION BY GENDER

Percentage

	2000	2001	2002	2003	2004
Women's clothing & accessories					
Female	87.0	88.5	89.8	90.7	90.7
Male	13.0	11.5	10.2	9.3	9.3
Total	100.0	100.0	100.0	100.0	100.0
Men's clothing & accessories					
Female	28.3	28.5	27.6	25.5	24.3
Male	71.7	71.5	72.4	74.5	75.7
Total	100.0	100.0	100.0	100.0	100.0

Source(s):   'FashionTrak', Taylor Nelson Sofres, 52 weeks ending July.

SELECTED CLOTHING ITEMS BOUGHT IN PAST YEAR

Percentage

	None	<£50	£50–£74	£75–£99	£100+
Womenswear					
Skirts	70.0	21.8	4.8	2.0	1.4
Blouses/tops	54.7	28.1	9.3	4.1	3.8
Cardigans & jumpers	62.5	24.3	7.3	3.4	2.5
Trousers	34.8	41.6	13.8	4.9	4.8
Sports clothing	62.5	21.8	7.5	3.6	4.7
Boots	76.3	12.6	5.9	2.9	2.3
Children's wear					
Clothing	30.9	6.9	4.3	3.0	6.7
Shoes	35.3	6.4	4.0	2.3	3.7

	None	<£20	£20–49	£50–74	£75+
Menswear					
Shirts	51.6	23.0	15.4	6.3	3.8
Jumpers & pullovers	64.2	16.7	12.0	4.5	2.5

Source(s):   Target Group Index © BMRB 2003 (April 2003 – March 2004).

TOP UK PHARMACEUTICAL CORPORATIONS, 2003

Rank	Corporation	Primary care[1] sales (£m)	Primary care[1] market share (%)	Hospital sales (£m)	Hospital market share (%)	Total market sales (£m)	Total market share (%)
1	Pfizer	1,151	13.2	132	5.3	1,282	11.4
2	GlaxoSmithKline	885	10.2	204	8.2	1,089	9.7
3	Astrazeneca	499	5.7	77	3.1	576	5.1
4	Wyeth	482	5.5	80	3.2	562	5.0
5	Merck & Co	507	5.8	32	1.3	539	4.8
6	Novartis	325	3.7	134	5.4	459	4.1
7	Aventis	326	3.7	119	4.8	446	4.0
8	Sanofi Synthela	299	3.4	40	1.6	340	3.0
9	Roche	194	2.2	145	5.8	339	3.0
10	Lilly	225	2.6	77	3.1	303	2.7
11	Johnson & Johnson	198	2.3	57	2.3	255	2.3
12	Bristol-Myers Squibb	174	2.0	77	3.1	251	2.2
13	Boehringer Inge	134	1.5	45	1.8	179	1.6
14	Novo Nordisk	138	1.6	17	0.7	155	1.4
15	Abbott	83	1.0	67	2.7	150	1.3
16	Schering Plough	70	0.8	71	2.8	141	1.3
17	Bayer	84	1.0	41	1.7	126	1.1
18	Schering Ag	56	0.6	41	1.7	97	0.9
19	Ivax	83	1.0	8	0.3	91	0.8
20	Eisai	71	0.8	10	0.4	82	0.7

Note(s): [1] Primary care sales are prescription and OTC medicines not dispensed in hospitals.
Source(s): Association of the British Pharmaceutical Industry.

TOP UK PHARMACEUTICAL PRODUCTS, 2002

Rank	Product	Manufacturer	Date of marketing authorisation	Primary sector[1] sales (£m)	Hospital sales (£m)	Total sales (£m)
1	Lipitor	Pfizer	Jan-97	317.71	6.95	324.66
2	Zoton	Wyeth	Apr-94	249.06	21.83	270.89
3	Simvastatin	Generic	May-03	198.95	1.07	200.02
4	Istin	Pfizer	Jan-90	188.57	4.31	192.88
5	Zocor	MSD	May-89	177.02	9.54	186.56
6	Seretide	GSK	Mar-99	158.90	6.15	165.05
7	Zyprexa	Lilly	Oct-96	119.21	28.31	147.52
8	Tritace	Aventis	Mar-90	137.20	4.65	141.85
9	Lipostat	BMS	Sep-90	124.90	3.59	128.49
10	Efexor	Wyeth	Jan-95	120.38	6.59	126.96
11	Plavix	BMS/Sanofi	Jul-98	102.67	10.60	113.27
12	Omeprazole	Generic	Apr-02	102.51	5.15	107.66
13	Serevent	GSK	Dec-90	100.43	2.97	103.40
14	Losec	AZ	Jun-89	92.92	8.27	101.19
15	Lisinopril	Generic	Oct-02	86.81	1.13	87.93
16	Fosamax	MSD	Sep-95	76.03	3.20	79.22
17	Cardura	Pfizer	Jan-89	77.78	1.28	79.05
18	Zoladex	AZ	Mar-87	65.76	12.42	78.19
19	Vioxx	MSD	May-99	74.91	2.78	77.69
20	Cozaar	MSD	Feb-95	74.34	1.44	75.78

Note(s): [1] Primary care sales are prescription and OTC medicines not dispensed in hospitals.
Source(s): Association of the British Pharmaceutical Industry.

ESTIMATED VALUE OF SOME PHARMACEUTICAL MARKETS, 2003

	Value, £m		Value, £m
Cough/cold/sore throat (total)	376	Paediatric analgesics	56
Cold/flu decongestants	185	Topical analgesics	48
Cough liquids	98	Oral lesions & toothache	26
Medicated confectionery	92	Skin treatments (total)	353
Eye care treatment	38	Anti-fungals	61
Gastro-intestinal	236	Anti-haemorrhoids	20
Anti-diarrhoeals	39	Antiseptic liquids	19
Indigestion remedies	115	Antiseptic creams	23
Irritable bowel syndrome	5	Cold sore treatments	25
Laxatives	47	Dry skin treatment	62
Stomach upset remedies	23	Insect bite/antiseptic sprays	12
Anti-allergy (hayfever)	79	Medicated skincare	85
Medicated mouthwash/sprays	23	Sleeping aids	28
Pain relief (total)	465	Smoking cessation	78
Adult oral analgesics	336	Vitamins & minerals (total)	296

Note(s): In view of the well-known difficulties of estimating market values, readers are advised to regard the figures as orders of magnitude only.
Source(s): PAGB; other trade bodies and research institutions.

MULTIPLE PHARMACY OUTLETS, 2003

	No. of outlets
Lloyds Pharmacy	1,349
Boots	1,150
Vantage Pharmacy	916
Moss Pharmacy	796
Co-op Pharmacy	429
L. Rowland & Co. (Various Fascia)	311
Cohens Chemist	115
Tims & Parker	78
Paydens (Various Fascia)	64
Bairds Chemists (Various Fascia)	49
Selles Dispensing Chemists	43
Manor Pharmacy	41

Source(s): Retail Locations.

PURCHASING OF ELECTRONIC EQUIPMENT: TVs

Working TVs per household

	%
None	2.5
1	18.5
2	33.6
3+	45.4

TV obtained

	Main set (%)	Second set (%)	Third set (%)
Within 12 months	20.7	8.8	6.0
1–2 years ago	24.4	16.8	8.2
Longer ago	49.2	49.6	29.2

Cost of TV set bought in last 12 months

<£250	4.0	5.6	4.3
£250–£499	5.7	1.1	0.5
£500–£749	3.4	0.4	0.1
£750–£999	2.3	0.1	0.1
£1,000+	2.2	0.1	. .

Most important factors when buying a TV set

	Most important (%)	Second most important (%)
Advertising	1.1	4.1
Company image	4.8	4.9
Features (eg. Nicam Stereo)	22.3	11.4
Personal experience	9.6	4.7
Personal recommendation	5.8	5.2
Price	36.3	22.3
Recommended by magazine/media	2.2	5.0
Reliability	27.0	16.3
Special offer	7.8	9.2

Source(s): Target Group Index © BMRB 2004 (April 2003 – March 2004).

VCRs & DVD PLAYERS

Working VCRs/DVD players per household

	%
Video recorder	91.8
DVD player	51.8
Neither	5.1

VCR/DVD player obtained

	VCR (%)	DVD player (%)
Within 12 months	14.1	27.5
1–2 years ago	22.0	16.6
Longer ago	52.0	6.4

Cost of VCR/DVD player

<£150	6.9	13.5
£150–£249	4.0	7.3
£250–£499	1.6	3.3
£500+	0.3	0.9

Source(s): Target Group Index © BMRB 2004 (April 2003 – March 2004).

COMPUTER SYSTEMS

	Own	Percentage Bought in last 12 months
Game Boy	6.6	0.7
Game Boy Advance	6.4	3.0
Nintendo GameCube	2.1	1.1
Nintendo 64	3.1	0.1
Sega Dreamcast	1.2	. .
Sony Playstation	11.4	1.3
Sony Playstation 2	14.7	6.7
Xbox	3.3	1.9
Others	5.1	1.3

Expenditure on computer systems and games

	Systems	Games
<£50	0.9	7.0
£50–£99	1.5	7.5
£100–£199	4.7	5.7
£200–£299	3.3	1.5
£300+	7.0	1.4

Source(s): Target Group Index © BMRB 2004 (April 2003 – March 2004).

AUDIO EQUIPMENT

Percentage

	Have/Own	Bought new in last 12 months	Bought for self	Bought for someone else
Midi system – pro-logic	13.7	3.1	1.3	0.4
Other midi systems	19.0	2.1	0.9	0.3
Mini system	14.6	2.8	1.0	0.5
Micro system	4.1	1.5	0.7	0.3
Mini disc player	8.9	2.4	0.9	0.6
CD player	19.0	2.8	1.1	0.5
Separate Hi-fi items	19.9	2.1	1.1	0.2
Electronic keyboard	7.7	0.9	0.3	0.3

Expenditure	<£150	£150–£299	£300–£499	£500–£699	£700+
Midi system – pro-logic	0.8	1.2	0.6	0.3	0.1
Other midi systems	1.1	0.5	0.2	0.1	..
Mini system	1.6	0.8	0.2	..	..
Micro system	0.9	0.4	..	..	..
Mini disc player	1.2	0.7	0.1	..	..
CD player	1.7	0.5	0.1	..	..
Separate Hi-fi items	0.5	0.5	0.4	0.2	0.3
Electronic keyboard	0.4	0.3	0.1	..	..

	Own	Bought new in last 12 months	Bought for self	Bought for someone else
Personal CD player	24.5	5.3	1.8	1.8
Personal cassette/radio cassette	12.3	1.0	0.3	0.3
Personal CD radio cass. recorder	17.3	3.0	1.3	0.7
Portable radio cassette recorder	5.9	0.4	0.1	0.1
Portable radio or cassette recorder	6.1	0.7	0.2	0.2
Portable mini disc player	3.7	0.9	0.4	0.2
MP3 player	2.5	1.1	0.5	0.2

Expenditure	<£25	£25–£49	£50–£99	£100–£199	£200+
Personal CD player	1.4	1.8	1.4	0.3	..
Personal cassette or radio cassette	0.5	0.2	0.2	0.1	..
Portable CD radio cassette recorder	0.8	1.1	0.7	0.2	..
Portable radio cass. recorder	0.1	0.1	0.1	..	..
Portable radio or cassette recorder	0.3	0.2	0.2	..	..
Port. mini disc player	0.1	0.1	0.1	0.3	0.1
MP3 player	0.2	0.2	0.2	0.2	0.1

Source(s): Target Group Index © BMRB 2004 (April 2003 – March 2004).

NEW TECHNOLOGY

Per household

	%
Recordable CD player	9.4
Web cam	6.6
Home cinema	6.4
DAB digital radio (for digital audio broadcasting)	2.7
Plasma screen	1.0

Source(s): Target Group Index © BMRB 2004 (April 2003 – March 2004).

THE BRITISH SHOPPER

DEMOGRAPHIC ANALYSIS OF MAIN SHOPPER BY RETAILER

Base (GB): All households = 100

	Aldi	Asda	Co-op	Iceland	Kwik Save	M&S
Social grade						
AB	79	90	84	71	66	117
C1	86	105	97	98	79	113
C2	112	104	110	107	111	85
D	127	109	113	117	135	79
E	112	90	101	121	138	93
Size of Household						
1	90	81	103	82	95	112
2	100	99	105	95	95	114
3–4	104	115	92	118	108	80
5+	125	122	101	129	114	59
Age						
16–34	94	113	98	105	92	75
35–44	97	111	90	110	99	93
45–64	110	97	102	97	104	104
65+	101	76	108	94	103	129
Working						
Not working	110	93	104	105	112	108
Full Time	83	103	94	86	83	97
Part Time	112	109	104	116	108	88

	Morrisons	Netto	Safeway	Sainsbury's	Somerfield	Tesco	Waitrose
Social grade							
AB	86	61	105	114	92	103	158
C1	98	78	103	112	96	103	106
C2	111	119	96	89	103	100	74
D	114	135	98	88	110	99	68
E	94	137	95	83	104	89	71
Size of Household							
1	86	73	92	98	90	93	94
2	101	99	105	104	105	102	120
3–4	108	117	101	96	102	103	92
5+	121	149	104	102	110	105	59
Age							
16–34	122	137	100	96	89	106	75
35–44	100	105	104	104	100	106	90
45–64	96	96	102	99	104	98	113
65+	87	82	98	97	107	90	115
Working							
Not working	97	105	98	95	106	95	102
Full Time	99	80	99	107	91	104	100
Part Time	108	126	106	98	105	103	97

Note(s): **Main Shopper**: Spends the largest proportion of grocery budget at given store.
Source(s): ACNielsen Homescan, 52 weeks ending December 2003.

LIFESTAGE COMPARISONS OF MAIN
SHOPPER BY RETAILER

Base (GB): All households = 100

	Pre-Family	New Family	Maturing Family	Established Family	Post Family	Older Couples	Older Singles
Aldi	63	105	112	102	98	114	98
Asda	105	125	120	115	95	93	72
Co-op	95	92	95	94	100	111	101
Kwik Save	70	106	106	112	99	109	97
Iceland	84	119	119	128	86	99	86
M&S	90	72	71	76	109	123	121
Morrisons	106	124	104	108	96	104	77
Netto	90	156	111	121	85	104	70
Safeway	98	97	104	100	105	103	91
Sainsbury's	111	98	98	95	101	101	95
Somerfield	84	102	93	112	96	114	97
Tesco	110	110	104	100	103	97	85
Waitrose	90	100	70	90	107	125	101

Note(s): **Main Shopper**: Spends the largest proportion of grocery budget at given store within a specified period.
Source(s): ACNielsen Homescan (52 weeks ending December 2003).

HOUSEHOLD PENETRATION BY RETAILER

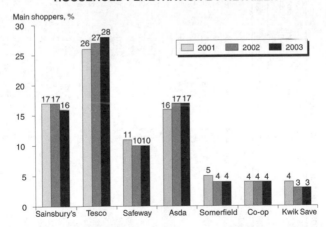

Note(s): **Main Shopper**: Spends the largest proportion of grocery budget at given store within a specified period. **Household penetration**: % of total households who shop at a store, at least once, within a given period.
Source(s): ACNielsen Homescan (52 weeks ending December 2003).

GROCERY PURCHASING PROFILES

ALL MAJOR SUPERMARKETS: All Shoppers

	Total GB H'holds (%)	H'holds Buying Brand (%)	Penetration (%)	Brand Expenditure £'000s (%)	Market Share (%)	Purchase Occasion per Buyer (No.)	Average Spend, £ (in retailer) per Buyer	Average Spend, £ (all sources) per Buyer	Loyalty to Retailer (%)
TOTAL PANEL	24,593,997	24,592,152	100.0	48,112,704	88.0	98.9	1,956.4	2,222.5	88.0
Social grade									
AB	22.3	22.3	100.0	23.7	88.1	91.9	2,077.2	2,358.5	88.1
C1	27.6	27.6	100.0	27.4	88.3	93.7	1,947.6	2,205.4	88.3
C2	19.3	19.3	100.0	21.5	89.4	99.0	2,176.9	2,434.2	89.4
D	17.4	17.4	100.0	17.5	87.9	108.4	1,968.8	2,238.6	87.9
E	13.4	13.4	99.9	9.9	84.4	108.6	1,439.9	1,705.8	84.4
Size of household									
1 member	28.8	28.8	100.0	16.5	85.8	89.7	1,123.5	1,309.0	85.8
2 members	34.9	34.9	100.0	36.0	86.5	103.0	2,017.3	2,330.8	86.6
3-4 members	29.7	29.7	100.0	37.1	90.1	99.7	2,449.4	2,718.0	90.1
5+ members	6.7	6.7	100.0	10.4	89.6	113.6	3,042.3	3,397.1	89.6
Age									
16-34	24.9	24.9	100.0	22.1	90.3	78.8	1,734.3	1,920.8	90.3
35-44	20.4	20.4	100.0	23.9	89.7	96.8	2,290.6	2,553.2	89.7
45-64	31.1	31.1	100.0	34.8	87.2	108.4	2,194.9	2,516.0	87.2
65+	23.6	23.6	100.0	19.1	84.9	109.4	1,587.7	1,868.5	85.0
Housewives' working status									
Not working	41.6	41.6	100.0	39.2	85.7	110.1	1,842.7	2,150.3	85.7
Full time	38.0	38.0	100.0	37.3	89.5	83.8	1,917.4	2,141.8	89.5
Part time	20.4	20.4	100.0	23.6	89.7	104.2	2,261.3	2,520.4	89.7

Presence of children									
Yes	29.8	29.8	100.0	37.0	90.2	98.0	2,427.9	2,690.5	90.2
No	70.2	70.2	100.0	63.0	86.8	99.3	1,756.2	2,023.8	86.8
Age of children									
0–4	12.0	12.0	100.0	14.5	89.1	95.2	2,356.2	2,643.6	89.1
5–10	15.4	15.4	100.0	19.5	90.7	97.1	2,471.8	2,725.4	90.7
11–15	13.5	13.5	100.0	18.4	90.5	104.6	2,659.3	2,937.2	90.5
Lifestage									
Pre-family	12.0	12.0	100.0	8.6	90.3	69.4	1,399.1	1,548.6	90.3
New family	7.9	7.9	100.0	8.5	89.1	90.7	2,099.8	2,355.4	89.1
Maturing families	14.4	14.4	100.0	18.6	90.6	97.3	2,519.3	2,780.2	90.6
Established families	9.7	9.7	100.0	13.1	90.7	106.4	2,637.4	2,907.8	90.7
Post families	19.0	19.0	100.0	18.3	86.5	95.4	1,878.0	2,170.0	86.5
Older couples	20.3	20.3	100.0	23.3	86.0	120.7	2,242.4	2,607.2	86.0
Older singles	16.6	16.6	100.0	9.7	84.7	98.3	1,142.5	1,349.1	84.7
Region									
London	19.3	19.4	100.0	20.3	87.5	93.3	2,055.1	2,347.7	87.5
South & South East	9.4	9.4	100.0	10.2	90.5	93.9	2,119.6	2,342.8	90.5
East of England	6.9	6.9	100.0	7.1	90.3	86.1	2,029.6	2,248.0	90.3
Central	15.8	15.8	100.0	16.1	88.2	101.8	1,986.7	2,253.3	88.2
South West	3.2	3.2	100.0	3.5	88.5	103.4	2,128.2	2,404.6	88.5
Wales & West	7.5	7.5	100.0	7.4	91.2	98.4	1,909.3	2,094.5	91.2
Yorkshire	10.5	10.5	100.0	9.8	87.4	98.1	1,841.4	2,106.5	87.4
North East	4.9	4.9	100.0	4.2	85.1	107.6	1,668.9	1,961.5	85.1
Lancashire/Borders	13.8	13.8	99.9	12.8	85.7	101.4	1,812.3	2,113.9	85.7
Central & North Scotland	8.6	8.6	100.0	8.6	87.2	112.6	1,956.0	2,242.5	87.2

Source(s): ACNielsen Homescan (52 weeks ending December 2003).

GROCERY PURCHASING PROFILES (Cont.)

TESCO: Main Shoppers

	Total GB H'holds (%)	H'holds Buying Brand (%)	Pene-tration (%)	Brand Expenditure £'000s (%)	Market Share (%)	Purchase Occasion per Buyer (No.)	Average Spend, £ (in retailer) per Buyer	Average Spend, £ (all sources) per Buyer	Loyalty to Retailer (%)
TOTAL PANEL	24,593,997	6,821,987	27.7	10,319,454	18.9	53.1	1,512.7	2,273.2	66.5
Social grade									
AB	22.3	22.9	28.4	22.9	18.2	54.3	1,511.1	2,267.6	66.6
C1	27.6	29.1	29.3	29.7	20.5	52.6	1,542.4	2,323.7	66.4
C2	19.3	21.0	30.1	23.5	21.0	52.2	1,694.2	2,498.9	67.8
D	17.4	16.9	27.0	16.4	17.7	51.8	1,466.7	2,176.3	67.4
E	13.4	10.1	20.8	7.5	13.8	55.4	1,130.0	1,832.7	61.7
Size of household									
1 member	28.8	26.2	25.2	15.0	16.7	51.7	865.2	1,312.7	65.9
2 members	34.9	36.2	28.8	36.1	18.6	54.3	1,507.3	2,331.8	64.6
3–4 members	29.7	31.2	29.2	39.6	20.6	53.5	1,917.3	2,780.1	69.0
5+ members	6.7	6.4	26.6	9.4	17.4	49.6	2,222.8	3,405.1	65.3
Age									
16–34	24.9	29.0	32.3	25.4	22.2	42.0	1,323.4	1,982.7	66.7
35–44	20.4	21.8	29.6	24.6	19.8	53.2	1,706.0	2,498.5	68.3
45–64	31.1	29.2	26.1	33.0	17.7	58.1	1,708.7	2,604.2	65.6
65+	23.6	20.0	23.5	17.0	16.2	61.6	1,289.5	1,964.3	65.6
Housewives' working status									
Not working	41.6	37.2	24.8	35.3	16.5	57.2	1,432.5	2,225.4	64.4
Full time	38.0	41.2	30.1	39.8	20.5	49.4	1,460.6	2,135.8	68.4
Part time	20.4	21.5	29.3	24.9	20.4	52.8	1,751.0	2,618.5	66.9

Presence of children									
Yes	29.8	32.3	30.1	39.9	20.9	49.7	1,867.2	2,750.2	67.9
No	70.2	67.7	26.8	60.1	17.8	54.7	1,343.6	2,045.7	65.7
Age of children									
0–4	12.0	13.0	30.1	15.4	20.4	47.5	1,790.2	2,713.9	66.0
5–10	15.4	16.5	29.6	20.9	20.9	48.6	1,919.6	2,822.5	68.0
11–15	13.5	13.6	27.8	18.0	19.0	51.7	2,008.0	2,950.6	68.1
Lifestage									
Pre-family	12.0	15.1	35.0	10.9	24.7	41.4	1,092.3	1,626.0	67.2
New family	7.9	9.3	32.4	10.2	22.8	48.2	1,659.8	2,473.3	67.1
Maturing families	14.4	15.1	29.0	19.4	20.3	49.5	1,942.9	2,863.3	67.9
Established families	9.7	9.5	27.1	12.3	18.4	53.8	1,969.6	2,851.1	69.1
Post families	19.0	18.5	27.1	17.3	17.6	53.2	1,414.3	2,156.9	65.6
Older couples	20.3	18.9	25.7	21.8	17.3	65.5	1,749.1	2,700.9	64.8
Older singles	16.6	13.6	22.8	8.0	15.0	55.4	890.8	1,364.6	65.3
Region									
London	19.3	22.0	31.5	23.8	22.0	51.2	1,638.6	2,417.0	67.8
South & South East	9.4	12.5	36.8	12.5	23.6	50.0	1,504.6	2,238.8	67.2
East of England	6.9	9.9	40.2	9.2	25.0	47.2	1,399.4	2,013.6	69.5
Central	15.8	14.1	24.8	13.8	16.3	53.3	1,477.4	2,311.8	63.9
South West	3.2	3.6	31.1	4.1	22.7	59.5	1,759.9	2,580.6	68.2
Wales & West	7.5	8.8	32.5	8.7	23.2	54.3	1,496.5	2,241.9	66.8
Yorkshire	10.5	6.9	18.3	7.0	13.2	52.4	1,528.2	2,234.3	68.4
North East	4.9	2.8	15.6	2.3	10.0	49.3	1,261.1	2,250.2	56.0
Lancashire/Borders	13.8	10.7	21.5	10.3	14.7	54.6	1,448.1	2,235.8	64.8
Central & North Scotland	8.6	8.7	28.1	8.4	18.3	64.4	1,456.0	2,183.8	66.7

Source(s): ACNielsen Homescan (52 weeks ending December 2003).

GROCERY PURCHASING PROFILES (Cont.)

SAINSBURY's: Main Shoppers

	Total GB H'holds (%)	H'holds Buying Brand (%)	Penetration (%)	Brand Expenditure £'000s (%)	Market Share (%)	Purchase Occasion per Buyer (No.)	Average Spend, £ (in retailer) per Buyer	Average Spend, £ (all sources) per Buyer	Loyalty to Retailer (%)
TOTAL PANEL	24,593,997	3,898,115	15.8	6,257.8267	11.4	50.4	1,605.3	2,454.9	65.4
Social grade									
AB	22.3	30.4	21.6	30.6	14.8	49.6	1,617.9	2,430.8	66.6
C1	27.6	31.2	17.9	32.4	13.6	48.1	1,667.0	2,457.8	67.8
C2	19.3	16.2	13.3	17.4	9.4	48.9	1,724.5	2,646.3	65.2
D	17.4	12.5	11.3	12.3	8.0	53.9	1,580.4	2,631.1	60.1
E	13.4	9.8	11.6	7.4	8.2	58.6	1,207.1	1,982.9	60.9
Size of household									
1 member	28.8	32.9	18.1	19.7	13.3	46.7	960.7	1,450.7	66.2
2 members	34.9	37.3	17.0	40.8	12.8	51.8	1,753.3	2,640.3	66.4
3–4 members	29.7	24.1	12.9	30.9	9.8	50.9	2,059.8	3,143.7	65.5
5+ members	6.7	5.7	13.5	8.6	9.7	61.7	2,438.2	4,130.6	59.0
Age									
16–34	24.9	22.3	14.2	17.7	9.4	40.4	1,276.8	1,978.1	64.5
35–44	20.4	21.6	16.8	23.3	11.3	47.4	1,724.9	2,845.4	60.6
45–64	31.1	30.3	15.5	36.5	11.9	54.8	1,933.9	2,827.4	68.4
65+	23.6	25.8	17.3	22.5	13.0	56.6	1,402.9	2,101.7	66.8
Housewives' working status									
Not working	41.6	39.7	15.1	37.9	10.8	54.8	1,532.3	2,453.0	62.5
Full time	38.0	42.7	17.8	42.5	13.3	45.8	1,596.4	2,304.3	69.3
Part time	20.4	17.6	13.7	19.6	9.7	51.9	1,792.4	2,825.6	63.4

Presence of children									
Yes	29.8	22.6	12.0	28.0	8.9	51.0	1,984.8	3,231.8	61.4
No	70.2	77.4	17.5	72.0	12.9	50.3	1,494.4	2,227.8	67.1
Age of children									
0–4	12.0	9.2	12.1	11.0	8.8	46.4	1,926.8	3,136.6	61.4
5–10	15.4	11.4	11.7	14.0	8.5	51.3	1,978.6	3,204.4	61.7
11–15	13.5	11.1	13.1	15.0	9.6	58.3	2,158.1	3,686.6	58.5
Lifestage									
Pre-family	12.0	14.3	19.0	9.6	13.2	38.4	1,073.9	1,624.3	66.1
New family	7.9	6.1	12.2	6.9	9.3	43.8	1,795.4	2,802.7	64.1
Maturing families	14.4	10.3	11.3	13.1	8.3	52.1	2,051.2	3,294.9	62.3
Established families	9.7	8.2	13.5	11.1	10.0	54.8	2,162.8	3,511.9	61.6
Post families	19.0	21.3	18.2	21.4	13.2	46.5	1,578.2	2,367.2	66.7
Older couples	20.3	21.3	16.6	26.3	12.6	58.8	1,982.3	2,948.3	67.2
Older singles	16.6	17.9	17.1	11.6	13.1	54.2	1,037.8	1,552.0	66.9
Region									
London	19.3	34.1	27.9	32.4	18.1	50.4	1,523.6	2,254.7	67.6
South & South East	9.4	11.3	19.0	12.3	14.2	50.4	1,747.2	2,524.0	69.2
East of England	6.9	8.5	19.5	10.1	16.7	55.9	1,923.3	2,858.6	67.3
Central	15.8	16.3	16.4	17.7	12.6	51.1	1,737.1	2,812.4	61.8
South West	3.2	3.4	17.2	3.7	12.3	58.5	1,725.9	2,527.3	68.3
Wales & West	7.5	5.1	10.8	5.2	8.4	41.3	1,631.4	2,317.7	70.4
Yorkshire	10.5	6.5	9.8	5.5	6.4	47.1	1,369.0	2,233.4	61.3
North East	4.9	1.1	3.5	0.9	2.3	38.3	1,279.9	2,471.8	51.8
Lancashire/Borders	13.8	9.0	10.3	8.0	6.9	48.0	1,421.6	2,296.3	61.9
Central & North Scotland	8.6	4.6	8.6	4.2	5.6	54.8	1,458.4	2,472.2	59.0

Source(s): ACNielsen Homescan (52 weeks ending December 2003).

GROCERY PURCHASING PROFILES (Cont.)

ASDA: Main Shoppers

	Total GB H'holds (%)	H'holds Buying Brand (%)	Pene-tration (%)	Brand Expenditure £'000s (%)	Market Share (%)	Purchase Occasion per Buyer (No.)	Average Spend, £ (in retailer) per Buyer	Average Spend, £ (all sources) per Buyer	Loyalty to Retailer (%)
TOTAL PANEL	24,593,997	4,170,161	17.0	5,831,656,574	10.7	47.7	1,398.4	2,121.3	65.9
Social grade									
AB	22.3	18.9	14.4	19.9	9.0	47.7	1,472.7	2,255.4	65.3
C1	27.6	27.0	16.6	25.2	9.8	45.6	1,308.0	2,073.0	63.1
C2	19.3	21.0	18.4	23.7	11.9	50.2	1,578.7	2,352.5	67.1
D	17.4	21.5	20.9	22.1	13.4	48.4	1,434.9	2,075.9	69.1
E	13.4	11.7	14.7	9.1	9.5	46.5	1,095.6	1,683.5	65.1
Size of household									
1 member	28.8	22.9	13.5	13.1	8.2	48.2	800.3	1,185.5	67.5
2 members	34.9	34.8	16.9	34.5	10.1	47.8	1,386.7	2,196.9	63.1
3–4 members	29.7	34.4	19.6	41.5	12.2	46.2	1,690.1	2,469.4	68.4
5+ members	6.7	7.9	20.2	10.8	11.4	52.3	1,910.7	2,979.4	64.1
Age									
16–34	24.9	33.0	22.5	30.5	15.1	41.3	1,290.0	1,917.0	67.3
35–44	20.4	23.1	19.1	25.9	11.8	46.7	1,572.4	2,352.7	66.8
45–64	31.1	28.9	15.8	31.8	9.7	53.2	1,538.5	2,348.1	65.5
65+	23.6	15.0	10.8	11.8	6.3	52.6	1,099.6	1,778.4	61.8
Housewives' working status									
Not working	41.6	37.2	15.1	35.3	9.4	50.8	1,327.5	2,078.0	63.9
Full time	38.0	41.8	18.6	41.2	12.0	45.0	1,380.7	2,065.4	66.9
Part time	20.4	21.1	17.5	23.5	10.8	47.6	1,558.7	2,308.6	67.5

Presence of children									
Yes	29.8	38.1	21.7	45.4	13.4	45.9	1,664.8	2,474.9	67.3
No	70.2	61.9	15.0	54.6	9.1	48.8	1,234.4	1,903.7	64.8
Age of children									
0–4	12.0	17.6	24.8	20.4	15.2	47.0	1,624.1	2,403.3	67.6
5–10	15.4	19.7	21.7	24.5	13.9	46.4	1,743.8	2,563.9	68.0
11–15	13.5	15.9	19.9	19.9	11.9	46.0	1,753.2	2,629.9	66.7
Lifestage									
Pre-family	12.0	14.5	20.5	10.6	13.5	37.5	1,020.3	1,533.0	66.6
New family	7.9	11.5	24.4	12.4	15.7	47.6	1,511.8	2,263.7	66.8
Maturing families	14.4	18.6	21.9	23.5	13.9	45.0	1,766.6	2,566.2	68.8
Established families	9.7	10.7	18.7	12.4	10.5	46.0	1,623.7	2,506.4	64.8
Post families	19.0	18.0	16.1	17.8	10.2	52.0	1,383.6	2,116.5	65.4
Older couples	20.3	15.6	13.0	17.0	7.6	54.6	1,522.0	2,419.3	62.9
Older singles	16.6	11.2	11.4	6.3	6.7	50.6	792.1	1,216.5	65.1
Region									
London	19.3	10.9	9.5	10.8	5.6	42.4	1,386.9	2,143.9	64.7
South & South East	9.4	7.8	13.9	7.8	8.3	52.7	1,402.0	2,200.5	63.7
East of England	6.9	3.2	7.9	3.6	5.6	41.7	1,574.0	2,492.2	63.2
Central	15.8	15.5	16.6	16.0	10.7	47.9	1,445.8	2,140.8	67.5
South West	3.2	1.5	8.2	1.6	4.8	55.1	1,411.0	2,249.2	62.7
Wales & West	7.5	8.3	18.6	7.6	11.4	42.6	1,278.4	1,936.6	66.0
Yorkshire	10.5	12.2	19.8	13.4	14.4	46.1	1,532.8	2,306.9	66.4
North East	4.9	8.6	29.7	7.3	17.9	46.4	1,186.6	1,787.0	66.4
Lancashire/Borders	13.8	19.8	24.2	19.2	15.6	48.8	1,361.4	2,064.1	66.0
Central & North Scotland	8.6	12.2	24.2	12.7	15.7	53.7	1,455.3	2,181.5	66.7

Source(s): ACNielsen Homescan (52 weeks ending December 2003).

GROCERY PURCHASING PROFILES (Cont.)

SAFEWAY: Main Shoppers

	Total GB H'holds (%)	H'holds Buying Brand (%)	Pene-tration (%)	Brand Expenditure £'000s (%)	Market Share (%)	Purchase Occasion per Buyer (No.)	Average Spend, £ (in retailer) per Buyer	Average Spend, £ (all sources) per Buyer	Loyalty to Retailer (%)
TOTAL PANEL	24,593,997	2,339,693	9.5	3,362,414	6.2	59.7	1,437.1	2,290.4	62.7
Social grade									
AB	22.3	25.0	10.7	28.7	7.5	62.1	1,650.6	2,499.7	66.0
C1	27.6	27.0	9.3	24.7	5.6	55.4	1,312.5	2,261.5	58.0
C2	19.3	18.6	9.2	20.3	5.9	51.9	1,562.4	2,413.2	64.7
D	17.4	14.5	7.9	17.7	6.2	77.2	1,755.4	2,748.0	63.9
E	13.4	14.8	10.5	8.6	5.1	56.5	835.3	1,388.2	60.2
Size of household									
1 member	28.8	31.3	10.3	17.8	6.4	53.8	815.6	1,266.8	64.4
2 members	34.9	31.9	8.7	35.3	5.9	68.5	1,588.7	2,544.7	62.4
3–4 members	29.7	30.1	9.6	34.2	5.8	53.0	1,635.5	2,695.0	60.7
5+ members	6.7	6.7	9.6	12.7	7.7	76.4	2,721.1	4,035.1	67.4
Age									
16–34	24.9	17.9	6.8	12.0	3.4	36.7	967.0	1,653.2	58.5
35–44	20.4	20.2	9.4	25.7	6.7	65.6	1,833.5	2,777.0	66.0
45–64	31.1	34.3	10.5	38.7	6.8	64.3	1,620.2	2,670.3	60.7
65+	23.6	27.7	11.2	23.6	7.3	64.7	1,224.7	1,875.9	65.3
Housewives' working status									
Not working	41.6	42.8	9.8	40.6	6.2	64.9	1,362.3	2,132.8	63.9
Full time	38.0	35.3	8.8	34.2	5.7	52.5	1,391.9	2,240.8	62.1
Part time	20.4	21.9	10.2	25.3	6.7	61.4	1,656.1	2,678.0	61.8

Presence of children								
Yes	29.8	27.1	8.7	31.5	5.4	57.6	1,667.6	2,743.3	60.8
No	70.2	72.9	9.9	68.5	6.6	60.5	1,351.4	2,121.9	63.7
Age of children								
0–4	12.0	8.2	6.5	10.8	4.6	64.4	1,895.8	2,878.9	65.9
5–10	15.4	16.7	10.3	20.6	6.7	58.9	1,772.3	2,787.5	63.6
11–15	13.5	13.1	9.2	18.5	6.4	70.4	2,036.4	3,171.3	64.2
Lifestage								
Pre-family	12.0	8.6	7.0	5.3	3.9	35.7	858.7	1,368.2	62.8
New family	7.9	3.9	4.6	3.1	2.2	50.9	1,142.2	2,403.7	47.5
Maturing families	14.4	16.4	10.8	20.3	6.9	57.6	1,782.2	2,774.3	64.2
Established families	9.7	10.5	10.3	15.2	7.4	60.6	2,086.1	3,310.8	63.0
Post families	19.0	18.0	9.0	16.9	5.6	57.8	1,349.4	2,148.1	62.8
Older couples	20.3	22.9	10.7	27.6	7.1	74.0	1,734.0	2,790.7	62.1
Older singles	16.6	13.6	11.2	11.7	7.1	58.8	853.8	1,279.3	66.7
Region								
London	19.3	16.6	8.1	14.7	4.4	54.0	1,272.5	2,154.9	59.0
South & South East	9.4	9.7	9.8	14.8	9.1	68.0	2,191.5	2,860.3	76.6
East of England	6.9	5.8	8.1	6.6	5.8	52.2	1,623.6	2,854.3	56.9
Central	15.8	16.2	9.8	15.9	6.1	58.1	1,407.7	2,241.8	62.8
South West	3.2	3.8	11.5	5.5	9.8	62.6	2,059.4	3,147.2	65.4
Wales & West	7.5	5.7	7.2	5.4	4.6	63.2	1,344.0	2,147.8	62.6
Yorkshire	10.5	7.2	6.5	5.9	3.6	47.0	1,178.3	1,973.3	59.7
North East	4.9	6.5	12.5	4.9	6.9	59.6	1,076.3	1,798.4	59.8
Lancashire/Borders	13.8	10.8	7.4	10.1	4.7	58.8	1,340.1	2,295.3	58.4
Central & North Scotland	8.6	17.6	19.6	16.4	11.6	68.7	1,335.3	2,130.4	62.7

Source(s): ACNielsen Homescan (52 weeks ending December 2003).

GROCERY PURCHASING PROFILES (Cont.)

KWIK SAVE: Main Shoppers

	Total GB H'holds (%)	H'holds Buying Brand (%)	Pene- tration (%)	Brand Expenditure £'000s (%)	Market Share (%)	Purchase Occasion per Buyer (No.)	Average Spend, £ (in retailer) per Buyer	Average Spend, £ (all sources) per Buyer	Loyalty to Retailer (%)
TOTAL PANEL	24,593,997	733,907	3.0	740,968	1.4	64.6	1,009.6	1,856.3	54.4
Social grade									
AB	22.3	5.2	0.7	3.7	0.2	52.9	716.8	1,548.6	46.3
C1	27.6	17.1	1.8	14.8	0.7	56.6	876.7	1,817.9	48.2
C2	19.3	24.5	3.8	28.5	1.8	54.3	1,175.1	2,142.7	54.8
D	17.4	29.9	5.1	32.7	2.5	73.4	1,104.1	1,982.1	55.7
E	13.4	23.4	5.2	20.4	2.7	72.4	878.0	1,493.5	58.8
Size of household									
1 member	28.8	29.6	3.1	17.8	1.4	59.7	606.0	1,079.0	56.2
2 members	34.9	28.5	2.4	26.6	1.0	64.8	940.7	1,786.0	52.7
3–4 members	29.7	33.6	3.4	43.5	1.6	66.4	1,307.5	2,394.9	54.6
5+ members	6.7	8.3	3.7	12.2	1.6	73.6	1,485.4	2,699.9	55.0
Age									
16–34	24.9	18.5	2.2	18.3	1.1	60.0	994.3	1,917.0	51.9
35–44	20.4	14.4	2.1	19.8	1.1	73.6	1,390.0	2,444.9	56.9
45–64	31.1	45.6	4.4	44.8	1.7	64.1	993.5	1,769.8	56.1
65+	23.6	21.5	2.7	17.1	1.2	63.4	802.6	1,593.8	50.4
Housewives' working status									
Not working	41.6	46.6	3.3	43.8	1.5	66.7	949.2	1,711.7	55.5
Full time	38.0	22.9	1.8	25.3	0.9	56.5	1,111.2	1,853.9	59.9
Part time	20.4	30.5	4.5	31.0	1.8	67.4	1,025.5	2,079.3	49.3

Presence of children									
Yes	29.8	30.3	3.0	39.9	1.5	70.7	1,332.4	2,400.3	55.5
No	70.2	69.7	3.0	60.1	1.3	61.9	869.5	1,620.3	53.7
Age of children									
0–4	12.0	7.6	1.9	8.5	0.8	56.8	1,133.4	2,070.7	54.7
5–10	15.4	17.2	3.3	20.8	1.5	58.9	1,222.9	2,347.9	52.1
11–15	13.5	19.1	4.3	28.4	2.2	73.8	1,475.5	2,594.4	56.9
Lifestage									
Pre-family	12.0	4.2	1.1	1.7	0.3	40.8	416.0	1,154.4	36.0
New family	7.9	5.4	2.0	6.3	1.0	66.7	1,178.0	1,966.2	59.9
Maturing families	14.4	16.4	3.4	20.5	1.5	57.1	1,262.7	2,431.8	51.9
Established families	9.7	11.8	3.6	18.8	2.0	86.6	1,617.7	2,640.8	61.3
Post families	19.0	19.0	3.0	13.6	1.0	66.8	723.6	1,393.1	51.9
Older couples	20.3	26.3	3.9	28.1	1.6	65.8	1,077.7	2,011.2	53.6
Older singles	16.6	-6.9	3.0	10.9	1.5	57.1	651.1	1,172.4	55.5
Region									
London	19.3	1.4	0.2	3.0	0.2	55.8	2,186.0	2,759.6	79.2
South & South East	9.4	:	:	:	:	:	:	:	:
East of England	6.9	0.5	0.2	0.5	0.1	36.0	1,091.4	1,570.5	69.5
Central	15.8	25.7	4.8	32.2	2.7	66.3	1,267.9	2,110.0	60.1
South West	3.2	2.1	2.0	2.3	0.9	50.0	1,134.0	2,620.6	43.3
Wales & West	7.5	19.7	7.8	15.6	3.0	50.1	796.2	1,586.2	50.2
Yorkshire	10.5	10.8	3.1	13.1	1.8	79.5	1,221.3	2,003.5	61.0
North East	4.9	8.4	5.1	6.2	1.9	89.4	741.7	1,838.1	40.4
Lancashire/Borders	13.8	28.5	6.1	25.2	2.6	63.3	892.0	1,709.0	52.2
Central & North Scotland	8.6	2.9	1.0	1.9	0.3	50.1	652.8	1,464.1	44.6

Source(s): ACNielsen Homescan (52 weeks ending December 2003).

GROCERY PURCHASING PROFILES (Cont.)

ALDI: All Shoppers

	Total GB H'holds (%)	H'holds Buying Brand (%)	Pene-tration (%)	Brand Expenditure £'000s (%)	Market Share (%)	Purchase Occasion per Buyer (No.)	Average Spend, £ (in retailer) per Buyer	Average Spend, £ (all sources) per Buyer	Loyalty to Retailer (%)
TOTAL PANEL	24,593,997	4,500,455	18.3	681,774	1.2	9.4	151.5	2,164.9	7.0
Social grade									
AB	22.3	17.6	14.5	14.9	0.8	7.4	128.2	2,204.5	5.8
C1	27.6	23.6	15.7	26.3	1.2	9.7	169.2	2,096.2	8.1
C2	19.3	21.6	20.5	25.2	1.5	9.5	176.4	2,498.8	7.1
D	17.4	22.1	23.2	20.2	1.4	9.7	138.4	2,182.3	6.3
E	13.4	15.1	20.5	13.4	1.6	10.4	134.5	1,720.5	7.8
Size of household									
1 member	28.8	26.0	16.5	16.2	1.2	7.8	94.3	1,221.8	7.7
2 members	34.9	34.9	18.3	32.9	1.1	9.6	142.7	2,197.3	6.5
3–4 members	29.7	30.8	19.0	40.1	1.4	10.5	197.2	2,694.2	7.3
5+ members	6.7	8.4	22.9	10.9	1.3	9.0	197.8	3,010.0	6.6
Age									
16–34	24.9	22.3	16.4	17.6	1.0	6.7	119.4	2,096.7	5.7
35–44	20.4	19.8	17.7	20.9	1.1	8.4	160.1	2,542.1	6.3
45–64	31.1	34.1	20.1	35.5	1.3	10.0	157.8	2,335.3	6.8
65+	23.6	23.8	18.5	26.0	1.6	11.7	165.4	1,672.5	9.9
Housewives' working status									
Not working	41.6	45.7	20.1	53.6	1.7	11.8	177.5	2,072.2	8.6
Full time	38.0	31.5	15.2	26.2	0.9	7.2	126.3	2,099.8	6.0
Part time	20.4	22.8	20.5	20.2	1.1	7.4	134.1	2,440.6	5.5

Presence of children									
Yes	29.8	32.4	19.9	38.9	1.3	9.4	181.7	2,642.6	6.9
No	70.2	67.6	17.6	61.1	1.2	9.3	137.0	1,936.0	7.1
Age of children									
0–4	12.0	12.5	19.0	11.5	1.0	7.2	139.5	2,540.4	5.5
5–10	15.4	17.6	20.9	21.3	1.4	10.1	183.2	2,626.2	7.0
11–15	13.5	15.4	20.9	24.2	1.7	11.6	238.1	2,912.8	8.2
Lifestage									
Pre-family	12.0	7.5	11.5	3.2	0.5	4.0	65.4	1,548.8	4.2
New family	7.9	8.3	19.2	6.4	0.9	6.6	116.0	2,468.2	4.7
Maturing families	14.4	13.2	20.6	19.1	1.3	9.7	178.6	2,594.4	6.9
Established families	9.7	9.9	18.7	16.1	1.6	11.3	246.4	2,827.6	8.7
Post families	19.0	18.7	18.0	10.3	0.7	6.4	83.4	2,148.3	3.9
Older couples	20.3	23.1	20.8	31.8	1.7	13.1	208.8	2,341.8	8.9
Older singles	16.6	16.3	17.9	13.0	1.6	9.7	121.3	1,228.6	9.9
Region									
London	19.3	7.2	6.9	5.8	0.4	7.0	121.9	2,248.6	5.4
South & South East	9.4	4.3	8.2	3.6	0.4	9.2	127.0	2,206.1	5.8
East of England	6.9	5.9	15.7	5.0	0.9	7.8	127.5	1,989.5	6.4
Central	15.8	22.5	26.1	21.0	1.6	8.7	141.1	2,231.3	6.3
South West	3.2	1.5	8.4	1.1	0.4	7.8	116.0	3,029.1	3.8
Wales & West	7.5	8.2	20.0	8.1	1.4	9.3	149.1	1,912.2	7.8
Yorkshire	10.5	10.9	19.0	8.5	1.1	7.8	119.1	2,155.5	5.5
North East	4.9	7.2	26.6	10.1	2.9	12.9	213.7	2,191.2	9.8
Lancashire/Borders	13.8	25.0	33.1	30.3	2.9	10.8	183.6	2,060.7	8.9
Central & North Scotland	8.6	7.3	15.5	6.4	0.9	8.9	133.2	2,453.2	5.4

Source(s): ACNielsen Homescan (52 weeks ending December 2003).

GROCERY PURCHASING PROFILES (Cont.)

SOMERFIELD: Main Shoppers

	Total GB H'holds (%)	H'holds Buying Brand (%)	Penetration (%)	Brand Expenditure £'000s (%)	Market Share (%)	Purchase Occasion per Buyer (No.)	Average Spend, £ (in retailer) per Buyer	Average Spend, £ (all sources) per Buyer	Loyalty to Retailer (%)
TOTAL PANEL	24,593,997	935,749	3.8	1,146,258	2.1	68.0	1,225.0	2,076.0	59.0
Social grade									
AB	22.3	19.3	3.3	24.8	2.2	59.4	1,575.8	2,495.0	63.2
C1	27.6	21.8	3.0	18.8	1.4	60.9	1,054.3	1,797.9	58.6
C2	19.3	19.0	3.7	16.1	1.6	63.7	1,040.3	2,063.9	50.4
D	17.4	17.2	3.8	21.4	2.6	73.9	1,521.0	2,446.0	62.2
E	13.4	22.6	6.4	18.9	3.8	81.4	1,020.4	1,715.9	59.5
Size of household									
1 member	28.8	30.2	4.0	19.0	2.4	72.9	773.8	1,227.3	63.1
2 members	34.9	34.7	3.8	31.6	1.8	65.5	1,115.7	1,973.7	56.5
3–4 members	29.7	33.4	4.3	48.4	2.8	67.4	1,775.5	2,970.2	59.8
5+ members	6.7	1.8	1.0	1.0	0.2	45.0	673.2	1,677.3	40.1
Age									
16–34	24.9	18.5	2.8	16.6	1.6	61.0	1,093.5	2,086.1	52.4
35–44	20.4	15.0	2.8	17.6	1.6	48.3	1,441.0	2,363.0	61.0
45–64	31.1	31.8	3.9	36.8	2.2	73.0	1,419.3	2,331.7	60.9
65+	23.6	34.7	5.6	29.0	3.1	75.7	1,023.7	1,712.2	59.8
Housewives' working status									
Not working	41.6	51.2	4.7	46.3	2.4	71.3	1,108.3	1,957.2	56.6
Full time	38.0	34.5	3.4	34.5	2.0	59.7	1,224.9	1,997.2	61.3
Part time	20.4	14.4	2.7	19.2	1.7	76.1	1,640.1	2,688.0	61.0

Presence of children								
Yes	29.8	25.8	3.3	34.5	2.0	64.8	1,642.9	2,665.7	61.6
No	70.2	74.2	4.0	65.5	2.1	69.2	1,080.0	1,871.5	57.7
Age of children								
0–4	12.0	8.5	2.7	9.3	1.4	63.2	1,334.6	2,351.3	56.8
5–10	15.4	10.5	2.6	14.3	1.6	59.4	1,667.4	2,755.0	60.5
11–15	13.5	13.9	3.9	22.8	2.7	64.7	2,004.0	2,908.9	68.9
Lifestage								
Pre-family	12.0	7.8	2.5	4.8	1.2	49.8	755.8	1,574.5	48.0
New family	7.9	5.2	2.5	4.3	1.1	62.0	1,006.1	1,848.5	54.4
Maturing families	14.4	10.4	2.7	14.3	1.7	59.0	1,679.4	2,774.1	60.5
Established families	9.7	11.4	4.5	17.2	2.9	71.4	1,849.3	2,891.5	64.0
Post families	19.0	17.6	3.5	18.8	2.1	68.0	1,307.3	2,108.2	62.0
Older couples	20.3	25.6	4.8	27.6	2.4	67.7	1,321.5	2,388.8	55.3
Older singles	16.6	22.0	5.0	13.1	2.7	78.8	726.5	1,165.9	62.3
Region								
London	19.3	13.3	2.6	15.8	1.6	64.9	1,450.5	2,709.2	53.5
South & South East	9.4	12.2	4.9	14.4	3.0	87.0	1,442.7	2,126.6	67.8
East of England	6.9	5.5	3.1	5.4	1.6	53.8	1,189.4	2,013.6	59.1
Central	15.8	16.3	3.9	12.9	1.7	52.0	973.3	1,790.8	54.4
South West	3.2	11.7	14.0	10.8	6.6	72.2	1,138.3	1,729.4	65.8
Wales & West	7.5	14.5	7.3	16.9	5.0	67.1	1,433.6	2,066.6	69.4
Yorkshire	10.5	7.3	2.6	6.2	1.3	76.8	1,041.9	2,018.3	51.6
North East	4.9	1.4	1.1	1.6	0.8	113.7	1,364.3	2,333.1	58.5
Lancashire/Borders	13.8	8.8	2.4	8.0	1.3	61.2	1,115.4	2,374.0	47.0
Central & North Scotland	8.6	9.1	4.0	8.0	1.9	73.0	1,083.4	1,804.1	60.1

Source(s): ACNielsen Homescan (52 weeks ending December 2003).

GROCERY PURCHASING PROFILES (Cont.)

WAITROSE: All Shoppers

	Total GB H'holds (%)	H'holds Buying Brand (%)	Penetration (%)	Brand Expenditure £'000s	Market Share (%)	Purchase Occasion per Buyer (No.)	Average Spend, £ (in retailer) per Buyer	Average Spend, £ (all sources) per Buyer	Loyalty to Retailer (%)
TOTAL PANEL	24,593,997	3,791,539	15.4	1,714,380	3.1	19.1	452.2	2,616.7	17.3
Social grade									
AB	22.3	35.2	24.3	57.8	7.7	25.4	742.4	2,728.3	27.2
C1	27.6	29.1	16.3	26.7	3.1	20.2	414.8	2,742.0	15.1
C2	19.3	14.3	11.4	5.7	0.8	9.2	179.9	2,632.9	6.8
D	17.4	11.9	10.5	5.4	1.0	14.3	204.5	2,551.4	8.0
E	13.4	9.5	10.9	4.4	1.3	13.9	210.4	1,876.2	11.2
Size of household									
1 member	28.8	27.0	14.5	20.4	3.8	18.5	341.6	1,566.5	21.8
2 members	34.9	41.9	18.5	38.7	3.3	17.6	418.5	2,714.8	15.4
3–4 members	29.7	27.2	14.1	36.3	3.1	21.7	603.6	3,289.3	18.4
5+ members	6.7	3.9	9.1	4.5	1.4	22.4	522.6	4,140.5	12.6
Age									
16–34	24.9	19.4	12.0	10.5	1.5	13.4	244.7	2,031.8	12.0
35–44	20.4	18.5	13.9	16.9	2.3	11.2	414.5	2,858.2	14.5
45–64	31.1	35.1	17.4	47.0	4.2	25.8	605.3	3,113.1	19.4
65+	23.6	27.0	17.7	25.6	4.0	20.0	427.5	2,225.4	19.2
Housewives' working status									
Not working	41.6	42.3	15.7	45.5	3.5	21.3	486.1	2,484.3	19.6
Full time	38.0	37.9	15.4	32.9	2.8	15.1	392.6	2,564.0	15.3
Part time	20.4	19.8	15.0	21.6	2.9	22.2	493.6	3,000.1	16.5

Presence of children									
Yes	29.8	24.3	12.5	21.0	1.8	17.2	391.2	3,095.6	12.6
No	70.2	75.7	16.6	79.0	3.9	19.8	471.7	2,463.4	19.1
Age of children									
0–4	12.0	10.6	13.5	12.0	2.6	23.2	514.7	2,974.6	17.3
5–10	15.4	10.7	10.7	8.9	1.5	14.9	376.5	3,286.5	11.5
11–15	13.5	9.9	11.4	5.4	1.0	11.6	246.1	3,338.0	7.4
Lifestage									
Pre-family	12.0	10.7	13.8	2.5	1.0	8.1	106.4	1,739.7	6.1
New family	7.9	8.0	15.4	8.7	3.3	22.6	495.9	2,656.1	18.7
Maturing families	14.4	10.0	10.7	8.5	1.5	15.1	383.0	3,344.9	11.5
Established families	9.7	8.7	13.9	8.5	2.1	17.1	439.2	3,281.4	13.4
Post families	19.0	20.4	16.5	26.2	4.4	21.1	581.0	2,644.1	22.0
Older couples	20.3	25.4	19.3	28.5	3.7	22.2	506.3	3,080.1	16.4
Older singles	16.6	16.8	15.5	17.1	5.3	21.1	462.6	1,641.0	28.2
Region									
London	19.3	42.0	33.5	53.0	8.1	24.0	569.7	2,609.4	21.8
South & South East	9.4	19.7	32.1	23.2	7.3	24.6	533.5	2,561.6	20.8
East of England	6.9	8.3	18.5	6.0	2.7	10.2	328.1	2,341.1	14.0
Central	15.8	13.1	12.7	6.7	1.3	12.1	231.0	2,694.0	8.6
South West	3.2	4.9	23.9	4.5	4.1	13.5	415.7	2,978.1	14.0
Wales & West	7.5	5.8	11.9	6.1	2.7	16.5	472.6	2,573.3	18.4
Yorkshire	10.5	3.2	4.7	0.4	0.1	3.6	61.1	2,306.0	2.7
North East	4.9	0.4	1.3	..	..	3.2	18.8	2,935.4	0.6
Lancashire/Borders	13.8	2.3	2.6	0.1	..	1.4	13.7	3,497.3	0.4
Central & North Scotland	8.6	0.2	0.4	..	..	1.3	7.0	2,373.8	0.3

Source(s): ACNielsen Homescan (52 weeks ending December 2003).

GROCERY PURCHASING PROFILES (Cont.)

NETTO: All Shoppers

	Total GB H'holds (%)	H'holds Buying Brand (%)	Penetration (%)	Brand Expenditure £'000s (%)	Market Share (%)	Purchase Occasion per Buyer (No.)	Average Spend, £ (in retailer) per Buyer	Average Spend, £ (all sources) per Buyer	Loyalty to Retailer (%)
TOTAL PANEL	24,593,997	2,462,814	10.0	444,891	0.8	12.9	180.6	2,053.5	8.8
Social grade									
AB	22.3	13.5	6.1	9.9	0.3	14.0	132.3	2,018.6	6.6
C1	27.6	21.6	7.9	17.4	0.5	10.5	145.8	2,049.8	7.1
C2	19.3	22.9	11.9	23.0	0.9	12.0	181.2	2,293.8	7.9
D	17.4	23.6	13.6	25.8	1.2	12.5	197.8	2,207.1	9.0
E	13.4	18.4	13.8	23.9	1.9	16.7	234.3	1,588.9	14.7
Size of household									
1 member	28.8	20.9	7.3	11.6	0.6	11.6	100.2	1,127.4	8.9
2 members	34.9	34.4	9.9	35.3	0.8	13.4	185.3	2,016.6	9.2
3 – 4 members	29.7	34.7	11.7	37.7	0.8	11.6	195.8	2,426.5	8.1
5+ members	6.7	10.0	15.0	15.5	1.2	18.5	280.6	2,825.4	9.9
Age									
16–34	24.9	29.6	11.9	19.3	0.7	9.0	117.9	1,836.0	6.4
35–44	20.4	21.5	10.5	26.5	0.9	11.2	223.4	2,383.4	9.4
45–64	31.1	29.7	9.6	35.5	0.8	15.1	216.3	2,270.5	9.5
65+	23.6	19.3	8.2	18.6	0.8	17.7	174.5	1,686.2	10.3
Housewives' working status									
Not working	41.6	43.9	10.6	49.1	1.0	15.5	202.1	1,952.0	10.4
Full time	38.0	30.4	8.0	27.6	0.6	9.7	163.8	1,992.6	8.2
Part time	20.4	25.7	12.6	23.4	0.8	12.3	163.9	2,298.5	7.1

Presence of children									
Yes	29.8	37.8	12.7	42.8	1.0	13.2	204.7	2,427.2	8.4
No	70.2	62.2	8.9	57.2	0.7	12.8	166.0	1,826.9	9.1
Age of children									
0–4	12.0	18.6	15.5	21.6	1.2	14.7	209.7	2,515.7	8.3
5–10	15.4	16.5	10.7	15.9	0.7	11.0	173.4	2,449.7	7.1
11–15	13.5	17.4	12.9	24.0	1.1	13.4	249.3	2,546.9	9.8
Lifestage									
Pre-family	12.0	10.8	9.0	6.0	0.6	6.2	100.5	1,284.4	7.8
New family	7.9	12.4	15.7	10.8	1.0	13.1	157.0	2,265.9	6.9
Maturing families	14.4	16.0	11.1	18.6	0.8	12.4	210.4	2,449.5	8.6
Established families	9.7	11.7	12.1	17.0	1.1	14.0	261.5	2,548.6	10.3
Post families	19.0	16.3	8.6	13.6	0.5	10.5	150.7	2,122.6	7.1
Older couples	20.3	21.2	10.4	25.9	0.9	16.1	220.9	2,197.8	10.1
Older singles	16.6	11.6	7.0	8.1	0.7	16.3	126.3	1,138.6	11.1
Region									
London	19.3	11.3	5.8	9.0	0.4	12.5	143.8	1,835.5	7.8
South & South East	9.4	2.5	2.6	2.4	0.2	12.5	175.7	2,408.4	7.3
East of England	6.9	7.2	10.5	8.7	1.0	11.0	216.8	1,966.8	11.0
Central	15.8	13.5	8.6	10.4	0.5	9.3	138.5	2,303.9	6.0
South West	3.2	0.1	0.5	0.0	0.0	1.0	0.4	3,114.1	0.0
Wales & West	7.5	0.7	1.0	0.1	0.0	1.4	15.2	1,267.9	1.2
Yorkshire	10.5	30.8	29.5	39.5	3.2	15.2	231.8	1,988.9	11.7
North East	4.9	10.3	20.9	7.4	1.4	12.0	129.4	2,151.7	6.0
Lancashire/Borders	13.8	23.1	16.7	22.6	1.4	14.0	176.9	2,080.6	8.5
Central & North Scotland	8.6	0.4	0.5	·	·	1.0	13.4	1,114.4	1.2

Source(s): ACNielsen Homescan (52 weeks ending December 2003).

GROCERY PURCHASING PROFILES (Cont.)

CO-OP: Main Shoppers

	Total GB H'holds (%)	H'holds Buying Brand (%)	Pene-tration (%)	Brand Expenditure £'000s (%)	Market Share (%)	Purchase Occasion per Buyer (No.)	Average Spend, £ (in retailer) per Buyer	Average Spend, £ (all sources) per Buyer	Loyalty to Retailer (%)
TOTAL PANEL	24,593,997	883,459	3.6	919,808	1.7	71.3	1,041.1	1,786.1	58.3
Social grade									
AB	22.3	14.6	2.4	12.4	0.9	70.1	884.1	1,531.1	57.7
C1	27.6	28.6	3.7	25.3	1.6	68.1	919.3	1,620.9	56.7
C2	19.3	22.7	4.2	31.7	2.5	76.3	1,450.2	2,308.5	62.8
D	17.4	16.0	3.3	14.2	1.4	66.6	921.7	1,750.5	52.7
E	13.4	18.0	4.8	16.5	2.7	75.2	951.9	1,627.3	58.5
Size of household									
1 member	28.8	43.7	5.5	31.0	3.1	65.3	737.9	1,210.8	60.9
2 members	34.9	31.1	3.2	34.9	1.6	71.0	1,165.6	2,062.3	56.5
3 – 4 members	29.7	19.3	2.3	25.0	1.2	83.1	1,348.3	2,402.4	56.1
5+ members	6.7	5.8	3.1	9.1	1.5	78.6	1,634.2	2,584.5	63.2
Age									
16–34	24.9	19.4	2.8	16.3	1.3	57.4	872.8	1,478.1	59.0
35–44	20.4	15.5	2.7	16.9	1.2	66.3	1,136.0	2,087.6	54.4
45–64	31.1	32.0	3.7	37.3	1.8	66.9	1,213.8	2,072.4	58.6
65+	23.6	33.0	5.0	29.5	2.5	86.2	928.4	1,548.3	60.0
Housewives' working status									
Not working	41.6	43.3	3.7	40.8	1.7	79.3	981.1	1,747.5	56.1
Full time	38.0	38.0	3.6	34.4	1.6	59.0	942.1	1,601.5	58.8
Part time	20.4	18.7	3.3	24.8	1.8	77.7	1,381.8	2,250.7	61.4

Presence of children									
Yes	29.8	21.3	2.6	28.0	1.3	75.5	1,368.0	2,320.3	59.0
No	70.2	78.7	4.0	72.0	1.9	70.2	952.6	1,641.4	58.0
Age of children									
0–4	12.0	5.8	1.7	7.5	0.9	64.3	1,345.8	2,176.8	61.8
5–10	15.4	13.9	3.2	17.2	1.5	74.0	1,292.8	2,174.1	59.5
11–15	13.5	8.5	2.3	12.7	1.2	87.0	1,556.4	2,752.9	56.5
Lifestage									
Pre-family	12.0	8.9	2.7	4.2	0.8	41.7	488.0	982.7	49.7
New family	7.9	3.9	1.7	3.6	0.7	73.8	964.6	1,421.5	67.9
Maturing families	14.4	12.3	3.1	16.3	1.5	70.0	1,382.1	2,441.0	56.6
Established families	9.7	7.5	2.8	10.6	1.4	77.4	1,471.8	2,443.0	60.2
Post families	19.0	21.1	4.0	20.7	1.9	59.1	1,019.8	1,772.2	57.5
Older couples	20.3	19.2	3.4	24.7	1.7	88.3	1,340.9	2,409.6	55.6
Older singles	16.6	27.2	5.9	19.9	3.3	77.0	763.5	1,191.4	64.1
Region									
London	19.3	9.2	1.7	8.4	0.7	90.0	955.6	1,883.9	50.7
South & South East	9.4	7.3	2.8	6.1	1.0	52.6	870.1	1,693.3	51.4
East of England	6.9	8.0	4.2	9.9	2.4	70.6	1,297.5	1,807.3	71.8
Central	15.8	20.7	4.7	20.7	2.2	72.6	1,041.8	1,788.8	58.2
South West	3.2	3.1	3.5	3.0	1.5	67.5	1,023.1	1,787.6	57.2
Wales & West	7.5	7.8	3.7	5.4	1.3	80.2	724.5	1,466.1	49.4
Yorkshire	10.5	14.1	4.9	10.9	1.8	64.6	800.2	1,506.2	53.1
North East	4.9	7.8	5.7	7.5	2.9	75.4	1,005.4	1,770.0	56.8
Lancashire/Borders	13.8	9.7	2.5	9.2	1.2	66.5	985.3	1,639.0	60.1
Central & North Scotland	8.6	12.3	5.2	18.8	3.7	71.1	1,587.5	2,399.3	66.2

Source(s): ACNielsen Homescan (52 weeks ending December 2003).

GROCERY PURCHASING PROFILES (Cont.)

MARKS & SPENCER: All Shoppers

	Total GB H'holds (%)	H'holds Buying Brand (%)	Penetration (%)	Brand Expenditure £'000s (%)	Market Share (%)	Purchase Occasion per Buyer (No.)	Average Spend, £ (in retailer) per Buyer	Average Spend, £ (all sources) per Buyer	Loyalty to Retailer (%)
TOTAL PANEL	24,593,997	8,488,868	34.5	1,104,818	2.0	9.4	130.1	2,495.7	5.2
Social grade									
AB	22.3	26.0	40.2	30.5	2.6	10.0	152.6	2,672.4	5.7
C1	27.6	31.2	39.1	34.6	2.6	9.5	144.3	2,435.7	5.9
C2	19.3	16.5	29.5	12.8	1.2	7.2	101.2	2,749.7	3.7
D	17.4	13.7	27.2	9.5	1.1	8.8	90.3	2,492.3	3.6
E	13.4	12.5	32.2	12.5	2.5	11.1	130.0	1,947.6	6.7
Size of household									
1 member	28.8	32.3	38.8	25.1	3.0	9.4	101.1	1,455.9	6.9
2 members	34.9	39.9	39.4	48.1	2.7	10.6	156.9	2,696.9	5.8
3–4 members	29.7	23.8	27.7	22.0	1.2	7.2	120.4	3,271.3	3.7
5+ members	6.7	4.0	20.5	4.7	0.9	9.0	156.0	4,297.6	3.6
Age									
16–34	24.9	18.2	25.3	10.6	1.0	5.4	75.8	2,148.6	3.5
35–44	20.4	19.0	32.1	17.2	1.5	7.4	117.6	2,776.6	4.2
45–64	31.1	32.3	35.9	40.5	2.3	10.4	163.0	2,912.9	5.6
65+	23.6	30.4	44.5	31.7	3.2	11.8	135.7	2,085.2	6.5
Housewives' working status									
Not working	41.6	45.0	37.4	46.4	2.3	11.1	134.0	2,375.0	5.6
Full time	38.0	37.0	33.6	36.1	2.0	7.5	127.0	2,450.8	5.2
Part time	20.4	18.0	30.5	17.5	1.5	8.9	126.8	2,890.0	4.4

Presence of children									
Yes	29.8	21.4	24.8	17.9	1.0	6.7	108.8	3,255.8	3.3
No	70.2	78.6	38.6	82.1	2.6	10.1	136.0	2,288.6	5.9
Age of children									
0–4	12.0	8.8	25.3	5.4	0.8	5.6	79.6	3,331.4	2.4
5–10	15.4	11.0	24.6	9.0	1.0	6.0	107.2	3,298.8	3.3
11–15	13.5	9.5	24.3	10.2	1.2	8.0	139.1	3,475.5	4.0
Lifestage									
Pre-family	12.0	10.8	31.1	7.4	1.8	6.4	89.5	1,683.3	5.3
New family	7.9	5.7	24.9	2.6	0.6	4.6	59.3	3,097.6	1.9
Maturing families	14.4	10.2	24.5	8.7	1.0	6.3	110.1	3,321.4	3.3
Established families	9.7	7.4	26.4	8.3	1.3	9.2	146.9	3,402.2	4.3
Post families	19.0	20.8	37.7	25.2	2.7	9.0	157.8	2,481.1	6.4
Older couples	20.3	24.9	42.3	29.9	2.5	12.0	156.1	2,909.6	5.4
Older singles	16.6	20.1	41.8	17.9	3.6	10.9	115.5	1,507.6	7.7
Region									
London	19.3	26.0	46.4	30.0	3.0	10.6	150.1	2,560.1	5.9
South & South East	9.4	9.8	35.6	7.2	1.5	7.1	96.5	2,743.6	3.5
East of England	6.9	5.6	28.2	3.3	0.9	7.2	75.5	2,512.5	3.0
Central	15.8	14.2	31.0	12.0	1.5	8.1	110.0	2,534.9	4.3
South West	3.2	2.7	29.0	2.0	1.2	6.2	99.2	2,884.5	3.4
Wales & West	7.5	5.7	25.9	4.8	1.4	8.6	110.3	2,143.5	5.1
Yorkshire	10.5	8.6	28.3	10.7	2.2	11.6	161.6	2,433.7	6.6
North East	4.9	4.7	32.7	3.9	1.8	10.2	109.3	1,985.7	5.5
Lancashire/Borders	13.8	13.4	33.4	13.8	2.1	9.1	134.1	2,432.5	5.5
Central & North Scotland	8.6	9.4	38.0	12.3	2.9	10.6	169.5	2,493.7	6.8

Source(s): ACNielsen Homescan (52 weeks ending December 2003).

GROCERY SHOPPING PATTERNS OF ALL SHOPPERS
BY DAY OF WEEK AND RETAILER

Weekly expenditure, %

	Mon	Tues	Wed	Thur	Fri	Sat	Sun
Tesco	13.1	12.8	11.4	13.8	18.4	20.8	9.7
Sainsbury's	13.7	13.2	11.5	14.2	17.7	21.3	8.5
Safeway	11.9	10.7	16.4	15.8	16.1	20.8	8.3
Asda	12.6	13.2	13.3	15.2	17.8	18.2	9.8
Somerfield	12.9	12.9	14.5	14.6	18.0	18.9	8.3
Kwik Save	13.6	11.7	12.2	15.2	20.4	18.5	8.3
Co-op	14.0	14.3	13.9	15.1	17.1	18.2	7.4
All Stores	**13.0**	**13.0**	**12.7**	**14.5**	**17.5**	**20.5**	**8.9**

Penetration, %

	Mon	Tues	Wed	Thur	Fri	Sat	Sun
Tesco	28.6	28.9	28.3	28.1	29.3	32.3	21.1
Sainsbury's	18.4	19.6	18.1	17.6	19.1	20.6	13.1
Safeway	12.9	13.2	15.4	14.4	13.7	14.9	10.0
Asda	16.7	17.5	16.9	16.9	18.3	19.8	13.7
Somerfield	8.1	8.6	8.9	8.6	8.8	9.6	5.1
Kwik Save	6.7	7.1	6.9	6.9	7.4	7.4	3.9
Co-op	11.3	11.9	11.4	10.1	10.9	11.8	7.1
All Stores	**79.6**	**81.6**	**81.8**	**81.5**	**84.4**	**85.7**	**63.5**

Average spend per visit, £

	Mon	Tues	Wed	Thur	Fri	Sat	Sun
Tesco	26.1	24.7	24.0	27.6	31.8	30.5	28.4
Sainsbury's	26.1	26.1	26.0	30.0	31.8	33.6	29.0
Safeway	18.7	17.5	20.3	23.3	24.1	25.9	21.8
Asda	26.9	27.2	27.6	30.1	32.3	31.0	28.7
Somerfield	12.8	12.5	13.6	14.0	16.4	16.6	17.6
Kwik Save	10.7	10.1	10.6	13.5	15.2	12.6	15.1
Co-op	9.0	8.8	9.7	11.1	11.4	10.7	9.3
All Stores	**15.7**	**15.0**	**15.7**	**17.3**	**18.7**	**18.8**	**20.9**

Regional expenditure, %

	Mon	Tues	Wed	Thur	Fri	Sat	Sun
London	13.1	12.8	12.6	13.4	16.1	21.8	10.2
South & South East	13.3	14.6	13.6	15.3	16.5	19.1	7.6
East of England	13.4	12.6	11.6	13.7	18.4	20.5	9.8
Central	13.1	12.6	13.5	14.5	17.2	20.5	8.5
South West	12.2	11.8	13.9	12.1	18.5	23.6	7.9
Wales & West	12.9	12.3	13.2	16.0	17.7	19.6	8.3
Lancashire	12.5	13.0	12.1	15.4	18.0	20.5	8.5
Yorkshire	13.0	13.6	11.7	14.9	18.7	20.2	8.0
North East	12.6	12.6	12.5	14.1	18.9	20.6	8.8
Scotland	13.0	12.8	12.9	14.7	18.4	18.3	9.9
GB	**13.0**	**13.0**	**12.7**	**14.5**	**17.5**	**20.5**	**8.9**

Source(s): ACNielsen Homescan (52 weeks ending December 2003).

TRENDS IN EXPENDITURE BY DAY OF THE WEEK

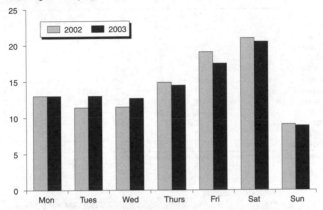

Percentage of weekly expenditure in all stores

Source(s): ACNielsen Homescan (12 weeks ending December 2003).

SHOPPING TRIPS BY BASKET SIZE

By retailer   Percent of total trips by retailer

	1–5	6–10	11–20	21–30	31–50	50+
Sainsbury's	18	19	25	14	15	9
Tesco	18	18	22	14	17	11
Safeway	22	24	26	14	10	4
Somerfield	35	27	21	7	7	3
Asda	14	17	21	14	20	14
Kwik Save	36	26	21	9	7	2
Co-op	46	27	18	5	3	1
Waitrose	24	22	23	13	13	4
Iceland	41	26	20	7	5	2
Aldi	19	18	26	16	14	7
Netto	22	21	24	13	14	7
Morrisons	13	17	22	14	19	15
All Grocers	**27**	**21**	**22**	**11**	**12**	**7**

Source(s): ACNielsen Homescan (52 weeks ending December 2003).

All grocers

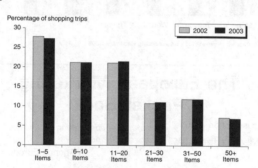

Percentage of shopping trips

AVERAGE NUMBER OF SHOPPING TRIPS

	2000	2001	2002	2003
Sainsbury's	51	52	52	51
Tesco	51	54	52	53
Safeway	60	63	62	60
Asda	46	46	46	48
Somerfield	66	63	68	68
Co-op	72	70	70	71
Kwik Save	64	66	63	65

Source(s): ACNielsen Homescan (52 weeks ending December 2003).

CONSIDERING WHERE TO SHOP

The Most Important Factor

Percentage

All Respondents	All Households	ABC1	C2DE	Pre-Family	New Family	Maturing Family	Established Family	Post Family	Older Couples	Older Singles
All Respondents	**100.0**	**49.9**	**50.1**	**12.0**	**7.9**	**14.4**	**9.7**	**19.0**	**20.3**	**16.6**
Value for money	34.6	31.3	37.9	32.4	41.5	39.9	37.0	32.2	35.7	28.0
Quality fresh produce	17.2	17.7	16.6	11.5	13.6	15.0	13.1	17.1	22.4	20.6
Convenient location	11.4	13.5	9.3	13.3	9.3	7.7	10.1	14.3	9.4	14.1
Good range of products	9.7	10.6	8.8	12.8	7.4	11.4	12.5	11.3	8.0	6.1
High quality products	8.7	9.3	8.1	9.8	7.3	7.6	7.0	8.6	9.1	10.1
Ease of parking	6.3	7.2	5.3	2.8	2.5	3.1	3.7	6.3	9.1	11.2
Low prices	5.6	4.3	7.0	10.8	11.1	6.9	8.4	4.0	1.9	3.2
Special in-store promotions	2.7	2.6	2.7	2.4	4.2	4.6	4.2	1.8	1.0	2.6
Good quality own label	2.1	1.7	2.4	0.9	2.3	2.6	1.9	2.6	1.9	1.9
Other	1.0	0.9	1.4	2.3	0.5	1.1	1.1	0.8	0.9	1.5
Store is clean and tidy	0.7	0.9	0.5	1.0	0.3	0.1	1.0	1.0	0.6	0.7

Note(s): **Question**: Which of the following factors do you consider to be the most important when choosing where to do your grocery shopping?
Source(s): ACNielsen Homescan Survey, November 2003.

ATTITUDES TO RETAILERS

The Attitudes to Retailers survey is compiled by ACNielsen using its Consumer Panel members. Panel members are asked to vote for a pre-defined list of retailers as either best or second best on five key attributes, this information is then used to calculate 'overall performance'.

Which Retailer Performs the Best Overall, Calculated Measured Index

1	Asda	8.2
2	Tesco	6.4
3	Sainsbury's	4.5
4	Marks & Spencer	3.7
5	Morrisons	2.9
6	Iceland	1.5
7	Safeway	1.5
8	Waitrose	1.5
9	Kwik Save	1.0
10	Co-op	0.8
11	Somerfield	0.6

Which Retailer Performs the Best Overall, by Region

London	Anglia	South	South West	Wales & West	Midlands	Lancs. & Borders	Yorkshire	Tyne Tees	Central & N. Scotland
Tesco	Tesco	Tesco	Tesco	Asda	Asda	Asda	Asda	Asda	Asda

Retailer Rankings by Key Attribute

	Overall	Price	Range	Quality	Service	Stock Levels
1st	Asda	Asda	Asda	M&S	Asda	Asda
2nd	Tesco	Tesco	Tesco	Asda	Tesco	Tesco
3rd	Sainsbury's	Morrisons	Sainsbury's	Sainsbury's	M&S	Sainsbury's

Note(s): Results are based on a sample of statistically weighted households which are representative of all GB Households.
Source(s): ACNielsen Homescan, 2004.

FOOD FOCUS GROUPS

Food Focus is an attitudinal segmentation based on expressed attitudes to cooking and eating.

Based on the sample of households drawn from the ACNielsen Homescan Panel, the households are weighted to represent the GB household population. In addition, the wealth of information, including purchasing history, is used to profile each of the segments.

Food Focus Summary By Segment

Food Focus Group	Characteristics	All households (%)	% of expenditure
No Bother Fodder	'If only there was a pill that could replace food, I really can't be bothered with this cooking lark.'	13.7	12.8
Chore Cooks	'I hate cooking but I will if I have to.'	14.4	13.7
Frenzied Families	'Life is so hectic with work, the kids and household chores, convenience meals and snacks are how I cope.'	14.9	15.1
Three Square Mealers	'I'm a meat and two veg type of person. I have no interest in these foreign foods.'	16.7	16.8
Nut Roast Nutritionists	'Meat is not an important part of my diet, I also like to eat healthily and be nutritionally aware.'	12.3	11.4
Eager Organics	'I really enjoy cooking and believe that an organic alternative really improves the quality and taste of a meal.'	14.0	15.3
Gourmet Go-Getters	'Food is my greatest pleasure in life. I love spending time in my kitchen cooking up culinary delights for my friends and family.'	14.1	15.0

Source(s): ACNielsen Homescan, 52 weeks ending December 2003.

IMPORTANCE OF SEGMENT TO RETAILER

	Tesco	Safeway	Sainsbury's	Asda	Somerfield	Kwik Save
					Base expenditure (GB): All households	
No Bother Fodder	111	109	83	111	82	69
Frenzied Families	81	103	88	121	89	174
Three Square Mealers	94	81	95	94	129	120
Nut Roast Nutritionists	109	79	111	74	107	68
Gourmet Go-Getters	119	102	111	110	70	22
Chore Cooks	93	122	107	107	91	173
Gourmet Go-Getters	97	104	105	79	125	65

Source(s): ACNielsen Homescan (52 weeks ending December 2003).

HEALTH & FITNESS

Do you do anything to maintain or improve your general health? (%)	
Yes	51.1
No	48.9

In the last year have you felt overweight (%)	
Yes	54.7
No	41.3

By how much have you felt overweight?

1–3 Kg	13.0	9–20 Kg	17.6
4–8 Kg	19.1	Over 20 Kg	4.4

How often do you diet either to slim/lose weight or for other health reasons? (%)

Often	13.2	Rarely	16.6
Sometimes	17.7	Never	31.2

Source(s): Target Group Index © BMRB 2004 (April 2003 – March 2004).

FOOD FOCUS GROUPS

Food Focus Summary By Segment

Food Focus Group	Characteristics	All households (%)	% of expenditure
Don't Snack, Won't Snack	'I never snack thank you very much, now it's time for my cup of tea and biscuit.'	13.6	12.8
Healthy Greys	'I watch what I eat nowadays, so I'll choose fruit over chocolate.'	13.3	13.5
Swift Snacking Singles	'I am often so busy I don't have time to have a proper meal, so I'll just have a hot snack instead.'	14.0	12.3
Pie and a Pint	'I like a pie and a can of beer while watching the footy on the box.'	11.0	10.9
Snack Police	'I keep a strict control on what my family can and can't eat.'	5.8	6.8
Lunchbox Planners	'My other half and I always prepare a proper packed lunch to take to work and school.'	12.5	13.9
Self Service Planners	'Everyone gets home at different times so we all just help ourselves.'	15.3	14.4
Comfort Snackers	'I just love to curl up in front of the TV with my favourite snack treats.'	14.5	15.4

Source(s): ACNielsen Homescan (52 weeks ending December 2003).

DIETING

Percentage of households

'Which of the following have you ever tried?'

Weight Watchers	22.0	High Protein	2.0
Slim Fast	13.0	Herbalife	2.0
Slimming World	11.0	Blood Type	1.0
Rosemary Conley	8.0	Other Low Carbohydrate	4.0
Atkins	7.0	Other Low Fat	15.0
Cabbage Soup	7.0	Other Diet	19.0
Grapefruit	3.0	Never Dieted	37.0

'Which if the following is most likely to improve your diet?'

Drink more water	53.0	Eat calorie controlled food	14.0
Eat 5 portions of fruit & veg	51.0	Eat functional foods	5.0
Eat less	37.0	None of these	11.0
Eat low fat versions	33.0		

Source(s): ACNielsen Homescan (12 weeks ending December 2003).

VALUE SALES GROWTH BY CATEGORY

Percentage change yr-on-yr

	Total category	Healthy sector/low fat or diet	
	%	%	Definition
Tea	−3.0	5.9	Decaffeinated, fruit & herbal
Butter	0.9	12.0	Nutriceuticals
Soft drinks	10.9	9.0	Diet carbonates
Dairy desserts	7.4	1.2	Diet yogurts
Dairy desserts	7.4	20.7	Bio & probiotic yogurts
Crisps	0.4	−8.1	Reduced fat
Salad accompaniments	7.4	8.5	Reduced fat

Source(s): ACNielsen Scantrack.

VALUE SALES OF DEFINED ORGANIC PRODUCTS THROUGH GROCERY MULTIPLES – ROLLING MAT[1]

Organic Food Sales vs. Total Business Performance

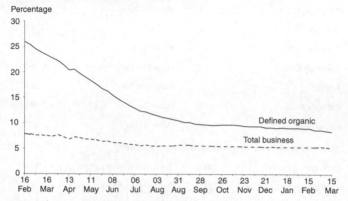

Percentage

Note(s): [1] 52 week period stated compared to equivalent 52 week period a year ago.
Source(s): ACNielsen Scantrack rolling moving annual totals to period end, year to March 2003.

Organic Food Sales as a Percentage of Total Business

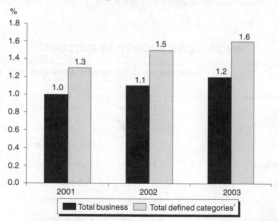

%

Note(s): [1] A category where an organic alternative is available.
Source(s): ACNielsen Scantrack (52 weeks ending March).

HOUSEHOLD PENETRATION OF ORGANIC GOODS

	GB Households (%)	Pack Sales (%)
Low (1–5 occasions)	49.6	9.9
Medium (6–30 occasions)	24.3	34.7
Committed (31 or more occasions)	4.8	55.4

Source(s): ACNielsen Homescan, (52 weeks ending February 2003).

CONSUMER ATTITUDES TO ORGANIC FOOD

Percentage

	All Households	Social Class ABC1	Social Class C2DE
Households agreeing to statement			
'I always look to see whether an organic alternative is available when choosing grocery products.'	13.0	14.8	11.1
'Organic products taste better than non-organic.'	31.2	33.6	28.7
'I buy more organic products now than I did a year ago.'	23.1	27.2	19.0
'It is worth paying extra for organic food.' 1	9.4	23.2	15.8

Source(s): ACNielsen Homescan Survey, February 2003.

CONSUMER MOTIVATIONS FOR PURCHASING ORGANIC FOOD

Percentage

	All households[1]
'Why do you personally purchase organic products?'	
No pesticides	59.5
Healthier	58.5
Better for the environment	55.7
Do not contain GM ingredients	51.0
Better quality	38.5
Trust organic production methods	30.8
Less likely to have a food allergy reaction	21.3
Other household member prefers it	7.3

Note(s): [1] Responses from consumers who have 'ever' purchased an organic food product.
Source(s): ACNielsen Homescan Survey, February 2003.

TRENDS IN CONSUMER PROMOTION

					Percent expenditure on items with offer
	1999	2000	2001	2002	2003
Total GB	**22.9**	**23.7**	**26.1**	**26.2**	**26.1**

Source(s): ACNielsen Homescan (12 weeks ending December 2003).

CONSUMER PROMOTION BY TYPE

	Percent of total
Price reduction	40.5
Multi-buy/save	44.2
Additional quantity in pack	5.8
Coupon used	1.0
Banded pack	3.1
Any other offer	5.4

Source(s): ACNielsen Homescan (12 weeks ending December 2003).

CONSUMER PROMOTION EXPENDITURE BY PRODUCT CATEGORY

	Percent of total expenditure by product category		
Liquor	41.0	Household	24.1
Soft drinks	35.1	Delicatessen	22.9
Defined frozen	36.6	Bakery	19.4
Confectionery	35.9	Dry grocery	20.5
Toiletries	23.6	Dairy	13.7

Source(s): ACNielsen Homescan (12 weeks ending December 2003).

CONSUMER PROMOTION BY TYPE AND PRODUCT CATEGORY

	Percent of total consumer promotions			
	Multi-buys	Store price reductions	Additional quantity in pack	Coupons
Dry grocery	48.6	31.8	7.9	1.1
Soft drinks	60.3	26.2	1.7	0.6
Household	25.8	33.9	24.9	2.0
Defined frozen	70.0	22.3	2.9	0.5
Delicatessen	44.1	43.3	4.4	0.4
Dairy	53.7	30.3	2.2	2.3
Liquor	29.9	59.5	2.6	1.0
Toiletries	58.8	23.4	4.3	3.9
Bakery	47.4	38.0	5.8	0.5
Confectionery	60.4	26.9	6.2	0.7

Source(s): ACNielsen Homescan (12 weeks ending December 2003).

TRENDS IN CONSUMER PROMOTION BY RETAILER

				Percent expenditure on items with offer	
	1999	2000	2001	2002	2003
Tesco	19.5	19.4	22.0	23.4	23.4
Sainsbury's	30.0	26.9	28.7	29.3	30.9
Safeway	29.5	37.4	43.1	43.5	46.5
Asda	20.2	20.0	20.8	20.6	16.7
Somerfield	32.1	35.3	37.2	38.4	38.6
Kwik Save	19.5	23.2	25.1	29.3	28.4
Total GB	**22.9**	**23.7**	**26.1**	**26.2**	**26.1**

Source(s): ACNielsen Homescan (12 weeks ending December 2003).

TRENDS IN CONSUMER PROMOTION BY TYPE AND RETAILER

		Percent of total consumer promotions by retailer			
		Multi-buys	Price Reductions	Additional quantity in pack	Coupons used
Tesco	end 2001	41	42	7	3
	end 2002	48	36	6	3
	end 2003	53	31	6	3
Sainsbury's	end 2001	41	41	8	2
	end 2002	41	39	8	1
	end 2003	48	39	6	1
Safeway	end 2001	6	81	5	4
	end 2002	12	76	5	. .
	end 2003	30	59	4	. .
Asda	end 2001	44	33	10	2
	end 2002	66	29	5	1
	end 2003	54	32	2	1
Somerfield	end 2001	19	66	9	1
	end 2002	29	53	11	. .
	end 2003	32	53	9	1
Kwik Save	end 2001	3	70	15	1
	end 2002	4	70	13	. .
	end 2003	9	71	10	. .
Total GB	**end 2001**	**32**	**49**	**8**	**2**
	end 2002	**38**	**45**	**7**	**1**
	end 2003	**44**	**41**	**6**	**1**

Source(s): ACNielsen Homescan (12 weeks ending December 2003).

PROMO* FOCUS GROUPS

Promo* is an attitudinal segmentation based on expressed attitudes to pricing and promotion activity.

Based on the sample of households drawn from the ACNielsen Homescan Panel, the households are weighted to represent the GB household population. In addition, the wealth of information, including purchasing history, is used to profile each of the segments.

Food Focus Summary By Segment

Food Focus Group	Characteristics	All households (%)
Branded EDLP Seekers	'I'm not prepared to compromise, even though I'm a bit short I know what brands I like and I'll search about for them at the lowest price.'	17.4
Low Price Fixture Ferrets	'I know where I'm going to shop and I'll look about for the lowest price when I get there.'	14.2
Promotion Junkies	'I've no need to be thrifty but I love it – I get a buzz out of getting the most groceries for the lowest price. Coupons appeal to me.'	15.1
Stock-pilers	'Well, it seemed silly not to buy it – it was such a good buy and even though I've got an awful lot of it, well it's our favourite brand.'	13.4
Budget Bound	'I hate shopping because I have to be so careful. Money is very tight.'	13.8
Promotion Opportunist	'I love promotions and am prepared to buy more to get a bargain. Saving money is key.'	11.9
Promotionally Oblivious	'So what's a promotion then?'	14.2

Source(s): ACNielsen Homescan (52 weeks ending December 2003).

IMPORTANCE OF SEGMENT TO RETAILER

					Base expenditure (GB): All households	
	Tesco	Safeway	Sainsbury's	Asda	Somerfield	Kwik Save
Branded EDLP Seekers	92	112	106	93	88	75
Low Price Fixture Ferrets	87	80	88	105	133	134
Promotion Junkies	109	71	108	120	96	69
Stock-Pilers	101	98	75	106	91	145
Budget Bound	95	115	146	74	88	84
Promotion Opportunist	103	117	103	87	102	60
Promotionally Oblivious	112	109	83	110	103	115

Source(s): ACNielsen Homescan (52 weeks ending December 2003).

COUPON DISTRIBUTION AND REDEMPTION

	1999	2000	2001	2002	2003
Distribution (billions)	**4.7**	**5.0**	**6.0**	**5.0**	**5.9**
Share of coupon redemption by media (%)					
Newspapers	2.6	3.3	0.9	0.6	1.7
Magazines	4.9	4.5	1.9	1.8	2.6
Door-to-door	19.4	3.4	1.1	1.1	2.1
In/on pack	4.7	23.7	6.0	6.0	2.5
In store	24.6	24.7	3.9	4.6	2.8
Direct mail	37.7	33.3	80.2	76.7	75.8
Other	6.1	7.1	6.0	9.2	12.3
Redemptions (millions)	**487**	**531**	**569**	**452**	**524**
Average redemption rates by media (%)					
Newspapers	3.2	3.3	1.8	0.9	3.7
Magazines	1.5	1.5	1.4	1.1	1.9
Door-to-door	4.8	3.3	2.1	3.4	5.3
In/on pack	26.8	26.5	28.8	21.6	8.8
In store	16.8	16.2	3.1	6.7	5.5
Direct mail	20.1	20.9	10.5	8.2	11.3
Other	15.8	14.4	12.1	14.1	21.5
Average face value (pence)	**57**	**46**	**53**	**99**	**79**
Recommended manufacturers' handling allowance to retailers					
(pence per 100 coupons)	360	360	360	360	360

Note(s): Excluding retailer tailor-made promotions.
Source(s): NCH Marketing Services Ltd.

THE PRINCIPAL RETAIL ENTERPRISES

SUMMARY OF MULTI-SECTOR RETAIL GROUPS
(details under individual trades in following section)

The arrangement by number of outlets does not imply ranking by turnover

		Approx. no. of outlets
Arcadia	541 Men's clothing; 1,514 Women's clothing; 12 Mixed clothing	2,067
Boots	1,150 Chemists; 297 Opticians; 249 Variety; 6 Toiletry	1,702
Whitbread	631 Restaurants/Pubs; 313 Coffee shops; 122 Health & fitness; 406 Hotels	1,472
Alexon	53 Men's clothing; 784 Women's clothing; 208 Mixed clothing; 166 Footwear	1,211
Dixons	710 Electrical; 287 Telecommunications; 137 Computers	1,134
J. Sainsbury	447 Supermarkets/Savacentres; 235 Petrol stations	715
HMV Media Group	192 Bookshops; 171 Music/entertainment	363
Monsoon	158 Women's clothing; 3 Children's clothing; 190 Haberdashery/accessories; 1 Drapery/soft furnishings	352
Next	335 Mixed clothing; 12 Discount stores	347
Austin Reed	17 Men's clothing; 203 Women's clothing; 59 Mixed clothing	279
John Lewis Partnership	25 Department stores; 2 Furniture stores; 165 Supermarkets; 6 Petrol stations	198

MULTIPLE RETAILERS BY NUMBER OF BRANCHES

The arrangement by number of outlets does not imply ranking by turnover

Trade	Retailer	Approx. no. of outlets
FOOD & DRINK Bakers	Greggs The Bakers (incl. 14 concessions)	1,022
	Baker's Oven (The)	234
	Three Cooks	228
	Sayers (incl. 1 concession)	121
	Hampsons	111
	Warren (W T) & Son	59
	Cooplands	57
	Firkin (M)	53
	Birds	46
	Percy Ingle	45
	Skelton Bakery	45
	Ferrari's Bakery	41
	Greenhalgh's Craft Bakery	38
	Milligans Bakers	35
	Delifrance	35
	Ainsleys	32
	Waterfields	32
	Woodhead	32
	Martins Craft Bakers & Sandwiches	29
	Simmons Bakers	24
	Forfars Bakers (incl. 2 concessions)	23
	Coughlans Patisserie	21
	Pearces	20
	Staniforth's	19
	Stuart (R T)	19
	Chatwins	18
	Chalmers Bakery	18
	Goodfellow and Steven	14
	Sparks	13
	Oddie (W H)	13
	Maison Blanc	13

	Bennetts Family Bakers	11
	Wenzels	11
Freezer centres, separate	Iceland (incl. 17 concessions)	749
	Farmfoods	264
	Heron	116
	Jack Fulton	65
	Cooltrader	11
Grocers	Tesco (incl. 74 Extra Stores, 87 Metro Stores, 54 Tesco Express, 118 concessions, 4 World of Wine stores)	682
	Somerfield (incl. 2 Essential, 2 Market Fresh, 88 concessions)	656
	Kwik Save (incl. 1 concession)	654
	Sainsbury's (incl. 6 Central Stores, 2 Market Stores, 11 Savacentres 53 local stores, 6 local concessions)	506
	United Co-op	488
	Safeway (incl. 4 Megastores)	456
	Lidl	346
	Aldi	268
	Asda (incl. 12 Supercentres)	265
	Co-operative (South East)	248
	Co-operative (Eastern/Central)	238
	Co-operative (Scottish)	187
	Waitrose (incl. 5 Food & Home, 2 concessions)	165
	Co-operative (NE & Cumbrian)	149
	Co-operative (South West)	148
	Midlands Co-op	135
	Netto	135
	Morrisons	133
	Co-operative (Wales & Borders)	127
	Co-operative (Northern)	121
	Budgens	110
	Oxford, Swindon & Gloucester Co-op	83
	Southern Co-operatives	83
	Lincoln Co-op	77
	Ipswich & Norwich Co-op	75
	Scotmid (Scottish Midland Co-op)	66
	Centra Foodmarket	57
	Food Weighouse (The)	56
	Plymouth & South West Co-op	52
	West Midlands Co-op	51
	Lothian Borders & Angus Co-op	45
	Anglia Co-op	43
	Colchester & East Essex Co-op	42
	Supervalu	37
	Marks & Spencer (Food Store)	36
	Heart Of England	35
	Co-operative (Northern Ireland)	33
	Booths	27
	Chelmsford Star Co-op	24
	Sheffield Co-op	24
	Leeds Co-op	22
	Channel Islands Co-op	16
	Rainbow (Anglia Co-op)	16
	Tamworth Co-op	15
	Stampers	12
	Smith (GT) & Sons	11
	Centra Quick Stop	10
	Le Riches	10
Convenience stores	Spar (Symbol Group)	2,494
	Londis (Symbol Group)	2,236
	Costcutter (Symbol Group)	1,158
	One Stop Convenience Stores	793
	Mace (Symbol Group) (incl. 113 Aberness Foods; 391 Northern Ireland)	504
	Alldays	482
	Spar (Tates)	188
	McColls Convenience	168
	Balfour	119
	Budgens (incl. 22 Express Stores, 36 Local Stores, 7 Quickstops, 23 concessions)	118

	Jacksons Family Food Store	105
	Forbuoys Convenience Stores	84
	Marks & Spencer Simply Food	69
	Bells Stores	54
	Spar Foodstores (Lang C J)	54
	Morning Noon & Night	50
	Thorougoods	41
	Botterills	37
	Martin Convenience	36
	Whistlestop Food & Wine	36
	Europa Foods (incl. 8 Crispins; 2 Super Foods & Wine)	29
	Cullens (incl. 7 Franchises; 11 Managed Stores)	18
	Woolworths General Store	17
	David Sands	16
	R S McColls Convenience	16
	Rusts	12
	Harts The Grocer	10
	Smile	6
Tea & coffee	Whittard	107
Health foods	Holland & Barrett	454
	Julian Graves (incl. 15 concessions)	212
	GNC	50
	Dr & Herbs	49
	Herbal Inn	34
	Dr China	27
	Herbmedic	26
Herbs & spices	Culpeper	16
Off-licenses	Thresher Wine Shops	1,002
	Victoria Wine Company (The)	703
	Bargain Booze	387
	Unwins	387
	Booze Buster	271
	Drinks Cabins	232
	Oddbins (incl. 8 Fine Wine; 13 Ultimate Wine Stores)	227
	Wine Rack	209
	Haddows	178
	Majestic Wine Warehouses	107
	Bottoms Up (incl. 9 Wine Shops)	82
	Winemark	70
	Hutton's	68
	Wine Cellar	58
	G101 Off Sales	50
	Russells Cellars	43
	Alpha Retail	42
	Rhythm & Booze	30
	Nicolas	21
	Airey's Wine Stores	20
CLOTHING, FOOTWEAR		
Clothing, men's	Burton (incl. 25 concessions)	386
	Top Man (incl. 44 concessions)	156
	Officers Club (The)	150
	Greenwoods	101
	Jaeger Man (incl. 22 concessions)	92
	Moss (incl. 2 concessions, 1 hire concession)	84
	Suits You	58
	Envy	53
	Ciro Citterio	51
	Cecil Gee (incl. 2 concessions)	32
	Baron Jon (incl. 1 Baron Jon Suits)	31
	Blue Inc	28
	Petroleum Menswear	26
	High and Mighty (incl. 1 concession)	25
	Van Heusen	25
	Scotts	22
	Austen Reed Menswear (incl. 15 concessions)	17
	Slater Menswear	17
	Hackett (incl. 4 concessions)	16
	Oxford Menswear	14
	Suit Co	13
	Blakes	12
	Lewin (T M)	11
	Suits Plus	11

	Kurt Muller	10
	Gieves & Hawkes (incl. 1 concession)	10
Clothing, women's	Dorothy Perkins (incl. 98 concessions)	541
	New Look	522
	Evans (incl. 29 concessions)	319
	Bon Marche (incl. 2 concessions)	304
	Ethel Austin	251
	Mackays (incl. 1 concession)	245
	Planet Shop (incl. 206 concessions)	221
	Select (incl. 32 concessions)	219
	Windsmoor Shop (The) (incl. 199 concessions)	219
	Precis Petit (incl. 202 concessions)	205
	Principles (incl. 147 concessions)	205
	Country Casuals (incl. 65 concessions)	199
	Etam (incl. 6 concessions)	198
	Warehouse (incl. 117 concessions)	179
	Viyella (incl. 125 concessions)	170
	Jacques Vert (incl. 137 concessions)	168
	Oasis (incl. 67concessions)	161
	Monsoon	158
	Alexon (incl. 147 concessions)	152
	Dash (incl. 127 concessions)	139
	Anne Harvey (incl. 76 concessions)	126
	Miss Selfridge (incl. 62 concessions)	126
	Romans Originals (incl. 72 concessions)	104
	Laura Ashley (incl. 6 Garments Stores)	102
	Coast (incl. 83 concessions)	92
	Elvi (incl. 69 concessions)	90
	Pilot	90
	Contessa	78
	Phase Eight (incl. 29 concessions)	72
	Happitt (incl. 22 concessions)	68
	Karen Millen (incl. 11 concessions	66
	Jane Norman (incl. 28 concessions)	59
	Kookai (incl. 29 concessions)	59
	Internacionale	52
	Morgan (incl. 26 concessions)	46
	East	44
	Quizz (incl. 1 concession)	40
	Episode (incl. 25 concessions)	35
	Hobbs (incl. 4 concessions)	34
	Size Up	34
	Whistles (inol. 19 concessions)	32
	Klrkwood Fashions	29
	Giant (incl. 26 concessions)	28
	Long Tall Sally (incl. 1 concession)	25
	Krisp	23
	Nightingales	23
	Logo	21
	Mango (incl. 1 concession)	17
	Talbots (incl. 11 concessions)	17
	Autonomy	16
	Menarys	16
	Esprit (incl. 13 concessions)	15
	Jaeger (incl. 55 concessions)	14
	Miss Sixty	14
	Nicole Farhi (incl. 2 concessions)	11
	Tammy	11
	Vestry (The)	10
Clothing, mixed	Peacocks (incl. 29 concessions)	405
	Next (incl. 7 concessions)	335
	Edinburgh Woollen Mill (incl. 16 concessions)	285
	Matalan	185
	Bewise (incl. 3 concessions)	184
	River Island	184
	QS	182
	MK One	164
	Jumper (incl. 62 concessions)	141
	Maxx (T K)	132
	Gap (incl. 15 Gap Body)	123
	Mexx (incl. 72 concessions)	100
	D2	86

	H & M (Hennes)	80
	Primark	80
	French Connection (incl. 4 concessions)	73
	Cromwell's Madhouse	65
	Gant (incl. 56 concessions)	65
	Austin Reed (incl. 7 concessions)	59
	Benetton	56
	Factory Shop (The)	51
	Eisenegger	49
	Ted Baker (incl. 23 concessions)	46
	Cotton Traders (incl. 4 concessions)	42
	USC	41
	Elle (incl. 24 concessions)	40
	Jigsaw	36
	Bay Trading (incl. 60 concessions)	32
	Designer Room (The)	30
	Hawkshead (incl. 13 concessions)	27
	Jean Scene	27
	Reiss	27
	Aquascutum (incl. 19 concessions)	26
	Crew Clothing Co	26
	Zara	26
	Bennett (L K)	25
	Burberry (incl. 1 concessions)	23
	Republic	23
	Marks & Spencer (incl. 18 Outlet Stores)	22
	Sisley (incl. 5 concessions)	22
	Leading Labels (incl. 1 concession)	21
	YHA Adventure Shops	21
	Bank	20
	Joseph (incl. 5 concessions)	20
	Active Venture	18
	Damart	18
	Alexandra	17
	Foxhole	17
	Pink (incl. 1 concessions)	17
	Capo	16
	Surprise Surprise	15
	Diesel (incl. 3 concessions)	14
	Orvis	14
	Richleys	14
	Base Menswear/Boys Base	13
	Best Jeanswear	13
	Choice	13
	Outfit (The)	13
	First Choice	12
	Next To Nothing	12
	Tommy Hilfiger	11
	Proibito	10
Clothing, children's	Adams (incl. 175 concessions)	490
	National Schoolwear Centres	28
	Pumpkin Patch	9
	Morleys	4
Maternity, babywear	Mothercare (incl. 62 Mothercare World, 7 concessions)	235
	Baby Gap	93
	Mamas & Papas Superstore	18
Underwear	Ann Summers	93
	La Senza (incl. 14 concessions)	78
	Knickerbox (incl. 25 concessions)	46
	Camille Lingerie	8
Accessories, haberdasheries	Claire's Accessories	409
	Accesorize (incl. 1 concession)	190
	Mr Minit (incl. 38 concessions)	179
	Tie Rack	124
	Jane Hilton (incl. 81 concessions)	88
	Sock Shop (incl. 10 concessions)	71
	Minit (incl. 42 concessions)	51
	Gullivers	32
	Baggage Company (incl. 28 concessions)	31
	Salisbury's (incl. 7 concessions)	27
	Links of London (incl. 3 concessions)	19
	Mikey (incl. 5 concessions)	18

	Girl Heaven	16
	Saddlers (incl. 1 concession)	15
	Lockeys (incl. 1 concession)	15
	Case London (incl. 6 concessions)	14
	Mulberry (incl. 6 concessions)	12
Leisurewear Footwear	See '*Other Non-Food Specialists: Camping, Leisurewear, Sports Goods*'	
	Clarks Shop (The) (incl. 85 Franchises, 65 concessions, 29 clearance shops)	537
	Barratts (incl. 313 concessions)	524
	ShoeFayre (incl. 5 ShoeFayre Extra; 69 concessions)	310
	Stead & Simpson (incl. 7 concessions)	243
	Faith Shoes (incl. 141 concessions)	193
	Dolcis (incl. 103 concessions)	166
	Shoe Zone (incl. 5 concessions)	160
	Rohan (incl. 120 concessions)	142
	Brantano	129
	Shoe Studio (The) (incl. 98 concessions)	99
	Shoe Collection (concession)	90
	Priceless Shoes	85
	Shoe Express	83
	Jones Bootmaker (various fascias)	74
	Scholl (incl. 1 concession)	55
	Shuh (incl. 2 concessions)	48
	Ravel	47
	Jonathan James	43
	Russell & Bromley (incl. 2 concessions)	42
	Kurt Geiger (incl. 35 concessions)	42
	Pavers (incl. 6 concessions)	36
	Original Shoe Co	32
	Bacons Shoes	32
	Sole Trader	31
	Peter Briggs	29
	Dune (incl. 1 concession)	29
	Carvela Shoes (concessions)	29
	Discount Shoe Zone	28
	Feet & Co	27
	D E Shoes	27
	Raw (incl. 1 Raw XS)	26
	Shoestop	24
	Moda In Pelle (incl. 7 concessions)	23
	Office London	22
	Medina Shoes (incl. 12 concessions)	21
	Wynsors World Of Shoes	21
	Charles Clinkard	19
	Lilley & Skinner (incl. 2 concessions)	17
	Nine West	16
	Tylers (incl. 10 Express Stores)	16
	Timberland (incl. 1 concession)	16
	Ecco	16
	Deichmann Shoes	14
	Bally (incl. 1 concession)	14
	Church's Shoes	13
	Shellys	13
	Soled Out	11
	Broughton Shoe Warehouse	11
	Feet Inc	10

HOME IMPROVEMENT, APPLIANCES
Decorating, DIY hardware, etc.

	B&Q (incl. 37 Mini Warehouse; 97 Warehouse)	318
	Homebase	277
	Focus Do It All (incl. 233 Focus for DIY & Gardening; 1 Wickes Warehouse)	253
	Topps Tiles (incl. 1 concession)	210
	Mica Hardware (Members)	178
	Wickes (incl. 2 Wickes Extra)	170
	ICI Dulux Decorator Centre	144
	Crown Trade Decorator Centre	106
	Brewer (C) & Sons	98
	Floors-2-Go	98
	Tiles R Us	94
	Leyland Trade Centres	92
	Robert Dyas	74

Machine Mart	44
Cargo Homeshop	37
Glyn Webb Home Improvements	25
Porcelanosa	22
Amy's Cook & Dine (incl. 1 concession)	13
Maxwells DIY	13
Cane Adam	11
Tile Market	10
BHK	10
Arnold Laver DIY Timberworld	10

Electronics, photographic
(see also TV rental; video rental)

Euronics Centres (Members)	608
Currys (incl. 296 Superstores)	386
Dixons (incl. 5 Dixons XL)	324
Klick Photopoint (incl. 23 concessions)	272
Comet	250
Supasnaps (incl. 69 concessions)	224
Max Spielmann	160
New Powerhouse (incl. 109 Super Stores)	133
Sony Centre (incl. 3 concessions)	124
Snappy Snaps	119
Maplin Electronics	80
Bang & Olufsen (incl. 3 concessions)	78
Hydro-Electric	53
Richer Sounds	45
Sevenoaks Sound & Vision	44
Colorama	42
Hughes Electrical	35
Bonus Print	29
Photo Factory	28
Miller Brothers	26
Audio T	16
Superfi	13
Apollo 2000	12
Ryness	10

Furnishers, household equipment
household
equipment

Rosebys (incl. 3 concessions)	350
Carpet Right (incl. 2 concessions)	348
Moben Kitchens (incl. 100 concessions)	285
Sharps (incl. 153 concessions)	247
MFI	214
Magnet (incl. 11 concessions)	206
Allied Carpets	190
Harveys	169
Bensons Bed Centres (incl. 99 concessions)	141
Hygena (concessions)	134
Brighthouse	116
Ponden Mill (incl. 12 concessions)	111
Walmsley's Furniture Superstore (incl. 53 Suite Superstores; 1 Furniture Centre)	103
Dreams Superstores	102
Hammonds (incl. 91 conesions)	95
Courts (incl. 65 Mammoth Superstores)	94
Laura Ashley (incl. 62 concessions; 29 Home Furnishings)	91
Au Naturale	81
DP Furniture Express	80
Sleepmasters (incl. 46 concessions)	78
Apollo Window Blinds	75
DFS	67
Dunelm Mill Shop	66
SCS	59
Multiyork	58
Klaussner Furniture (incl. 1 concession)	56
Land Of Leather	54
Habitat	40
Paul Simon (incl. 21 concesions)	40
In-Toto Kitchens	39

	Fabric Warehouse (incl. 1 concession)	37
	Mostyns (incl. 19 concessions)	36
	Aga Shop (The)	34
	Futon Company	33
	London Bed Company (The) (incl. 32 concessions)	33
	Harry Corry	33
	Furniture Village	29
	Sofa Workshop	29
	Pier (The) (incl. 2 concessions)	26
	Lakeland Limited	26
	Traesko	25
	Reid	25
	Furnitureland	22
	Linens Direct	21
	Wesley-Barrell	20
	General George	20
	Spacemaker	19
	Storey Carpets (incl. 2 concessions)	19
	And So to Bed (incl. 1 So to Bed Studio)	18
	Iron Bed Company (The)	17
	Texstyle World Home	17
	Clive Christian	15
	Matthews Office Furniture	15
	Allders At Home	15
	Bed And Bath Works	15
	Carpet-World	14
	Kingdom Of Leather	13
	Mutual	12
	New Heights (incl. 1 concession)	12
	IKEA	12
	Essex Beds (incl. 1 concession)	11
	Design House	11
	Delcor Furniture	10
	Sofas UK	10
	Harris Carpets	10
	Fabric Land	10
Tableware	National Trust	220
	Waterford Wedgwood (incl. 127 concessions)	146
	Royal Doulton (incl. 134 concessions)	135
	Edinburgh Crystal (incl. 104 concessions)	117
	Past Times	83
	Swarovski (incl. 25 concessions)	37
	Lawleys (incl. 1 concession)	36
	Natural World	30
	Dartington Crystal (incl. 18 concessions)	25
	Gift Company (The)	23
	Hobbycraft	20
	Professional Cookware Company	17
	Evolution	16
	Nauticalia	12
	Oliver Bonas	12
	Martin Dawes	18
TV rental	Sportizus	11
	Bennetts	11
Video rental & sales	Video Stores (independents)	0,120
	Blockbuster Superstores (incl. 472 Express Stores)	721
	Global Video	225
	Choices Video	220
	Apollo Video	91
	Xtra-Vision	54
	Video Drive In	33
	Prime Time Video	20
	Vid Biz	15
	Hollywood Video	15
	Video Solent	11
	Silverscreen DVD Entertainment	6
	Video Stop (The)	6
OTHER NON-FOOD SPECIALISTS		
Booksellers	Waterstone's (incl. 1 concession)	192
	Works (The)	150
	Ottakar's (incl. 2 concessions)	123
	Blackwell's (various trade names)	66
	County Bookshops	49
	Wesley Owen	38
	Books Etc	35
	Bookworld	30
	Booksale	30

	Eason	26
	SPCK Bookshops	25
	Borders	25
	Book Depot	21
	CLC	20
	Just Books	12
	Bookcase (The)	11
	Bookends (Sound & Media)	10
	Samedaybooks.co.uk At Methvens	8
	James Thin	8
	Banana Bookshop	7
Camping, leisureware, sports goods	JJB Sports (incl. 3 Soccer Dome; 227 Superstores)	436
	All:Sports	280
	JD Sports	262
	Millets (incl. 2 concessions)	243
	Intersport (Members)	122
	Sports Soccer	105
	Gilesports (incl. 2 concessions)	80
	Fat Face	77
	Blacks	67
	Hargreaves Sports (incl. 1 concession)	59
	American Golf Discount Centre	55
	Yeomans Army Stores	52
	Foot Locker	43
	Tog 24	42
	First Sport	38
	Free Spirit	37
	Nevada Bob	28
	Camping & Outdoor Centres	26
	Mountain Warehouse (incl. 1 concession)	24
	Legends	23
	Quiksilver Boardrider Club	23
	White Stuff	19
	Sweatshop (incl. 11 concessions)	18
	Streetwise Sports	17
	Reebok	17
	Field & Trek	15
	Donnay International	15
	Trespass	15
	Lifestyle Sports	14
	Adidas	14
	Cotswold	14
	Athleisure	14
	Size? (incl. 2 concessions)	14
	Ellis Brigham	12
	Sports World (incl. 1 concession)	12
	Supersport	12
	Up & Running	12
	Tiso (incl. 1 concession)	11
	Just Add Water	10
	O'Neill (incl. 1 concession)	10
Car accessories	See *'The Retail Motor Trade'*, p. 110	
Chemists, drug stores, toiletries	Lloyds Pharmacy (incl. 5 concessions)	1,349
	Boots (incl. 24 Healthcare Stores, 14 concessions, 6 toiletries)	1,150
	Vantage Pharmacy (incl. 880 franchises)	916
	Moss Pharmacy (incl. 13 concessions)	783
	Co-op Pharmacy (incl. 128 Co-op Healthcare)	429
	Rowland (L) & Co (incl. 2 concesions)	311
	Cohens Chemist	115
	Tims & Parker	78
	Paydens (various fascias)	64
	Bairds Chemists (various fascias)	49
	Selles Dispensing Chemists (incl. 1 concession)	43
	Manor Pharmacy	41
	Howard & Palmer	41
	Weldricks Pharmacy	36
	Gordons Chemists	33
	Taylor Chemists (Various Fascia)	27
	Munro Chemists (incl. 1 concession)	26
	Lindsay & Gilmour	23

	Gordon Davis	21
	Walter Davidson And Sons	20
	Sheppard (A & J M)	19
	McParland Pharmacies (various fascias)	18
	Houghton And Lappin	16
	Murray (J N)	14
	Safedale	14
	Dean & Smedley	10
	Pharmacy Plus	10
	Lifestyle Pharmacy	7
Note(s):	*Many supermarkets now operate in-store pharmacies.*	17
Computers,		
computer games	Game (incl. 30 concessions)	339
	Gamestation (incl. 35 concessions)	199
	PC World	137
	Computer Shop (The) (incl. 1 concession)	130
	Chips	23
	Evesham.Com	17
	Specialist Computer Centres	13
	Computer Exchange	10
Confectioners,		
tobacconists,		
newsagents	Thorntons (incl. 7 concessions; 203 franchises)	559
	Martin The Newsagent	396
	Forbuoys	338
	Stars News Shops	190
	Dillons (CTNS)	172
	R S McColls	140
	Supercigs	121
	Smith (W H)-Bookstalls (incl. 93 Station/Airport Bookshops)	121
	Mills Newsagents	84
	Gt Retail	74
	United News Shops	63
	Mercury News Shops	63
	Newshops	54
	Arden News	44
	Gibbs	30
	Maxwell & Kennedy	18
	Finlays	18
	More	16
	Sweet Factory (incl. 2 concessions)	13
Decorative gifts	Prices Candles	16
Garden centres	Calor Dealers	526
	Wyevale Garden Centres	122
	Countrywide Stores	32
	Dobbies Garden Centres	17
	Notcutts Garden Centres	14
	Hillier Garden Centres	13
	William Strike	11
	Squires	10
Note(s):	*Many DIY chains operate garden centres.*	13
Greetings cards,		
stationers	Clinton Cards	742
	Birthdays (incl. 13 concessions)	499
	Card Warehouse	205
	Cardfair	189
	Stationery Box	129
	Ryman	91
	Partners The Stationers	84
	Paperchase (incl. 44 concessions)	61
	Card Factory	55
	British Bookshops Sussex Stats	49
	Art	37
	Athena	33
	Card Crazy	31
	Osborne Office Stationers	25
	Pen Shop (The) (incl. 9 concessions)	23
	Celebrations	21
	Cards Galore	17
	Cards	16
	Paper Mill Shop (The)	13
	Art Factory (The)	10

Jewellers	Samuel (H)	413
	Ernest Jones	180
	Goldsmiths Group Jewellers	166
	Warren James	112
	Hinds (F)	106
	Half Price Jewellers	70
	Ciro (incl. 52 concessions)	55
	Harvey & Thompson	52
	Beaverbrooks	51
	Fraser Hart (various fascias)	28
	Henderson The Jewellers	22
	Symingtons The Genuine H P (incl. 1 concession)	21
	Mappin and Webb (incl. 4 concessions)	21
	Herbert Brown	20
	Leslie Davies	17
	Watches Of Switzerland (incl. 1 concession)	14
	Chapelle Jewellery	12
	Ortak	12
	Toko	10
Music, entertainment	HMV (incl. 2 concessions)	171
	Virgin Megastores (incl. 54 Virgin Express)	150
	MVC	86
	Music Zone	48
	XS Music & Video	21
	Andys Records	20
	Fopp	15
Opticians, optical superstores, eyeware	Specsavers (incl. 14 concessions)	448
	Dollond & Aitchison	383
	Boots Opticians (incl. 1 concession)	297
	Vision Express Optical Lab	191
	Optical Express (incl. 3 concessions)	163
	Rayner	76
	Batemans Opticians	68
	Scrivens	65
	Sunglass Hut/Watch Station	60
	Leightons	45
	Melson Wingate Opticians	38
	David Clulow (incl.5 concessions)	33
	Crown Optical Centre	30
	Direct Specs Factory Outlet	26
	Black & Lizars	23
	Eye Clinic	21
	Direkt Optik International	20
	Conlons Opticians	17
	Lancaster And Thorpe	17
	Blow (D I)	14
	Optica (incl. 1 concession)	10
Photographic	*See under, 'Electronics, Photographic'.*	
Pet shops	Pets At Home	151
	Petworld (concessions)	39
	Jollye's Petfood Superstores	31
Telephones, communications	Carphone Warehouse (The) (incl. 17 concessions)	477
	Phones 4 U	349
	Vodafone Retail	315
	Link (The)	287
	Orange	254
	O2	198
	T-Mobile	132
	MPC Mobile Phone Centre	56
	KJC Mobile Phones	45
	Jag	41
	Fonehouse	28
	Chitter Chatter	13
	Mobile Phones Direct	13
Toys	Early Learning Centre (incl. 54 concessions)	265
	Toyworld Toymaster (incl. 166 members; 22 concessions)	210
	Games Workshop	114
	Gadgetshop.Com	68
	Toys R Us	64
	Disney Store (The)	61
	Discovery Store (The) (incl. 7 concessions)	57
	Entertainer (The)	35
	Formative Fun (incl. 3 concessions)	33

	Bear Factory (The)	31
	Warner Brothers Studio Stores	20
	Gamleys Toy Shops	19
	Modelzone	17

DEPARTMENT & VARIETY STORES

Department stores	Debenhams	102
	Hughes (T J) & Co	37
	Dunnes Stores	33
	Boyes Stores	27
	Allders	26
	John Lewis	21
	House Of Fraser	17
Variety stores	Woolworths	788
	WHSmith	559
	Poundstretcher	334
	Marks & Spencer	270
	Boots-Large Stores	249
	Wilkinson	220
	Your More Store (incl. 7 concessions)	192
	Bhs	161
	Littlewoods/Littlewoods Extra	120
	Poundland	102
	Home Bargains	80
	Krackers 99p Store	25
	Big W	22
	Quids In	20
	Quality Save	19
	99p Stores	18
	Qd Stores	17
	Muji (incl. 2 concessions)	16
	B&M Bargain Madness	16
	Range Home & Leisure (The)	13

SERVICES

Bingo halls	Gala Clubs	169
	Mecca Bingo	124
	Castle Leisure	7
Dry cleaners	Johnsons (incl. 33 concessions)	458
	Sketchley (incl. 76 concessions)	221
	Munro-Klick	96
	Klick-Johnsons	40
	Brooks (incl. 2 concessions)	32
	City Of London Launderette	14
	Marlowe Cleaners	7
Health clubs, gyms	Health Clubs/Gyms Independents	996
	Fitness First	138
	Harpers Fitness/Leisure Connec	113
	Livingwell	83
	L A Fitness	64
	Esporta Health & Fitness Club	61
	Holmes Place (incl. 15 concessions)	54
	Cannons Family Clubs (incl. 46 concessions)	54
	David Lloyd	54
	Marriott Health & Fitness Club	50
	Leisure (D C)	49
	Spirit Health Clubs-Concessins	45
	Bannatyne's Health Club	31
	Club Motivation	31
	Poolside Leisure Club	27
	Dragons Health Club	21
	De Vere Leisure Club	21
	Choice Hotels Leisure Centre	20
	Ymca	19
	Sebastian Coe Health Club	18
	Swallow Leisure Club	18
	Total Fitness	17
	Holiday Inn Health Club	17
	Reviva	16
	Fitness Express	16
	Courtney's (concessions)	16
	Greens Health & Fitness	15
	Virgin Active	14
	Village Leisure	14
	Next Generation Clubs	11
Insurance, assurance	Swinton	267

	Co-op Insurance-District Office	127
	Prudential	127
	Endsleigh	123
	Royal London (The)	58
	CGU Insurance	58
	Royal Sun Alliance	52
	Legal & General	51
	Allied Dunbar	40
	AXA Insurance	40
	Liverpool Victoria Friendly Society	37
	Norwich Union	36
	Scottish Equitable	34
	Sun Life Of Canada	29
	Friends Provident	26
	AXA Sun Life	24
	Scottish Amicable	22
	Standard Life	20
	Scottish Life	18
	Zurich Insurance	18
	Royal Liver Assurance	17
	Nfu Mutual	14
	National Mutual Life	13
	Scottish Mutual Assurance	12
	Cornhill	12
Post offices	Post Office	16,495
Print & copy shops	Prontaprint	173
	Kall-Kwik	165
	Mail Boxes Etc.	79
	Service Point Uk	42
	PDC Copyprint	25
	Presto Print	10
Pubs/restaurants	Greene King Pub Partners	1,052
	Scottish & Newcastle Pubs	800
	Wolverhampton & Dudley (Managed)	794
	Wetherspoon (J D)	644
	Laurel Pub Company	479
	Burtonwood (41 managed; 409 tenanted)	450
	Greene King	413
	Pizza Hut	378
	Shepherd Neame	368
	Spirit Local	335
	Mitchells & Butlers	306
	Town/Bar Classics	301
	Wimpy	293
	Pizza Express	277
	Woodhouse Inns (94 managed; 162 tenanted)	256
	Charles Wells	255
	Brewers Fayre	246
	Ember Inns	230
	Vintage Inns	206
	Fullers	205
	Sizzling Pub Co.	201
	Spirit City	189
	Youngs Pubs	182
	Belhaven (65 managed; 109 tenanted)	174
	Beefeater Restaurant & Pub	162
	Brewsters	151
	Harvester	144
	Mr Q'S	143
	Arena	142
	Eldridge Pope	140
	Hungry Horse	136
	Chef & Brewer	134
	Yates's	130
	Everards	127
	Morrells	123
	Barras (John) & Co	117
	Brain (S A) & Co	114
	ASK	112
	George Gale	110
	Hogshead	100
	McMullen's	99
	Brakspear	98
	Innventures-Leased	97
	Bernard (T&J)	95

Two For One	93
Noble House Pubs	92
It's A Scream	91
Millers Kitchens	88
O'Neills	87
Frankie & Benny's Italian Diner	87
Nando's	85
Toby Carvery	82
Harry Ramsden's (Incl. 10 concessions)	79
Honeycombe	77
Country Carvery	77
Spirit Food (Big Steak) Pubs	77
Mitchell's of Lancaster (24 managed; 51 tenanted)	75
Q's	73
Hydes Anvil (41 managed; 31 tenanted)	72
Cafe Rouge	70
Chicago Rock Cafe	70
Regent Inns	69
Batemans	67
Ridleys	67
Pubs 'N' Bars	66
Caffe Uno	66
Litten Tree	65
Wizard Inns	62
Old English Inns & Hotels	61
Zizzi	60
Mill House Inns	59
Slug And Lettuce (The)	57
Smith & Jones	57
Barracuda Pub	55
Cafe Giardino (various fascias)	55
Bella Pasta	53
Davies & Sons (J T)	51
Deep Pan Pizza	49
All Bar One	48
Davys	47
Tom Cobleigh	45
Hook Norton	43
TGI Friday's	42
Goose	41
La Tasca	38
Thorley Taverns	34
Edwards	34
Bar Med	32
Arkell's	31
Old Orleans	31
Conran Restaurants	31
Sir John Fitzgerald	30
Out & Out Restaurant	30
Revolution	29
Flares	29
Pilcher & Piano	28
Ponti's (Various Fascias)	28
Po Na Na	27
Hobgoblins	27
Innkeepers Fayre	27
Garfunkels	27
Jennings (Tenanted)	26
Poacher's Pocket	26
Ye Olde Pub	24
Loch Fyne Restaurants	24
Chiquitos Mexican Restaurants	24
Varsity	23
Bar Room Bar	23
Ha!Ha! Bar & Canteen	23
Urbium	22
All Day Family Feast	22
Poppins	22
Ultimate Leisure	21
Est Est Est	21
Balls Brothers	18
Living Room (The)	17
Wagamama (incl. 1 concession)	17
Rat & Parrot	16

	Casa	16
	Jamies	16
	Browns Restaurant	16
	Brannigans	15
	Pleisure	15
	Bar 38	15
	Gastro Bars	15
	Cairns (R W)	15
	Jim Thompson's	14
	Yo! Sushi (incl. 3 concessions)	14
	Firkin Beer Co	14
	Herbies Pizza	13
	Simpsons Of Cornhill	13
	Blubeckers Restaurants	13
	Pizza Piazza	13
	Oak Inns	13
	Sterling Pub Company	12
	Ma Potter's	12
	Prezzo	12
	Arbuckles	12
	Chez Gerard	12
	Broken Foot Inns	12
	Puzzle	11
	Pancake Place (The)	11
	Strada	11
	Bella	11
	Henry's Cafe Bar	11
	Cafe Med	10
	Pizza Organic	10
Roadside eateries	Little Chef	382
	Moto	40
	Welcome Break	26
	Roadchef	22
Travel agents	Lunn Poly	766
	Worldchoice (Members)	631
	Thomas Cook (incl. 7 Thomas Cook Plus; 15 concessions)	623
	Going Places (incl. 11 concessions)	615
	Travelcare (incl. 63 concessions)	376
	First Choice Holiday Hypermarket (incl. 228 travel shops; 56 concessions)	320
	Co-op Travel (United Co-Op)	96
	Carlson Wagonlit	88
	Co-op Travel (Midlands)	84
	BTI UK (incl. 58 implants)	77
	American Express (15 representatives, 52 travel services, 1 concession)	68
	Travel House (The)	61
	STA Travel	60
	Bath Travel	54
	Flight Centre	53
	Travelworld	47
	Ilkeston Co-op Travel	39
	Lets Go Travel	32
	Callers Pegasus Travel Service	32
	Althams Travel Services	31
	Portman Travel	31
	Co-op Travel (West Midlands)	28
	Dawson & Sanderson (incl. 1 concession)	23
	Uniglobe Travel (various names)	23
	British Airways Travel Shops (incl. 4 concessions)	23
	Portman Travel-Implants	22
	Wallace Arnold Travel Shops	21
	Co-op Travel (Leeds Co-Op)	20
	Galaxy Travel	17
	Bowens	17
	Premier Travel Agency	15
	Yorks Travel	14
	Dr Holiday	13
	Tomorrows World Travel	12
	Tappers Travel	11
	Personal Service Travel	10
	Sibbald Travel	10

Note(s): To save space we have not necessarily shown each company's full style.
Data is accurate as of August 2004.
Source(s): Retail Locations.

CO-OPERATIVE OUTLETS

Outlets Summary

Type		Approx. no.
Large units	Superstores 27; major supermarkets 228	255
Food	Supermarkets 2,045; other grocers 69; other specialist food 14	2,128
Non-food	Department stores 94; small general stores 35; drapery (including menswear and textiles) 9; footwear 369; furnishings, hardware, jewellers, etc. 26; combined durable goods 15; radio, TV, electrical 14; pharmacy & drugs 594; optical 10	1,166
Services	Hairdressing salons 9; travel bureaux 658; restaurants 76; garages, petrol stations 182	925
Other	Post office 270; miscellaneous 34; in-store bakeries 63	367
Total		**4,841**

Source(s): Co-operative Union Ltd, 2002.

Major Societies

	Approx. no.		Approx. no.
The Co-operative Group	1,511	Southern Co-operatives (Portsmouth)	108
United Co-op	627	Anglia (Peterborough)	102
Shoefayre (Leicestershire)	366	West Midlands	00
Midlands (Lichfield)	298	Heart of England	84
National Co-op Chemists	287	Plymouth & South Devon	73
Yorkshire (Bradford)	216	Lothian & Borders (Galashiels)	65
Scottish Midland (Edinburgh)	204	Colchester & East Sussex	60
Lincoln	154	Ilkeston	58
Oxford, Swindon & Gloucester	114	Leeds	53
Ipswich & Norwich	110	Sheffield	52

Source(s): Co-operative Union Ltd, 2002.

CONVENIENCE STORES

There is no official definition of a convenience store but the following criteria provide a generally acceptable description:

- self-service;
- 1,000 to 3,000 square feet selling area;
- parking facilities;
- open seven days a week for long hours;
- a wide range of goods but limited brand choice, including groceries, CTN products, toiletries, OTC medicines, alcohol and stationery. Other products and services are take-away foods, DIY, toys, video hire, film processing and petrol.

This definition applies to specialist purpose-built convenience stores. Other convenience stores, which do not conform exactly to the full criteria, have developed from grocers, CTNs and petrol stations. Their product mix usually reflects their origin.

Leading operators, ranked in terms of number of outlets, include:

Specialists			Sainsbury[1]	540
Spar	2,800		Budgens	228
Londis	2,250		**Petrol Forecourts**	
Big Food Group	2,054		Esso	1,300
Iceland	754		Texaco	1,300
Premier	1,300		BP	1,250
Tesco[1]	1,995		TotalFina Elf	1,250
Co-operative Group	1,829		Shell	1,150
Somerfield Group	1,269		**Off Licences**	
Somerfield	589		Thresher Group	2,050
Kwik Save	680		**Pharmacies**	
TM Retail	1,260		Lloydspharmacy	1,363
Costcutter	1,200		Moss Pharmacy	795

Note(s): [1] Total UK stores, including supermarkets and hypermarkets.
Source(s): Verdict Research.

VOLUNTARY ASSOCIATIONS

Approximate number of retail members' outlets

Car accessories	A1 Motor Store (Association of Independent Motor Stores)	236
Chemists	AAH Pharmaceuticals	6,500
	Vantage	916
	Numark Ltd	1,650
CTN	Palmer & Harvey	555
Department stores	Associated Independent Stores	266[1]
Florists	Interflora	2,100
General students' supplies	NUS	750
Hardware	Fair & Square	320
Hotels	Best Western and Consort Hotels	314
Photographic	Image (Sangers Photographic)	4
Supermarkets	NISA/Today's	475
Toys	Toymaster	210

Note(s): [1] Includes some specialist shops.
Source(s): Retail Locations; companies concerned.

SOME CASH & CARRY ORGANISATIONS

Approximate number of depots

	Depots	Approx. av. sq. ft
Today's Supergroup[1]	346	30,000
Booker Cash & Carry	175	80,000
Landmark Cash & Carry	82	50,000
Sterling Supergroup[1]	50	16,000
Makro Self-Service Wholesalers (Metro)	33	150,000
Watson & Philip Food Service[2]	22	100,000
Batleys	18	17,000
Hancocks	15	50,000

Note(s): [1] Wholesale Marketing Group. [2] Also operates one specialist confectionery cash and carry depot under the Sovereign name.
Source(s): Retail Locations; companies concerned.

RETAILER LOYALTY CARDS

Which of the following Loyalty Cards do you have?[1]

	%
Tesco Clubcard	40.9
Nectar	34.0
Boots Advantage Card	32.9
WH Smith Clubcard	13.8
Shell Smart Card	2.1
Other	16.5

Note(s):   [1] Where reward points are collected when making purchases.
Source(s):   Target Group Index © BMRB 2004 (April 2003 – March 2004).

STORE, RETAIL & SERVICE CARDS

Which type of account card do you have?

	%
Option Account (pay when like)	21.4
Budget Account (fixed monthly sum)	2.7

Which Card(s) do you own?

	%
BHS	3.4
Burtons	0.6
Currys/Dixons	0.7
Debenhams	2.3
House of Fraser	3.1
John Lewis Partnership	3.3
Marks & Spencer	10.2
Sears Card	0.3
Time Card	0.8
Other Clothing Retailers	6.4
Other	10.4

Source(s):   Target Group Index © BMRB 2004 (April 2003 – March 2004).

DEPARTMENT STORES

In the past 3 months have you been to a department store to shop/look around?

	%
Yes	73.9
No	26.1

How often do you do that?

	Shop (%)	Look around (%)
Once a week or more	7.9	12.4
2–3 times a month	11.8	15.6
Once a month	14.8	17.9
Less often	17.8	18.8

Source(s): Target Group Index © BMRB 2004 (April 2003 – March 2004).

TOP 10 STORES SHOPPED AT FOR MEN'S CLOTHING

		Last 3 months (%)	Last 12 months (%)
1	Marks & Spencer	17.7	30.2
2	Asda	13.7	21.2
3	Next	11.2	18.5
4	Matalan	10.6	18.4
5	Tesco	9.6	13.4
6	Debenhams	8.4	16.4
7	Burtons	6.2	12.8
8	BHS	5.8	12.8
9	Littlewoods	4.3	7.9
10	TK Maxx	4.1	7.5

Source(s): Target Group Index © BMRB 2004 (April 2003 – March 2004).

TOP 10 STORES: WOMEN'S CLOTHING

		Last 3 months (%)	Last 12 months (%)
1	Marks & Spencer	18.4	28.5
2	Asda	11.6	17.9
3	Next	11.5	17.8
4	New Look	10.6	17.1
5	Matalan	9.8	16.6
6	Debenhams	8.0	14.5
7	Dorothy Perkins	7.9	13.9
8	BHS	7.1	13.6
9	Tesco	6.0	9.6
10	Top Shop	5.3	8.3

Source(s): Target Group Index © BMRB 2004 (April 2003 – March 2004).

TOP 10 STORES: SHOES

		Last 3 months (%)	Last 12 months (%)
1	Clarks	9.8	19.7
2	Marks & Spencer	5.3	11.0
3	Next	4.8	8.7
4	Asda	3.9	7.0
5	Shoe Express	3.1	6.1
6	Barratts	2.8	6.0
7	Stead & Simpson	2.1	4.6
8	Brantano/Shoe City	1.9	4.2
9	Debenhams	1.9	4.0
10	Dolcis	1.6	3.5

Source(s): Target Group Index © BMRB 2004 (April 2003 – March 2004).

TOP 10 STORES: CHILDREN'S CLOTHING

		Last 3 months (%)	Last 12 months (%)
1	Asda	11.1	15.6
2	Next	8.3	12.2
3	Tesco	7.5	10.3
4	Woolworths	7.3	12.0
5	Matalan	6.8	10.5
6	Adams	5.9	10.6
7	Marks & Spencer	5.8	9.8
8	Mothercare	4.7	7.5
9	BHS	3.7	6.6
10	Debenhams	3.0	5.6

Source(s): Target Group Index © BMRB 2004 (April 2003 – March 2004).

TOP 10 STORES: PERFUME & TOILETRIES

		Last 3 months (%)	Last 12 months (%)
1	Boots	27.6	37.3
2	Superdrug	18.0	25.0
3	Tesco	13.0	15.8
4	Asda	11.7	14.6
5	Marks & Spencer	4.3	7.4
6	Debenhams	3.4	6.5
7	House of Fraser	1.8	3.3
9	John Lewis	1.9	3.3
8	Co-op	2.0	2.9
10	Woolworths	1.1	1.8

Source(s): Target Group Index © BMRB 2004 (April 2003 – March 2004).

TOP 10 STORES: HOUSEHOLD FURNITURE & FURNISHINGS

		Last 3 months (%)	Last 12 months (%)
1	Argos	10.1	19.0
2	Ikea	6.9	14.7
3	Asda	3.0	5.8
4	John Lewis	2.6	5.7
5	Marks & Spencer	2.5	6.1
6	Index	2.3	5.1
7	Next	2.1	4.2
8	Debenhams	2.0	4.4
9	MFI/MFI Homeworks	1.9	5.0
10	Tesco	1.9	3.9

Source(s): Target Group Index © BMRB 2004 (April 2003 – March 2004).

TOP 10 STORES: ELECTRICAL APPLIANCES

		Last 3 months (%)	Last 12 months (%)
1	Argos	13.4	26.9
2	Currys	8.1	19.6
3	Comet	6.9	16.8
4	Dixons	3.9	9.9
5	Asda	3.9	7.8
6	Tesco	3.1	6.4
7	John Lewis	2.0	4.6
8	Index	2.0	4.5
9	Co-op	1.5	3.3
10	Powerhouse	1.2	3.6

Source(s): Target Group Index © BMRB 2004 (April 2003 – March 2004).

TOP 9 STORES: MUSIC

		Last 3 months (%)	Last 12 months (%)
1	HMV	21.0	36.0
2	Woolworths	17.8	29.8
3	Any supermarket	16.3	26.1
4	WH Smith	13.7	23.8
5	Virgin Megastores	11.9	22.0
6	MVC	5.2	9.7
7	Local Record Store	3.9	6.7
8	Tower Records	0.7	1.7
9	Sanity	1.0	1.4

Source(s): Target Group Index © BMRB 2004 (April 2003 – March 2004).

TOP 10 STORES: TOYS & GAMES

		Last 3 months (%)	Last 12 months (%)
1	Argos	12.4	22.6
2	Woolworths	12.1	20.3
3	Toys R Us	8.5	16.0
4	Early Learning Centre	7.1	13.0
5	Asda	6.1	10.2
6	Tesco	4.7	7.8
7	Any specialist toy shop	4.2	7.4
8	Any supermarket	4.1	7.4
9	Any department store	3.3	6.5
10	Mothercare	3.0	5.3

Source(s): Target Group Index © BMRB 2004 (April 2003 – March 2004).

TOP 5 STORES: DIY

		Last 3 months (%)	Last 12 months (%)
1	B&Q	41.8	60.9
2	Homebase	20.2	33.2
4	Argos	12.4	22.1
3	Focus	12.2	20.2
5	Wickes	10.6	19.4

Source(s): Target Group Index © BMRB 2004 (April 2003 – March 2004).

RETAILER PROFILES

THE BOOTS COMPANY PLC

Head Office

Group Headquarters, 1 Thane Road, Nottingham, NG2 3AA
Telephone: 0115 950 6111
Website: www.boots-plc.com

Subsidiary Companies

Various companies within the four divisions: Boots Retail, Boots Retail International, Boots Healthcare International, handbag.com.

Review of Operations

The year ending 31 March 2004 saw a new leadership team and senior management structure take shape for the Boots Company. Although turnover was very similar to previous years at £5,326, pre-tax profit was up by 18% from £494.9 to £581.0m. The restructuring initiative was implemented in order to improve efficiency and cut costs, resulting in the loss of 900 jobs across departments. Boots The Chemist continued to see good sales growth throughout the year, and Boots Healthcare International recorded sales of over £500m for the first time, capital spend on these two core businesses having been increased significantly. Huge structural changes were also made to the supply chain, again to increase efficiency and respond to demands by customers. The two largest warehouses were outsourced to Unipart and the management of Boots transport services transferred to Tibbett & Britten. This means stores will no longer have to hold unnecessary stock, and mileage will be greatly reduced. The launch of an instant Advantage Card proved successful with customers, with around a further one million people signing up.

Financial Overview

Year ended March

	2000	2001	2002	2003	2004
Group turnover £m	5,187.0	5,220.9	5,328.3	5,325.2	5,326.4
of which BTC	3,978.8	3,991.5	4,070.6	4,284.4	4,475.7
Group pre-tax profit, £m	561.7	492.2	595.8	494.9	581.0
Group operating profit, £m	542.9	552.6	630.0	544.1	550.1
of which BTC	491.6	526.1	–	568.6	531.1
Outlets at year end: (including those within BTC stores)					
Boots The Chemists	1,404	1,411	1418	1,429	1,428
Boots Opticians	298	298	297	296	–
Health & Beauty Experience	–	12	10	10	–
Dentalcare	–	48	54	54	54
Footcare	–	41	44	44	44
Hearingcare	–	–	47	47	–
LASIK Clinic	–	–	5	9	9

Source(s): Published company financial accounts.

Boots The Chemist

Although Boots The Chemist saw a decrease in pre-tax profit of 6.6%, its sales growth continued throughout the year and it had its best year since 2000. This decrease in profit

THE BOOTS COMPANY PLC (Cont.)

may have been due to lowered prices on around 2,000 product lines, which may also account for the increase of sales. The relaunch of the Prescription Collection Service secured loyalty, resulting in an increase in dispensing of 6.3%. The company was were also able to regain market leadership in vitamins.

A store modernisation programme saw 192 new-look customer centered pharmacies open during the year. For cost and efficiency reasons, Opticians and Dentalcare are now being integrated into BTC, rather than operating as stand-alone businesses. There were also around 6,000 touch-screen tills installed which are compatible with the new chip and PIN technology.

Boots Retail International

Originally, the company had planned to sell Boots own brand products and open stores internationally. This strategy has now been replaced by placing products in similar environments using a host retailer's store. The most successful example of this was in Hong Kong where there are over 30 implants in Watson's drugstores. This has resulted in a 20.8% increase in sales for Boots Retail International.

Boots Internet Ventures

Renamed last year, boots.com saw underlying sales increase by 59% to £14.8m, bringing the business close to break-even. A 67% increase over the Christmas period was a strong indication of the potential for further growth. This year, boots.com has developed its online services with the addition of pharmacy medicines and prescription fulfillment online. This will help them to benefit from the new NHS IT systems which will enable GP's to send their patients' prescriptions direct to pharmacies.

Boots Healthcare International

This was year two of a four year strategic plan through which Boots Healthcare International achieved 7.8% sales growth and 14.9% profit (at comparable exchange rates). This growth rate was twice that of the total OTC market. Its core brand sales are Nurofen, Clearasil and Strepsils, each of which saw a sales increase, with Nurofen leading at 15.3%. The company aim to become one of the top global players in analgesics, cough/cold medicines and skincare, as well as developing new brands.

THE BIG FOOD GROUP PLC

Head Office

Second Avenue, Deeside Industrial Park, Deeside, Flintshire, CH5 2NW
Telephone: 01244 830100
Website: www.thebigfoodgroup.co.uk

Subsidiary Companies

Bejam Group plc; BF Ltd; Booker Cash and Carry Ltd; Booker plc; Burgundy Ltd; Iceland Foods plc; Iceland Foods (Ireland) Ltd; Iceland Foodstores Ltd, Trans European Insurance Ltd; Woodward Foodservice Ltd.

Review of Operations

The financial year ending April 2004 was a vast improvement on the previous year for The Big Food Group. Although turnover was only slightly up from £5,060.9m to £5,151.6m, profit before tax and exceptional items rose by 35% from £37.1m to £50.1m. This was a marked change from 2003 when both turnover and pre-tax profit decreased. This change is attributed to a fully integrated food group and improved performance from new-format Iceland stores. The company's proposed acquisition of Londis was unable to progress, so it concentrate efforts on developing Premier fascia and extending relationships with independent convenience and neighbourhood stores.

During the year, Iceland continued to develop its new store format with the refurbishment of 100 new stores across the UK. The new stores have been designed to provide a more inviting shopping environment and include an extended fresh and chilled range. The stores have seen success, as like for like sales increased by 0.7% for the year and operating profit rose to £197.5%. Sales improved throughout the year, with an increase in Christmas trading due to the Party Fayre and Christmas Deal Range. The refurbishment programme will continue with an estimated further 150 stores converted this year. Iceland's Home Shopping and Home Delivery Service also continued to develop, with 80,000 deliveries being made a week and the Company intends to improve both of these services.

Booker enjoyed a successful year, despite a more demanding trading environment. Both sales and operating profit rose, £3,488m and £57.6m respectively. Continued growth of its Premier fascia as well as increased promotional activity and improved tobacco sales helped the company in this period of high trading. At the end of the year, 1,455 independent retailers were operating under the Premier fascia and it is now the third largest symbol group of independent retailers in the UK.

Although still in its development phase, sales for Woodward increased over the year by 24.0% to £119m. Its success was underpinned by the aquisition of new contracts from Jurys Doyle Hotels, Out of Town Resturants, London and Edinburgh Inns and Swallow Hotels.

Financial Overview

| | | | | Year ended December | |
	2000	2001	2002[1]	2003[1]	2004[2]
Group turnover, £m	1,917.7	4,949.7	5,220.4	5,060.9	5,151.6
Group pre-tax profit, £m	65.3	40.1	47.7	45.0	52.8
Iceland outlets	760	767	759	754	754
Booker outlets	–	180	177	178	173

Note(s): [1] Year ended March. [2] Year ended April.
Source(s): Published company financial reports.

KINGFISHER PLC

Head Office

Kingfisher plc, 3 Sheldon Square, Paddington, London, W2 6PX
Telephone: 020 7372 8008
Website: www.kingfisher.com

Subsidiary Companies

B&Q (China) B.V.; B&Q Ireland Ltd; B&Q plc; B&Q Properties Ltd; Euro Depot Espana; Castorama Dubois Investissments; Castorama France; Castorama Italia; Castorama Polska; Euro Depot S.A.; Halcyon Finance Ltd; Screwfix Direct Ltd.

Review of Operations

Kingfisher began a restructuring process three years ago which was completed last year. The electricals and furniture businesses were demerged, allowing the company to become a single sector business focused solely on home improvements. The main brands are now B&Q, Castorama, Brico Dépôt and Screwfix Direct. The remainder of the Castorama Dubois Investissements (CDI) were acquired and CDI was de-listed from Euronext Paris. There were also a number of disposals during the year; the home improvement businesses in Canada and Brazil, the NOMI home improvement business in Poland, the Dubois Matériaux builders merchant business in France and Castorama in Belgium and Germany.

These changes resulted in Group sales and pre-tax profit reduced by 18% and 13% respectively, however, sales on continuing operations were up 15% to £7bn while adjusted pre-tax profit was up 15% to £591m. The cost of the demerger of Kesa Electricals amounted to £5.3m, while Group restructuring costs of £9.8m included the restructuring of the Kingfisher plc head office, and the integration of the head offices at London and Lille.

The home improvement business made good progress during the year, with like for like sales growth of 5.1%. Twenty-eight new stores were opened, including the first Group store in Spain. A 14th store was opened in Beijing, China with over 20,000 square metres of sales space, making it the largest B&Q store in the world. An investment of £361m was put towards stores, supply chain and information systems, and a strong focus on staff training was implemented.

Profile of Retail Sectors

| | Year ended 1 February 2004 | | |
	UK & Ireland	France	Rest of the world
Turnover (£m)	4,117.4	2,327.8	593.0
Selling space ('000s sq. m.)	2,119.6	1,255.2	600.4
Employees (full time equivalent)	28,284	17,221	11,920

Source(s): Published company financial reports.

UK & Ireland

B&Q performed well in both the UK and Ireland. Sales were up 9.8% to £3.9bn, a like for like increase of 3.9%. Retail profit grew by 12.8% and the company increased its share of the UK's repair, maintenance and improvement market from 13.5% to 14.4%. These increases were

KINGFISHER PLC (Cont.)

attributed to ongoing sales space expansion, extensive range innovation and an emphasis on value for money. Efficiency initiatives also continued throughout the year, with the introduction of e-procurement and new in-store replenishment systems to improve the in-store ordering process. There has also been a number of new product ranges introduced during the year and the range of 'Special Order' products in-store has also been extended.

A total of nine new warehouses and four new mini-warehouses were opened during the year and selling space increased by 7% to 144,100 square metres. The mini-warehouse conversion programme continued, with 16 stores being converted during the year. This has allowed greater accessiblity B&Q's product range, in turn improved margins. A further 20 stores, including 11 warehouses and 9 mini-warehouses are set to open this financial year and 25 supercentres are to be converted to mini-warehouses. B&Q Direct, which includes diy.com, moved into profitability, reaching sales of £37m and doubling those of the previous year.

Screwfix Direct

Screwfix Direct is the UK's leading supplier of tools and materials for the trade. It witnessed another successful year with sales growth of 19.6% to over £220m. The company provides next day delivery guaranteed on over 8,000 products. Sales growth was helped by screwfix.com, which accounts for nearly 30% of all sales. Due to this rapid growth, a 30,000 square metre semi-automated fulfilment centre in Stoke-on-Trent is currently under construction. There was a one-off cost associated with the new site of £2.7m, however retail profit still rose to £19.1m, an increase of 6%.

International development

In France, Castorama had an increase in sales of 2.7% to £1.5bn, while profits rose over 20% to £126m (on a constant currency basis). Three new Castorama stores were opened during the year and these are set to provide the template for the entire Castorama estate. The Strategic Supplier Management Programme is now in place and will ensure better deals from suppliers. There was also continued growth at Brico Dépôt in France, with sales up 26% and profits up 38% to £60m and four new stores opening during the year. Profits were ahead in all other international countries, with sales of £593m, up 28% on the previous year and retail profit up 63% to £62m. Over 40% of sales are now outside the UK and the company intends to continue international growth, as potential new markets for Europe and Asia come under review this year.

Financial Overview

Year ended February

	2000	2001	2002	2003	2004
Group turnover (£m)	10,885.0	12,134.2	11,238.1	10,710.6	8,798.6
Group pre-tax profit (£m)	712.8	691.2	28.0	493.4	426.7
Outlets at year end:					
B&Q	297	301	314	320	359
Castorama	–	–	–	–	142
Brico Dépôt	–	–	–	–	60
KOCTAS	–	–	–	–	5

Source(s): Published company financial reports.

JOHN LEWIS PARTNERSHIP PLC

Head Office

John Lewis Partnership, 171 Victoria Street, London, SW1E 5NN
Telephone: 020 7828 1000
Website: www.johnlewis.co.uk

Subsidiary Companies

Bainbridge & Co Ltd; Bonds Ltd; Buy.com Ltd; Cavendish Textiles Ltd; Cole Brothers Ltd; Findlater Mackie Todd & Co. Ltd; Herbert Parkinson Ltd; J.H. Birtwhistle & Company Ltd; JLP Holdings BV; JLP Insurance Ltd; JLP Victoria Ltd; John Lewis Building Ltd John Lewis Construction Ltd; John Lewis Car Finance Ltd; John Lewis Card Services Ltd; John Lewis Overseas Ltd; John Lewis Properties plc; John Lewis Transport Ltd; Jonelle Jewellery Ltd; Jonelle Ltd; Leckford Estate Ltd; Leckford Mushrooms Ltd; Peter Jones Ltd; Stead, McAlpin & Company Ltd; Suburban & Provincial Contracts Ltd; Suburban & Provincial Stores Ltd; The Odney Estate Ltd; Waitrose Ltd; Waitrose Card Services Ltd.

Review of Operations

Sales for the Partnership increased by 8% to £5bn in the last financial year. This is the first time sales have exceeded £5bn, and marks an overall rise of 35% over the last five years for the company. Profit before tax was up 19% to £174m, the second year in succession to see growth rather than decline.

Waitrose

Waitrose sales increased by 12% to £2.7bn, with like-for-like sales up by 5%, despite a serious fire at Finchley. Three new stores were opened at Belgravia, Mill Hill and Portishead. This was the first full year for the new Food and Home branches at Canary Wharf and Cheltenham and their success has led to an announcement that a fifth Food and Home store will be unveiled at Maidstone in 2006. In March 2004 the company announced that it would be acquiring 19 supermarkets from William Morrison and the coming year will see the integration of these stores.

John Lewis department Stores

A successful Christmas season saw store sales increase by 3% over the 53 week trading year. Although the year did not get off to a good start, the company was able to gain market share in the second half-year, despite a late build up to Christmas. Refurbishment work was completed at Nottingham and Edinburgh and the benefit of the work was evident from the strong gains.

Customer Accounts

The company announced in June that it was transferring its customer accounts operation to HFC, a subsidiary of HSBC. This affected the division's profit significantly, since previously interest earned on customer accounts was included in divisional income.

Financial Overview

					Year ended January
	2000	2001	2002	2003	2004
Group turnover, £m	3,747.6	4,126.6	4,459.4	4679.3[1]	5,046.8
Group pre-tax profit, £m	194.7	149.5	141.5	145.5[1]	173.5
Outlets at year end					
John Lewis	25	25	26	26	26
Waitrose	121	136	136	141	144

Source(s): Published company financial reports.

MARKS & SPENCER PLC

Head Office

Marks & Spencer plc, Waterside House, 35 North Wharf Road, London, W2 1NW
Telephone: 020 7935 4422
Website: www.marksandspencer.com

Subsidiary Companies

Marks & Spencer comprises chain stores in the UK and Hong Kong. The group also has some financial subsidiaries.

Review of Operations

In the 52 weeks ending 3 April 2004, Group operating profit for the company rose by 6.5% to £822.9m, despite absorbing £59m for the launch of the '&more' credit and loyalty card. This was due to a strong performance from Menswear, Lingerie and women's casualwear. Its position as the leading provider of lingerie in the UK was consolidated with a 26.5% share. Although the image of their clothing market has increased over the past three years, the company experienced a 0.2% drop in clothing market share, while food maintained its market share with and recorded an increase of 1.6% in like-for-like sales. The decision to reduce its reliance on heavy discounting in the home sector led to a fall in sales, particularly in the fourth quarter. In February, the first Marks & Spencer Lifestore was opened in Gateshead.

The decline in the clothing market share was led mainly by Womenswear and Childrenswear. Although prices were reduced, core customers bought less in the last year and the clothing teams have now been strengthened in a bid to focus on those areas that performed badly. The launch of per una dué in May, aimed at a younger market was followed by the launch of Blue Harbour Vintage and Sp which also targets younger customers.

Marks & Spencer's food is positioned in relatively high growth areas, which allowed it to maintain market share last year, aided by the new Simply Food stores. Sales at Christmas and Valentine's Day however, were lower due to insufficient product innovation. Thirty-three new Simply Food stores were opened during the year, attracting 1.2 million customers each week.

The launch of the '&more' credit and loyalty card has created a base of over two million credit and loyalty card accounts and 2.7 million card holders, making Marks & Spencer one of the top ten credit card operators. The company plans to increase spending and balances so that the credit card moves into profit during 2006.

Financial Overview

Year ended March

	2000[1]	2001[1]	2002	2003	2004
Group turnover, £m	**8,195.5**	**7,342.6**	**7,619.4**	**8,019.1**	**8,154.8**
UK retail	6,482.7	6,293.0	6,575.2	7,027.1	7,159.8
Overseas retail[2]	1,348.2	686.5	693.4	662.1	665.0
Financial services	364.6	363.1	350.8	329.9	330.0
Group operating profit, £m	**543.0**	**480.9**	**629.1**	**773.0**	**822.9**
UK retail	420.1	334.8	505.2	643.8	728.1
Overseas retail	24.0	41.9	33.3	42.8	44.2
Financial services	115.9	96.3	84.2	86.4	50.6

Note(s): [1] 2000 data are based on a 53 week year. [2] Data for 2001 and 2002 reflect company restructuring.
Data for 2003 have been restated.

Source(s): Published company financial reports.

WM MORRISON SUPERMARKETS PLC

Head Office

Hilmore House, Thornton Road, Bradford, West Yorkhire, BD8 9AX
Telephone: 01274 494166
Website: www.morereasons.co.uk

Subsidiary Companies

Farmers Boy Ltd; Farock Insurance Company Ltd; Holsa Ltd; Wm Morrison Produce Ltd; Neerock Ltd; W. Todd (Potatoes) Ltd; Erith Pier Company Ltd; Lifestyle Wholesale Distribution Ltd; M1 Discount Stores Ltd; Nathanspire Ltd; Returnvital Ltd.

Review of Operations

It was an important year for Morrisons. After a 14 month period of investigation by the Office of Fair Trading, the company was given consent to bid for Safeway and the transaction took place on the 8th March 2004. Despite this diversion the company performed well, with record sales and profits. Total sales increased by 15.3% to £5.3bn while like for like sales were up 9.3%. This was attributed to new stores, an increase in the number of customers in each store and an increase in the average spend per customer. The average number of customers using the stores each week rose by 3.4% and the average spend increased by 3.9%. The operating profit for the company was £305.1m after taking into account £10.9m of advisory costs related to the Safeway acquisition.

Size Profile of Stores (Excluding Safeway)

				Year ended February	
	2000	2001	2002	2003	2004
Total sales area ('000s sq. ft.)	3,572	3,907	4,039	4,241	4,526
Number of outlets					
0–25,000 sq. ft.	10	11	9	9	9
25–40,000 sq. ft.	74	80	83	86	93
40,000 sq.ft +	17	19	21	24	24
Average store size '000s sq.ft.	35.4	35.5	35.7	35.6	36.2

Source(s): Published company financial reports.

A number of new stores were opened during the course of the year at Port Talbot, Ebbw Vale, Barrow, Liverpool, Bristol and Barnsley. Three large new replacements also began trading at Anlaby, Failsworth and Rotherham and petrol filling stations were added to the stores in Banbury, Failsworth, Keighley, Retford and Yeadon.

Financial Overview

				Year ended February	
	2000	2001[1]	2002	2003[2]	2004
Group turnover, £m	2,970.1	3,500.4	3,918.3	4,289.9	4,944.1
Group pre-tax profit, £m	189.2	219.1	243.0	282.5	319.9
Outlets at year end	101	110	113	119	479

Note(s): [1] 53 week year. [2] 2003 figures have been restated.
Source(s): Published company financial reports.

WM MORRISON SUPERMARKETS PLC (Cont.)

The company has been continuing its growth and development strategy over the financial year. On the first day of the financial year its first Scottish store opened at Kilmarnock, followed by a new store at Hartlepool. Future developments include major store projects and the rebuilding of existing stores and a 100 acre site has been acquired in Corby in order to increase packing capacity for fresh fruit and vegetables.

Safeway

A total of 149 stores and 194 petrol filling stations were added to the Morrison group when the company acquired Safeway Plc. Under the terms and conditions of the consent, it is required to dispose of 52 of these stores. Attentions have been turned to integrating the two fascias and implementing one culture throughout the whole company, thereby improving operating standards. The first 50 Safeway stores that will be converted to the Morrisons brand have been selected. By benchmarking all the own label products of both brands, the supply chain can be simplified and production efficiency maximised. The absence of firm information before the aquisition has been problematic but this is being overcome and plans are now in place to dispose of the Hayes office.

Size Profile of Stores

Size '000s sq. ft.	No. of outlets	Total sales area	Average store size
0–15,000	143	1,370	9.6
15–25,000	195	3,890	19.9
25–40,000	134	3,834	28.6
40,000 sq. ft. +	7	347	49.6
Total	479	9,441	19.7

Source(s): Published company financial reports.

J SAINSBURY PLC

Head Office

J Sainsbury plc, 33 Holburn, London, EC1N 2HT
Telephone: 020 7695 6000
Website: www.j-sainsbury.co.uk

Subsidiary Companies

Sainsbury's Supermarkets Ltd; Bells Stores; Jackson's Stores; Sainsbury's Bank plc.

Review of Operations

This was the final year of Sainsbury's modernisation programme and saw a host of changes take place. Both Shaw's Supermarkets and JS Development (JSD) were sold during the year, allowing the company to focus solely on Sainsbury's Supermarkets and Sainsbury's Bank. This was in a bid to simplify the Group structure and strengthen its UK market position. These changes had an impact on the Group performance for the year, with a downturn in profit from £695m to £675m, a reduction of 2.9%. Sales were slightly up by 2.4% to £15,517m from £15,147m. The Business Transformation Programme which started in October 2000, was completed in March 2004. It involved renewal of the company's distribution and supply chain, a complete re-platforming of all its IT systems and a large investment into upgrading and extending stores. The company also purchased Swan Infrastructure Holdings Limited as part of their IT outsourcing arrangements.

Profile of Main Stores

Year ended April 2004

	Sales (£m)	Operating profit (£m)	No. of stores	Sales space ('000s sq. ft.)	No. of employees ('000s)
Sainsbury's	15,297	564	583	15,570	147,500
Shaw's[1]	2,709	138	–	–	–
Sainsbury's Bank	220	26	–	–	–
JD Developments[1]	13	7	–	–	–

Note(s): Figures for 2003 have been restated. [1] Discontinued operation.
Source(s): Published company financial reports.

Sainsbury's Supermarkets

Sales for Sainsbury's Supermarkets increased by 2.2% to £15,297m. Underlying operating profit was down by 1.4%, as were like-for-like sales, dropping by 0.2%. The priority this year was the implementation of the Business Transformation Programme, which led to the renewal of its depot infrastructure and the relaunch of its non-food ranges. Although this has been disruptive to the store's operations, the company hopes that these changes will lead to improved operational efficiency, a stronger platform for growth and a lowering of costs in the future.

Ten new supermarkets were opened during the year and a further 16 were either refurbished or extended. This means that 80% of stores are either new, refurbished or extended. Two supermarkets were sold during the year, which generated a profit of £42m. In order to increase its position in the convenience store market, the company opened 25 new Locals and acquired

J SAINSBURY PLC (Cont.)

The Health and Beauty range has been extended in the larger stores. The new range of non-food products, including homewares and other general merchandise ranges in refitted stores, has been operating successfully.

Nectar

Nectar is the UK's largest loyalty programme with more than 50% of households currently participating. The number of partners issuing points increased from five to 13 over the past 12 months to March 2004. The number of customers that can be mailed has increased and collectors receive statements four times a year.

Sainsbury's Bank

Sainsbury's Bank, jointly owned with HBoS completed the first full year of its growth strategy. It is hoped the investment will provide future growth prospects and income. Customer numbers increased and it now has 1.9m customer accounts. New products were also launched during the year, including health insurance, life insurance and savings bonds. By March 2004 there were 50 in-store banking centres and the website had been re-launched enabling customers to access their accounts online. Two-hundred extra cash machines were installed in stores, bringing the total to 532. Deposit boxes are also being introduced in-store, so that customers can deposit cash and cheques.

Sainsbury's To You

The online home delivery service broke even in March 2004. This was as planned and represented a 19% growth, year-on-year. In a bid to reduce costs, it was announced that the Park Royal depot would be closed and transferred to a store based operation. New technology allows specialized picking orders from specific product areas, thus fulfilling orders with increased speed and accuracy.

Shaw's Supermarkets

This branch of the company was sold last year. This move was taken after it was decided that Sainsbury's should concentrate solely on the UK market to increase its market position. The sale was to Albertson's Inc. and was announced on 26 March 2004. Shaw Supermarkets did deliver profit growth for the year in dollars, despite very low like-for-like sales of 0.4%. A good price was realised for the sale of the business.

Financial Overview

					Year ended April
	2000	2001	2002	2003	2004
Group sales, £m[1]	17,414	18,441	18,206	18,144	18,239
Group pre-tax profit, £m	580	549	627	667	610
Outlets at year end:					
Sainsbury's	432	453	463	498	583
Shaw's[2]	168	185	185	185	–

Notes(s): [1] Including discontinued operations. [2] Discontinued operation.
Source(s): Published company financial reports.

SOMERFIELD PLC

Head Office

Somerfield plc, Somerfield House, Whitchurch lane, Bristol, BS14 OTJ
Tel: 0117 935 9359
Website: www.somerfield.plc.uk

Subsidiary Companies

Somerfield Stores Ltd; Somerfield Property Company Ltd; Kwik Save Stores Ltd; Colemans Ltd; KS Insurance Ltd

Review of Operations

Somerfield experienced its fourth year of profit growth in succession, proving that the investment it has made in modernising its stores and realigning its estates is paying off. Operating profit rose from £30.1m to £45.4m. However, like for like sales were only up slightly on the previous year at 1.1%, with the Somerfield fascia accounting for all of the growth. Due to a weak first half-year and despite an improvement in the second half, Kwik Save like for like sales were down 0.1%.

A Portfolio Strategy Group was established in 2003 in order to restructure the estates as a single portfolio. This led to the closure of 47 Kwik Save and Somerfield stores, and through this restructuring and disposal, £66.7m was generated for the company. A further £11.8m was generated by the sale of the company's North West distribution centre and the disposal of surplus depots. Capital investment was again increased for the year to £195m, £5m more than the previous year. Store investment is a high priority for the company, 33% of the Somerfield estate and 10% of the Kwik Save estate had been refitted by the end of the year. This process is to continue in order to increase group sales.

Somerfield

Somerfield completed its third year of the refit programme, over the last financial year. In those stores which have had the refit, sales per square foot were over £14, whereas in those still awaiting refit they were only £10. Eleven Kwik Save to Somerfield conversions were carried out, increasing both sales and margins for these stores. Eight new Somerfield convenience stores were developed during the year, making the total 28. Twelve stores were closed, bringing the final end of year store numbers for Somerfield to 634.

As part of the refit programme, Somerfield stores have developed an operational strategy to match store type with size, demographics and customer shopping needs. Somerfield Essentials is at the high-end range, with a convenience store format that is open long hours. It provides demonstrably better fresh food which has increased margins. Somerfield Market Fresh is designed for city-based customers. The two trial Market Fresh stores that were opened at Wanstead and Carshalton proved positive over the year. Finally, the Somerfield Progressive was launched in Standish, carrying standard Somerfield branding and catered to meet the needs of the local neighborhood. Two more trial stores are set to open in 2004.

Kwik Save

Refit strategy for Kwik Save was implemented later than for the Somerfield stores, hence a total of only 10% benefiting from the implementation at the year end. The Simply range was launched in January in 12,000 sq. ft. stores. This will lead to the extension of some smaller

SOMERFIELD PLC (Cont.)

stores and a few transferals across to Somerfield. The Group is optimistic that these changes will see the return in rising sales and profits in the following year.

Financial Overview

			52 weeks ending April 24 2004	
	Kwik Save 2004	Somerfield 2004	Group[1] 2003	Group[1] 2004
Turnover, £m	1,690.0	2,743.0	4,484.3	4,521.2
Operating profit, £m	–	–	30.1	45.5
Profit before tax, £m	–	–	124.0	140.4
Number of stores	634	634	–	1,268

Note(s): [1] Group totals of both years include stores of other fascias.

TESCO PLC

Head Office

Tesco House, New Delamare Road, Cheshunt, Hertfordshire, EN8 9SL
Tel: 01992 632 222
Website: www.tesco.com

Subsidiary Companies

Shopping Centres Ltd; BLT Properties Ltd; Tesco British Land Property Partnership; Tesco BL Holdings Ltd; Tesco Personal Finance Ltd; Tesco Personal Finance Life Ltd; Tesco Personal Finance Investments Ltd; Tesco Home Shopping Ltd; ivillage UK Ltd; DunnHumby Associates Ltd.

Review of Operations

As one of the top three international retailers in the world, Tesco enjoyed yet another successful financial year. Group sales rose by 18.7% to £33.6 billion, while pre-tax profit increased by 21.9% to £1,708m. Both the UK and international businesses performed well, with non-food business and retailing services.

Retailing Services

This year, Tesco had success in all areas of retail services. Tesco.com is the world's biggest online supermarket and achieved sales in excess of £577 million, aided by record breaking sales and deliveries over Christmas. The success of Tesco Personal Finance, which has developed a significant insurance business, led to the launch of Tesco Mobile in partnership with O2 and the Home Phone service.

UK Retail

It was an excellent year for the UK retail market, the highest since records began. Sales in the UK grew by 16.3% to £26,876m, with 6.7% coming from existing stores and the remaining 7.5% from new stores. Operating profit increased by 17.7% to £1,526m. Eight Extra stores, 20 Superstores four Metros, 30 Express and two T&S Stores were opened in the last 12 months and 71 stores were refreshed.

International Retail

International retail was again a very successful operation for the company, with sales up by 29% and profit up by 44%. Asia in particular out-performed with sales of £2,847m, up 31.1% on the previous year. Twenty-two new stores were opened in Asia, taking the total to 179. Two businesses were purchased over the financial year, Kipa, a small hypermarket business in Turkey and C Two-Network, a convenience store operator in Japan.

Financial Overview

					Year ended February
	2000	2001	2002	2003	2004
Group turnover, £m	20,358	22,773	25,654	28,280	30,814
UK	16,958	18,372	20,052	23,101	26,876
Rest of Europe	1,374	1,756	2,203	3,007	3,384
Asia	464	860	1398	2,172	2,847
Group pre-tax profit, £m	955	1,070	1,221	1,401	1,708
Outlets at year end	659	692	729	1,982	2,318

Note(s):   Turnover for 2003 has been restated.
Source(s):   Published company financial reports.

HOME SHOPPING

MAIL ORDER RETAILERS

Mail order specialists share of market, 2002   Per cent of total

	Market share %		Market share %
Childrenswear	17.4	Footwear	6.7
Menswear	12.4	Furniture/floorcoverings	4.5
Womenswear	12.8	Electrical appliances	4.8
Homewares	5.5	Other products	5.1

Source(s): Verdict Research.

Market shares by retailer, 2002   Per cent of total

	Market share %		Market share %
Shop Direct	17.0	Redcats UK	4.6
Littlewoods	12.2	Avon	3.0
Otto UK	8.4	Findel	1.9
Grattan	4.6	Betterware	0.6
Freemans	3.8	Other mail order	33.6
Next Directory	5.4	Other door-to-door	8.1
N Brown	5.2		

Source(s): Verdict Research.

Mail Order Business

	Mail order sales value £ million	Annual growth (%)	Mail order business vs. all retailer business		Mail order percent of total retail sales
			Index 2000 = 100		
			Mail order	All retailers	
1995	6,629	−4.0	85	80	4.0
1996	6,808	2.7	88	84	3.9
1997	7,134	4.8	92	89	3.8
1998	7,546	5.8	97	94	3.8
1999	7,678	1.8	99	97	3.8
2000	7,771	1.2	100	100	3.7
2001	8,020	3.2	103	105	3.7
2002	8,300	3.5	107	111	3.6
2003	7,616	−8.2	98	114	3.2

Source(s): 'Business Monitor SDM28 – Retail Sales', National Statistics © Crown Copyright 2004; WARC.

Some mail order houses

Great Universal Stores: Great Universal, Argos, Rock Bottom Clearance, Bargain Crazy.

Arcadia: Zoom (*www.zoom.co.uk*).

Littlewoods: Littlewoods, LX (Littlewoods Extra).

Otto Versand: Freemans, Grattan, Actebis-Gruppe.

Empire (Redcats UK): Empire, La Redoute, Daxon, Vertbaudet.

Historical Collections: Windrush Mill.

Source(s): Retail Locations; Companies concerned.

TOP INTERNET SITES BY CATEGORY

	Reach[1] (%)	Visitors[2] ('000s)		Reach[1] (%)	Visitors[2] ('000s)
Portals			**Entertainment**		
MSN	60.1	15,765	BBC	36.6	9,607
Google	51.7	13,576	Windowsmedia	13.3	3,487
Yahoo!	42.3	11,096	Channel 4	7.8	2,055
Wanadoo	22.8	5,992	BSkyB	6.7	1,766
AOL	20.0	5,234	Play.com	6.1	1,596
ISPs			**Business/Finance**		
BTOpenworld	13.3	3,476	Lloyds TSB	11.7	3,061
Demon	7.1	1,869	Paypal	8.8	2,308
Blueyonder	6.8	1,782	Barclays	6.7	1,748
BT Yahoo! Internet	5.1	1,328	Egg	6.6	1,720
AOL Broadband	3.2	827	Halifax	6.2	1,627
Services			**Travel**		
Microsoft Passport	30.7	8,064	Multimap.com	13.9	3,645
MSN Messenger Service	30.1	7,894	Expedia	7.5	1,968
AOL Instant Messenger	13.4	3,510	Streetmap	6.8	1,773
CentralNic	6.5	1,717	Virgin Travel	6.0	1,579
Bluestreak	6.4	1,690	The AA Travel and Leisure	4.9	1,285
Consumer electronics			**News/Information**		
Microsoft	60.4	15,854	BBC News	14.2	3,717
Real	17.8	4,670	BBC Weather	7.5	1,978
Apple	12.1	3,182	Yahoo! News	7.1	1,849
CNET	7.7	2,012	YELL.com	6.9	1,816
Macromedia	6.9	1,802	About.com	5.2	1,353
Commerce			**Family/Lifestyle**		
eBay	31.0	8,139	Tickle	3.9	1,035
Amazon	21.5	5,636	Boots	2.3	593
Kelkoo	13.1	3,434	AOL Health	2.2	586
Tesco	10.5	2,744	Ultralase	1.8	470
Argos	9.8	2,567			

Note(s): [1] "Reach" is the number of visits to a site expressed as a percentage of the total internet population.
[2] "Visitors" are the number of unique people that have visited the site at least once during the defined time period (April).

Nielsen//NetRatings is the leading global provider of Internet audience research, providing up-to-date, accurate and comprehensive information and analysis to help clients understand consumer behaviour and trends online, as well as advertising effectiveness and brand preferences. Nielsen//NetRatings regularly reports the behaviour of Internet users across the world, using its panels of over 130,000 people worldwide in 17 countries in North America, Australia, Asia and Europe. In addition to the Nielsen//NetRatings audience measurement service, the company also provides analytical reports on international markets and trends and operates the AdRelevance online advertising tracking service in the US.

Source(s): Nielsen//NetRatings, Home & Work Panel, April 2004.

USERS OF INTERNET RETAIL SITES

Internet users (%)	December 2001	December 2002	December 2003	June 2004
All adults (15+)	**47**	**51**	**58**	**58**
Male	53	57	60	63
Female	41	45	49	53
Age				
15–17	82	87	88	89
18–24	73	76	78	82
25–34	63	68	73	79
35–44	57	64	67	72
45–54	51	52	57	61
55–64	30	33	40	45
65+	9	12	14	14
TV area				
Scotland	43	44	51	56
North East	40	47	50	54
Lancashire	43	47	50	56
Yorkshire	44	46	49	50
Midlands	44	47	50	52
Wales & West	42	49	52	57
East Anglia	53	50	55	58
London	54	63	63	67
Southern	51	52	58	63
South West	46	48	50	61
Social grade				
AB	71	75	75	81
C1	58	65	68	72
C2	42	45	51	55
DE	25	27	32	34

Note(s):   Usage is based on the percentage of GB adult population using the internet in the last 12 months.
Source(s):   NOP Internet User Profile Survey, June 2004.

HOUSEHOLDS WITH HOME ACCESS TO THE INTERNET BY GOVERNMENT OFFICE REGION

Percentage

	1998–99	1999–00	2000–01	2001–02	2002–03[1]
North East	7	14	25	32	41
North West	9	18	32	39	43
Yorkshire & the Humber	8	15	29	34	42
East Midlands	9	19	31	41	49
West Midlands	8	20	33	34	41
Eastern	11	22	34	45	52
London	16	25	40	49	51
South East	13	24	38	48	52
South West	9	19	37	35	44
England	11	20	34	41	47
Wales	7	15	22	32	37
Scotland	8	14	24	37	42
Northern Ireland	5	11	20	31	35
UK	**10**	**19**	**32**	**40**	**46**

Note(s):   [1] Provisional data.
Source(s):   Family Expenditure Survey (April 1998 to March 2001); Expenditure and Food Survey (April 2001 onwards).

INTERNET GROCERY PURCHASING PROFILES

	Total GB h'holds (%)	H'holds buying via internet (%)	Penetration (%)	Total expenditure £'000s (%)	Market share (%)	Average frequency of purchase (No.)	Average spend £ (internet) per buyer	Average spend £ (all sources) per buyer	Loyalty to internet (%)
TOTAL PANEL	24,593,997	1,543,200	6.3	670,348	1.2	6.6	434.4	2,857.6	15.2
Social grade									
AB	22.3	25.9	7.3	28.0	1.4	7.1	470.0	3,118.4	15.1
C1	27.6	32.2	7.3	35.8	1.6	6.9	483.1	2,831.6	17.1
C2	19.3	24.1	7.8	23.7	1.4	6.6	428.7	2,880.0	14.9
D	17.4	12.2	4.4	8.2	0.6	4.3	292.8	2,675.9	10.9
E	13.4	5.7	2.7	4.3	0.5	6.8	325.1	2,119.9	15.3
Size of household									
1 member	28.8	16.4	3.6	6.6	0.5	4.1	175.7	1,574.5	11.2
2 members	34.9	33.9	6.1	38.4	1.3	8.0	492.9	2,688.5	18.3
3-4 members	29.7	39.2	8.3	40.2	1.4	6.2	444.9	3,330.5	13.4
5+ members	6.7	10.5	9.9	14.8	1.8	7.0	610.7	3,643.5	16.8
Age									
16-24	5.9	10.5	11.1	3.5	1.0	3.2	143.7	1,970.2	7.3
25-34	19.0	30.6	10.1	34.3	2.4	7.3	485.8	2,577.6	18.9
35-44	20.4	28.4	8.7	27.4	1.4	5.6	419.0	3,041.5	13.8
45-64	31.1	24.2	4.9	28.4	1.0	7.5	511.4	3,465.6	14.8
65+	23.6	6.3	1.7	6.5	0.4	9.5	441.5	2,539.6	17.4
Housewives' working status									
Not working	41.6	29.3	4.4	35.5	1.1	8.3	525.3	2,974.7	17.7
working Full Time	38.0	43.5	7.2	39.4	1.3	5.7	393.6	2,589.2	15.2
working Part Time	20.4	27.2	8.4	25.1	1.3	6.0	401.5	3,160.7	12.7

Presence of children									
Yes	29.8	46.7	9.8	52.6	1.8	6.6	490.0	3,162.4	15.5
No	70.2	53.3	4.8	47.4	0.9	6.5	385.7	2,591.1	14.9
Age of children									
0–4	12.0	24.6	12.8	29.0	2.5	6.9	510.6	3,146.9	16.2
5–10	15.4	26.4	10.8	35.2	2.3	7.4	579.4	3,215.3	18.0
11–15	13.5	14.8	6.9	14.7	1.0	5.5	430.8	3,379.2	12.7
Lifestage									
Pre-family	12.0	19.8	10.4	13.1	1.9	5.3	287.3	1,902.9	15.1
New family	7.9	14.7	11.6	12.0	1.7	5.0	354.3	2,937.1	12.1
Maturing families	14.4	24.8	10.8	32.9	2.2	7.5	576.9	3,222.4	17.9
Established families	9.7	8.8	5.7	9.8	0.9	6.9	480.6	3,573.6	13.4
Post families	19.0	18.9	6.2	21.6	1.4	7.2	498.2	2,857.5	17.4
Older couples	20.3	9.6	3.0	8.1	0.4	7.6	364.7	3,438.0	10.6
Older singles	16.6	3.5	1.3	2.6	0.3	6.2	322.5	1,931.2	16.7
Region									
London	19.3	28.6	9.3	36.0	2.2	7.9	545.9	2,804.0	19.5
South & South East	9.4	9.3	6.2	9.4	1.2	6.4	436.8	3,048.0	14.3
East of England	6.9	6.4	5.9	5.1	0.9	4.7	346.6	3,031.3	11.4
Central	15.8	21.3	8.5	15.5	1.2	5.5	315.6	2,769.7	11.4
South West	3.2	3.6	7.2	2.2	0.8	3.7	257.7	2,085.7	12.4
Wales & West	7.5	3.9	3.2	4.0	0.7	7.0	455.4	2,882.6	15.8
Yorkshire	10.5	9.7	5.8	9.3	1.2	7.0	414.9	2,834.2	14.6
North East	4.9	2.2	2.8	1.7	0.5	6.0	340.5	2,658.9	12.8
Lancashire/Borders	13.8	9.7	4.4	7.1	0.7	4.7	319.4	2,928.8	10.9
Central & North Scotland	8.6	5.2	3.8	9.7	1.4	10.8	807.2	3,471.4	23.3

Source(s): ACNielsen Homescan, 52 weeks ending December 2003.

INTERNET PURCHASING BY CATEGORY (%)

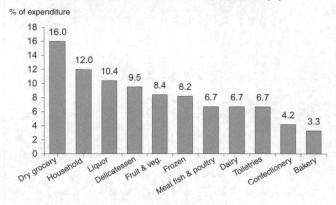

% of expenditure

Source(s):   ACNielsen Homescan, (52 weeks ending December 2003).

KEY FACTS BY RETAILER

	Penetration	Share of exp.	Freq. of purchase	% of repeat buyers	Loyalty	Ave. spend per visit, £
Internet Shopping	6.3	100.0	6.6	68.1	15.2	66.19
Tesco.com	3.5	52.2	5.8	66.5	77.8	69.90
Sainsbury's to you	1.9	33.3	7.0	70.5	71.2	70.53
Asda@home	0.6	2.9	5.1	59.1	57.5	54.34
Iceland.co.uk	0.6	6.2	2.4	37.5	43.1	56.98

Source(s):   ACNielsen Homescan, (52 weeks ending December 2003).

INTERNET GROCERY PURCHASING BY TYPE OF CONSUMER OFFER

		Percentage
	2002	2003
All Offers	20.4	23.5
Multibuy	56.6	67.5
Price reduction	25.4	20.2
Additional quantity	6.6	5.4

Source(s):   ACNielsen Homescan, (52 weeks ending December 2003).

CONSUMER HOME SHOPPING CONCERNS

	% of households who agree
'I would only use home shopping on brands I really trust'	
All households	51.6
ABC1	50.7
C2DE	52.5
Pre-Family	43.2
New Family	46.9
Maturing Family	50.0
Established Family	48.1
Post Family	49.9
Older Couples	60.0
Older Singles	54.8
	% of main shoppers who agree
Sainsbury's	55.2
Tesco	48.7
Safeway	51.2
Asda	51.8
Somerfield	50.3
Kwik Save	52.0

Source(s): ACNielsen Homescan Survey, November 2003.

INCIDENCE OF ONLINE SHOPPING

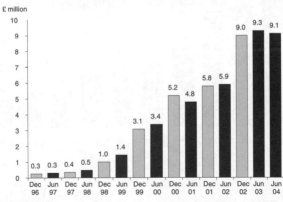

£ million

Dec 96	Jun 97	Dec 97	Jun 98	Dec 98	Jun 99	Dec 99	Jun 00	Dec 00	Jun 01	Dec 01	Jun 02	Dec 02	Jun 03	Jun 04
0.3	0.3	0.4	0.5	1.0	1.4	3.1	3.4	5.2	4.8	5.8	5.9	9.0	9.3	9.1

Source(s): NOP World.

FREQUENCY OF INTERNET PURCHASES, JUNE 2004

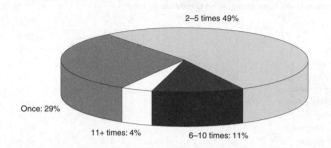

2–5 times 49%

Once: 29%

11+ times: 4%

6–10 times: 11%

Source(s): NOP World.

TOP 10 PURCHASES BY CATEGORY, JUNE 2004

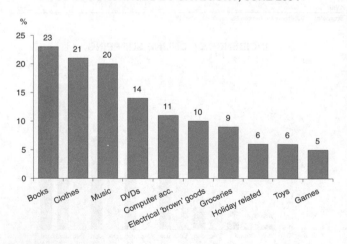

Source(s): NOP World.

AVERAGE SPEND ON ONLINE PURCHASES, JUNE 2004

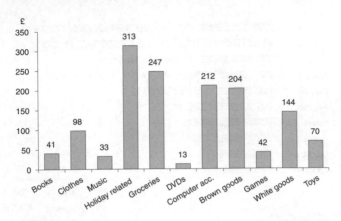

Source(s): NOP World.

TOP 10 SITES VISITED, JUNE 2004

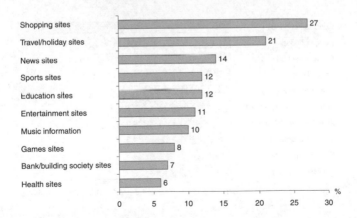

Source(s): NOP World.

TOP 10 SITES PURCHASED FROM, JUNE 2004

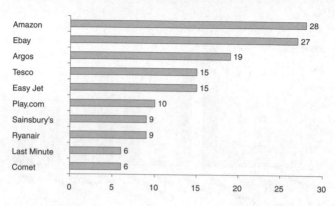

Source(s): NOP World.

MEAN SATISFACTION WITH ONLINE SHOPPING, JUNE 2004

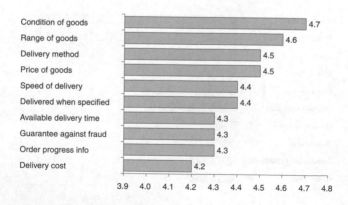

Note(s): 1 = very dissatisfied, 5 = very satisfied.
Source(s): NOP World.

RETAIL CRIME AND PREVENTION

COST OF CRIME

	%
Retail crime losses	
Customer theft	41
Staff theft	28
Fraud	6
Damage	1
Till snatch/burglary/robbery	12
Other	11
Total costs (£ million)	**1,000**
Crime prevention costs	
Security staff	28
Cash collection	7
Theft protection	8
Burglary protection	3
Hardware leasing & maintenance	13
Chip & PIN	2
Alarm systems	28
Alarm monitoring	6
Other	5
Total costs (£ million)	**960**
TOTAL COST OF RETAIL CRIME (£ million)[1]	**1,960**

Note(s): [1] Figures may not sum due to rounding errors.
Source(s): British Retail Consortium: Retail Crime Survey 2003.

TYPES OF CRIME

Theft by customers

	No. of incidents per 100 outlets	Average value of stolen goods per incident, £	Suspects detained % of incidents	No. of suspects detained per 100 outlets	No. of detainees passed to police per 100 outlets
Clothing & footwear	744	127	85	654	44
Mixed retailers	4,728	98	56	3,334	..
DIY & hardware	11,340	94	20	2,267	100
Electrical	422	222	41	174	8
Food & drink	1,889	65	25	905	14
Department stores	6,318	668	61	3,881	..
Other specialist non-food	117	234	38	61	55
All retailers	**2,866**	**162**	**45**	**1,712**	**33**

Source(s): British Retail Consortium: Retail Crime Survey 2003.

Staff Theft

	Known incidents per 1,000 staff	Average value of goods stolen per incident, £	% of suspects passed to police
Clothing & footwear	18	239	92
Mixed retailers	4	631	22
DIY & hardware	14	203	47
Electrical	34	156	91
Food & drink	11	722	58
Department stores	13	1,535	62
Other specialist non-food	6	1,117	45
All retailers	**9**	**852**	**58**

Source(s): British Retail Consortium: Retail Crime Survey 2003.

Burglary

	Completed burglaries per 100 outlets	Attempted burglaries per 100 outlets	Average cost of repair, £ per attempted/ completed burg.	Average stock loss, per completed burg. (£)
Clothing & footwear	4	3	1,035	4,744
Mixed retailers	28	12	2,344	5,246
DIY & hardware	102	25	44	1,088
Electrical	8	24	1,275	12,990
Food & drink	20	11	974	1,512
Department stores	20	8	2,997	32,174
Other specialist non-food	13	16	767	3,377
All retailers	**21**	**12**	**1,675**	**4,881**

Source(s): British Retail Consortium: Retail Crime Survey 2003.

Physical violence

	Incidents of violence per 100 outlets	Incidents of violence per 1,000 staff	Threats of violence per 100 outlets	Threats of violence per 1,000 staff
Clothing & footwear	71	34	404	195
Mixed retailers	62	6	258	20
DIY & hardware	103	15	2,458	307
Electrical	10	4	413	159
Food & drink	25	5	299	53
Department stores	59	4	62	2
Other specialist non-food	15	5	17	5
All retailers	**43**	**7**	**318**	**47**

Source(s): British Retail Consortium: Retail Crime Survey 2003.

Fraud

Per £ million total retail turnover	Cheque Fraud	Payment Card Fraud[1]	Application Fraud	Other[2]
Clothing & footwear	34	158	. .	240
Mixed retailers	82	75	. .	35
DIY & hardware	3	2	. .	71
Electrical	73	111	196	30
Food & drink	20	117	. .	8
Department stores	316	381	132	77
Other specialist non-food	215	124	10	65
All retailers	**88**	**119**	**52**	**23**

Note(s): [1] Includes card not present and credit/debit card fraud. [2] Includes counterfeit notes fraud.
Source(s):   British Retail Consortium: Retail Crime Survey 2003.

RISK RATES BY RETAIL CATEGORY (PER 100 OUTLETS), 2003

	Customer theft	Staff theft	Completed burglary	Criminal damage[1]	Robbery	Till snatches
Clothing & footwear	774	37	4	11	4	4
Mixed businesses	4,728	53	28	124	3	12
DIY & hardware	11,340	88	102	192	2	21
Electrical	422	85	8	62	1	1
Food & drink	1,889	70	20	34	18	10
Department stores	6,318	179	20	53	2	19
Other specialist non-food	117	20	13	15	2	4
Total retail	**2,866**	**65**	**21**	**55**	**8**	**10**

Note(s): [1] Criminal damage includes arson this year.
Source(s):   British Retail Consortium: Retail Crime Survey 2003.

RISK RATES BY RETAIL CATEGORY (PER £ MILLION TURNOVER): FRAUD, 2003

	Cheque fraud	Payment card fraud[1]	Application fraud	Counterfeit notes	Other fraud
Clothing & footwear	34	158	. .	240	. .
Mixed businesses	82	75	. .	33	2
DIY & hardware	3	2	1	54	18
Food & drink	20	117	. .	7	1
Department stores	316	381	132	. .	77
Other specialist non-food	215	124	10	31	35
Total retail	**88**	**119**	**52**	**13**	**10**

Note(s): [1] Payment card fraud includes credit/debit card fraud and card not present fraud.
Source(s):   British Retail Consortium: Retail Crime Survey 2003.

OWN LABEL OR RETAILER PRIVATE BRAND PRODUCTS MOST LIKELY TO BE STOLEN

2002–2003

Bed linen/textiles/bedding	Leather belts
Baby clothes	Leather jackets and other leather garments
Batteries	Leather wallets and purses
Beer	Light fittings
Cheese	Packaged meat
Children's clothes	Neckties
Coffee	Perfumes and fragrances
Cosmetics	Shoes
Costume jewellery and earrings	Sportswear
Costume accessories	Suits
Cushions	Sunglasses
Electrical beauty products	T-shirts
Female lingerie	Tea and coffee
Films	Sports footwear
Handbags and purses	Vitamins
Jackets	Wrist watches
Jeans	

Source(s): The European Retail Theft Barometer, Survey February–May 2003.

RETAIL ADVERTISING

ADVERTISING EXPENDITURE BY CATEGORY, 2003

	£m		£m
Motors	924	Mail order	206
Finance	823	Clothing & accessories	197
Retail	807	Business & industrial	145
Entertainment & the media	690	Household appliances	65
Telecomms	587	Property	52
Food	570	Multi advertisers	31
Cosmetics & toiletries	552	Gardening & agriculture	29
Leisure equipment	456	Online retail	23
Travel & transport	408	Miscellaneous	18
Computers	343	Office equipment & supplies	11
Gov't, social, political organisations	295	Tobacco & accessories	5
Household equipment	282	Electrical/electronics	..
Drink	281	Manufacturing	..
Pharmaceutical	280	Recruitment classified	..
Household stores	270	**Total**	**8,349**

Note(s): TV, Press, Radio, Cinema and Outdoor advertising expenditure.
Source(s): Nielsen Media Research.

RETAIL ADVERTISING EXPENDITURE BY STORE TYPE

£'000s

Store type	2002	2003	% change 02/03
Furniture & furnishings	140,321	157,420	12.2
Supermarket & grocery chains	127,097	138,248	8.8
Department stores	77,286	85,749	10.9
Chain restaurants	81,400	83,762	2.9
Electrical retailers	57,302	70,166	22.4
DIY stores	57,652	64,371	11.7
Other retail	43,910	39,679	–9.6
Mail order – catalogues	37,100	33,409	–9.9
Clothing (mail order)	29,007	24,618	–15.1
Opticians	18,932	22,682	19.8
Shopping centres	19,453	21,274	9.4
Chemists	22,241	19,294	–13.3
Giftware (mail order)	19,232	15,870	–17.5
Record & video stores	19,615	14,444	–26.4
Direct response – misc. (mail order)	19,822	14,140	–28.7
Jewellery & watches (mail order)	11,996	13,918	16.0
Media (excl. clubs) (mail order)	15,891	13,757	13.4
Leisure equipment (mail order)	11,034	11,248	1.9
Health/pharm. incl. condoms	9,336	10,761	15.3
Loyalty/reward cards	18,969	10,478	–44.8
Stationery stores	5,326	10,214	91.8
Office/home comms equip. (mail order)	12,457	9,857	–20.9
Fashion – unisex	16,638	9,821	–41.0
Household durables (mail order)	6,376	9,772	53.3
Jewellers	7,664	9,258	20.8
Book clubs (mail order)	9,815	9,122	–7.1
Toy stores	6,382	7,859	23.1
Household furnishings (mail order)	8,577	7,573	–11.7
Garden centres	6,842	6,966	1.8
Online bet/bookmaker/lottery	5,878	6,677	13.6
TOTAL RETAIL[1]	**1,028,234**	**1,043,907**	**1.5**

Note(s): TV, Press, Radio, Cinema and Outdoor advertising expenditure. [1] Includes online and mail order.
Source(s): Nielsen Media Research.

ADVERTISING EXPENDITURE: RETAIL TOP 50

£'000s

		2000	2001	2002	2003
1	McDonalds	42,466	41,790	42,166	40,924
2	Sainsbury's	30,686	27,919	36,899	39,237
3	DFS	23,650	28,591	33,410	34,075
4	B&Q	29,554	23,533	27,834	33,940
5	Currys	25,630	13,660	14,423	25,422
6	Tesco	19,484	18,945	17,413	24,412
7	JD Williams & Co.	21,398	21,687	19,759	23,824
8	Asda	17,840	19,536	19,720	23,375
9	Argos	12,715	15,382	18,635	22,891
10	Boots The Chemists	15,009	14,070	23,508	20,349
11	Courts	13,802	13,329	12,729	19,686
12	Homebase	25,200	16,359	19,039	19,508
13	Kentucky Fried Chicken	12,878	14,081	15,141	17,465
14	MFI	13,300	12,068	12,588	15,875
15	Comet	18,582	13,668	11,846	13,324
16	Woolworths	10,644	9,192	9,915	11,814
17	Debenhams	6,614	10,038	10,571	11,660
18	Shop Direct	7,999	7,132	9,838	11,541
19	Pizza Hut	7,286	7,465	9,362	11,147
20	Burger King	11,264	8,707	11,169	9,933
21	Dial A Phone	13,510	15,095	12,250	9,723
22	William Morrison	5,004	6,344	7,112	9,574
23	Dixons	13,375	8,568	7,898	9,198
24	WH Smith	3,561	2,028	2,750	9,178
25	Marks & Spencer	5,157	8,913	9,571	8,794
26	Cooperative Group	5,940	8,120	7,722	8,097
27	Specsavers	9,312	8,992	2,908	7,984
28	Iceland	14,907	13,897	11,267	7,785
29	Lidl	5,581	6,807	6,982	7,356
30	Matalan	2,362	6,185	10,786	7,033
31	Brooks & Bentley	7,631	6,113	6,492	6,985
32	BCA (Book Club Assoc.)	11,204	9,909	7,222	6,681
33	Waitrose	190	4,197	5,577	6,562
34	Harveys	2,582	4,552	4,005	6,263
35	Focus	6,932	4,413	6,640	5,953
36	Furniture Village	4,505	5,174	5,203	5,468
37	House Of Fraser	4,013	4,666	5,221	5,368
38	Virgin Megastores	2,190	3,357	2,790	5,367
39	Bristol	1,879	3,233	3,788	5,344
40	Ikea	7,644	4,676	5,645	5,294
41	Compton & Woodhouse	2,791	2,521	5,060	5,138
42	Toys 'r' Us	3,734	4,064	4,593	5,134
43	Somerfield	6,621	3,587	7,971	5,128
44	Loyalty Management	. .	. .	7,802	4,896
45	Boots Opticians	4,290	1,227	5,031	4,856
46	Blockbuster Entertainment	10,503	8,855	6,905	4,784
47	Aldi	3,043	3,833	4,153	4,711
48	JML Direct Priority Order Dept	701	5,054	4,821	4,282
49	Time Life International	1,567	4,799	5,589	3,927
50	Holland & Barrett	471	2,244	2,684	3,509
	Total	527,205	508,576	562,401	620,773
	Other stores	568,459	499,188	465,832	423,134
	Total retail[1]	**1,095,664**	**1,007,765**	**1,028,234**	**1,043,907**

Note(s): TV, Press, Radio, Cinema and Outdoor advertising expenditure. [1] Includes online and mail order.
Source(s): Nielsen Media Research.

TOP RETAIL ADVERTISERS BY RETAIL TYPE, 2003

	£'000s		£'000s
Bookshops		**Electrical retailers**	
Ottakars	140	Currys	25,330
Books Etc.	127	Comet	12,988
Waterstones Booksellers	104	Dixons	8,775
WH Smith	55	Powerhouse	3,368
W & G Foyles	48	Euronics Centre	1,942
Total	**792**	**Total**	**70,166**
Chain restaurants		**Men's fashion**	
McDonalds	40,924	Burton Group	978
Kentucky Fried Chicken	17,465	Hackett	296
Pizza Hut	11,147	Quiksilver Boardriding Company	197
Burger King	9,933	Crombie	118
Little Chef	1,410	Alfred Dunhill	101
Total	**83,762**	**Total**	**3,006**
Chemists		**Unisex fashion**	
Boots The Chemists	17,315	H&M Hennes	1,894
Superdrug Stores	976	GPS	1,594
Semi Chem	436	McArthur Glen	859
Gordons Chemists	128	Mango	401
Lloyds Pharmacy	92	Burberry	356
Total	**19,294**	**Total**	**9,821**
Computer retailers		**Women's fashion**	
Staples Office Superstore	558	New Look Fashion Stores	737
Dixons Stores Group	378	Monsoon	405
Comet Group	296	CI Clothing International	209
Canon	164	Wallis	192
Toys R Us	155	Elvi Fashions	148
Total	**2,802**	**Total**	**3,390**
Department stores		**Furniture & furnishings**	
Argos	21,198	DFS	34,075
Woolworths	11,072	Courts	19,686
Debenhams	10,953	MFI	15,875
Marks & Spencer	8,072	Harveys	6,263
House Of Fraser	5,115	Furniture Village	5,468
Total	**85,749**	**Total**	**157,420**
DIY stores		**Jewellers**	
B&Q	32,627	Ernest Jones Jewellers	1,390
Homebase	18,968	H Samuel	1,215
Focus Group	5,917	Graff Diamonds	728
Wickes Building Supplies	3,263	Boodle & Dunthorne	412
Maplin Electronics	255	Warren James Jewellers	262
Total	**64,371**	**Total**	**9,258**

TOP RETAIL ADVERTISERS BY RETAIL TYPE, 2003 (Cont.)

	£'000s		£'000s
Off-licences		**Sports shops**	
Thresher	783	JJB Sports Wear	1,529
Bargain Booze	238	Decathlon Sports Megastore	509
New Wine Ministries	43	JD Sports	316
Booze 2U	15	American Golf Discount	185
Berry Bros & Rudd Wine Cellars	12	American Golf Disc (Sunderland)	85
Total	**1,183**	**Total**	**3,997**
Opticians		**Stationery**	
Specsavers	7,978	WHSmith	8,825
Boots Opticians	4,856	Clinton Cards	1,039
Vision Express	3,278	Staples Office Superstore	108
Optical Express	2,287	Picture Palace Wedding Service	56
Dollond & Aitchison	1,506	Rymans Stationers	40
Total	**22,682**	**Total**	**10,214**
Online retail		**Supermarkets & grocery stores**	
Casino On Net	2,324	Sainsburys Supermarkets	35,839
Empire Direct	1,218	Tesco	23,278
Waitrose supermarkets	1,102	Asda Stores	23,056
Sainsbury's supermarkets	1,052	William Morrison Supermarkets	9,469
Paco	1,015	Iceland Frozen Foods	7,785
Total	**22,988**	**Total**	**138,248**
Petrol stations		**Toy shops**	
BP	1,053	Toys 'r' Us	4,829
Safeway	581	Argos	1,131
Shell	125	Woolworths	690
Total Fina Elf	122	Early Learning Centre	235
Autopia Motor Group	62	Asda Stores	220
Total	**2,014**	**Total**	**7,859**
Record & Video stores		**TV & video rental**	
Virgin	5,286	Forbes Direct	163
Blockbuster	4,776	Granada Boxclever	159
HMV	2,644	Musical Images	60
MVC	420	Choices Video	35
Emap	316	British Sky Broadcasting	29
Total	**14,444**	**Total**	**565**
Shopping centres			
Jones Lang Lasalle	1,221		
Mcarthur Glen	1,051		
Lend Lease Project	789		
Merry Hill Shopping Centre	761		
Trafford Centre	649		
Total	**21,274**		

Note(s): TV, Press, Radio, Cinema and Outdoor advertising expenditure. [1] Includes online and mail order.
Source(s): Nielsen Media Research.

ADVERTISING/SALES RATIOS, 2002

Rank by A/S Ratio	Product category	Nielsen Media Research Expenditure[1] £'000s	Advertising/ Sales Ratio %
Food			
	Bakery goods		
100	Biscuits	16,249	1.56
151	Bread & bakeries	13,723	0.87
213	Cakes & fruit pies	3,182	0.23
163	Cakes (frozen)	1,377	0.71
33	Crispbread/crackers	3,887	6.17
	Confectionery		
34	Chewing gum	18,291	5.81
53	Chocolate-bars & countlines	65,115	3.52
7	Chocolate-boxed	18,924	13.81
149	Chocolate-other	5,014	0.89
155	Ice cream & lollies	14,965	0.80
104	Sugar confectionery	22,364	1.43
	Cooking products & seasoning		
144	Cakes & pastry mixes	120	0.92
8	Cooking fats	2,441	13.56
234	Flour & baking powder	61	0.13
28	Sauces (cooking & mixes)	22,567	6.58
13	Sauces	17,766	10.97
243	Sugars	234	0.10
105	Artificial sweeteners	924	1.42
	Dairy products & substitutes		
70	Butter	7,929	2.46
90	Cheese	15,732	1.72
228	Cream & substitutes	467	0.16
182	Eggs	2,761	0.49
68	Margarine	12,471	2.51
225	Milk & milk products	3,412	0.17
98	Yoghurt/fromage frais	14,954	1.61
	Drinks & beverages		
84	Coffee (fresh)	1,694	1.90
63	Coffee (instant)	15,986	2.99
21	Tea	22,413	7.50
	Fruit, vegetables, pasta		
183	Fruit (canned)	682	0.46
127	Fruit (dried)	1,128	1.08
251	Fruit (fresh)	2,143	0.06
276	Fruit (frozen)	..	..
107	Rice & pasta (dried & fresh)	5,963	1.38
201	Vegetables & pasta (canned)	1,238	0.31
254	Vegetables (fresh)	1,244	0.06
141	Vegetables (frozen)	9,021	0.95
	Meat, fish & poultry		
212	Bacon	2,451	0.23
224	Fish (canned)	659	0.17

Rank by A/S Ratio	Product category	Nielsen Media Research Expenditure[1] £'000s	Advertising/ Sales Ratio %
145	Fish (fresh & frozen)	7,141	0.92
258	Slice meat, meat/fish spread, paté	1,713	0.04
138	Meat pies & sausages	5,081	0.96
216	Poultry (fresh & frozen)	4,086	0.23
	Prepared & convenience foods		
172	Baby foods	2,425	0.64
30	Cereals (ready to eat)	59,941	6.38
71	Cereals (requiring preparation)	5,029	2.43
191	Convenience desserts	5,989	0.40
237	Pizza – fresh	280	0.12
61	Pizza – frozen	10,902	3.05
72	Frozen ready to eat meals	14,037	2.42
147	Jam & spreads	772	0.91
169	Soup (canned)	1,656	0.66
58	Soup (packet) dry & fresh	5,255	3.26
129	Potato crisps & snacks	31,353	1.07
	Organic foods range	2,620	0.22
217	Organic Foods	2,620	0.22
Drink			
	Alcoholic drinks		
232	Beer	24,384	0.14
211	Stout	17,081	0.25
170	Lager	72,468	0.65
244	Brandy	561	0.10
221	Cider & perry	3,016	0.20
167	Gin	4,523	0.68
249	Port	88	0.08
159	Rum	5,230	0.75
181	Sherry	853	0.50
157	Vermouth	939	0.78
193	Vodka	6,131	0.36
175	Whisky/whiskey	14,405	0.59
£210	Champagne	2,104	0.25
222	Wines/sparkling wines	18,221	0.20
102	Liqueurs & spirits	20,681	1.46
	Soft drinks		
165	Soft drink mixer	714	0.69
69	Mineral water	10,350	2.49
79	Cordials	8,994	2.05
87	Fruit juices/still fruit drink	22,014	1.82
67	Other carbonated	47,509	2.53
Tobacco & Accessories			
	Tobacco range		
252	Cigarettes	7,621	0.06
195	Cigars	2,070	0.34
54	Tobacco	14,008	3.50
	Tobacco accessories		

Rank by A/S Ratio	Product category	Nielsen Media Research Expenditure[1] £'000s	Advertising/ Sales Ratio %
230	Lighters, matches, other accessories	310	0.14
Cosmetics & toiletries			
	Bath toiletries		
106	Bath additives	5,212	1.40
43	Soaps & shower gels	14,793	4.30
	Beauty aids & cosmetics		
44	Mass market eye make up	8,375	4.21
45	Mass market facial make up	10,278	4.18
32	Mass market lipstick	10,440	6.29
59	Nail polish/remover/care	2,081	3.25
22	Mass mkt women's facial S/C med.	5,387	7.28
116	Prem. women's facial S/C non med.	7,039	1.23
48	Premium mens skincare	523	4.02
	Hair products		
4	Hair colourants	30,051	15.98
131	Hair perms & curlers	52	1.04
91	Hair sprays	1,578	1.72
11	Shampoos only	31,563	11.48
66	Conditioners only	5,753	2.59
	Personal hygiene & health		
55	Dentalcare – denture cleaners	1,852	3.49
2	Dentalcare – centure fixatives	4,896	27.20
26	Dentalcare – toothbrushes	8,681	6.89
29	Dentalcare – toothpaste, polishes	22,205	6.51
17	Deodorants	42,899	9.43
37	Depilatories & bleach	5,731	5.16
40	Oral hygiene incl. mouth wash	3,836	4.92
83	Facial paper tissues	3,641	1.91
16	Sanitary protection	24,938	9.74
51	Shaving preparations	2,704	3.70
39	Wet razors & blades	10,501	5.02
	Men & womens fragrances	54,577	8.13
25	Prem. womens perfumes/fragrances	28,351	6.90
35	Premium mens fragrances/toiletries	13,979	5.38
Pharmaceutical			
	First aid		
18	Germicides & antiseptics	2,998	8.33
	Medication		
41	Analgesics	19,094	4.87
15	Asthma & hay fever remedies	6,703	9.86
12	Cold remedies	18,211	11.31
14	Cough remedies	9,523	10.58
6	Indigestion remedies	14,424	14.28
10	Laxatives	5,057	12.33
20	Vitamins & tonics	21,142	7.63
124	Eyecare/drops	436	1.15
274	Contact lens solutions	1	..

Rank by A/S Ratio	Product category	Nielsen Media Research Expenditure[1] £'000s	Advertising/ Sales Ratio %
	Chemist related		
1	Babycare products	31,852	39.82
185	Feminine products	2,560	0.45
56	Athletes health/energy drinks	10,957	3.46
36	Sleeping pills/aids	1,262	5.26
5	Smoking deterrents	11,074	15.38
	Family planning		
101	Contraceptives	1,382	1.52
	Health & fitness		
123	Prescrip frames/contact lenses	23,260	1.15
Clothing & accessories			
	Clothes (ready to wear)		
272	Babies clothing	72	0.01
246	Childrens wear	2,856	0.09
267	Coats	164	0.01
248	Knitwear	1,394	0.08
75	Mens fashions & outfitters	14,991	2.27
60	Sports and leisure wear	15,845	3.20
156	Jeans	11,729	0.79
266	Clothing & accessories	172	0.02
	Clothes (underwear & sleepwear)		
271	Sleepwear	85	0.01
265	Stockings & tights	91	0.02
146	Underwear & lingerie	7,914	0.91
160	Footwear	35,236	0.74
	Personal accessories		
197	Jewellery	9,503	0.34
50	Watches	27,568	3.74
46	Sunglasses (not prescription)	3,575	4.16
Household appliances			
	Large appliances		
121	Dishwashers	2,422	1.16
229	Extractor equipment	759	0.16
174	Refrigeration & freezers	5,980	0.60
128	Washing machines & driers	9,019	1.07
	Small household appliances		
108	Carpet sweepers, vacuums etc.	7,149	1.38
49	Electric hair appliances	4,424	3.75
220	Sewing & knitting machines	153	0.21
	Cookers		
85	Cookers – electric	3,224	1.89
179	Cookers – gas	1,185	0.51
209	Cookers – microwave	584	0.26
161	Cookers – gas & electric	2,872	0.71
	Heating appliances		
273	Heating – electric	90	0.01

Rank by A/S Ratio	Product category	Nielsen Media Research Expenditure[1] £'000s	Advertising/ Sales Ratio %
236	Heating – gas	4,330	0.12
187	Heating – other	2,512	0.44
276	Electric blankets	..	..
	Small bathroom appliances		
42	Electric & battery shavers	4,096	4.55
	Small kitchen appliances		
112	Electric irons	1,519	1.31
24	Food mixers & processors	2,721	6.98
82	Kettle, percolator, coffee maker	3,209	1.96
Household equipment			
	Soft furnishings		
166	Carpets & soft floor coverings	15,740	0.68
250	Curtains	459	0.08
142	Venetian & roller blinds	2,237	0.94
239	Bed & bath linens & towels	1,386	0.11
200	Furniture upholstery & fabric	11,018	0.31
	Furniture & fittings		
158	Beds	22,063	0.75
95	Furniture – kitchen	30,136	1.66
94	Furniture – lounge & dining	22,800	1.68
	Houseware		
92	Tableware	1,595	1.70
	House expansion & improvement		
148	Household security systems	1,502	0.89
Household stores			
	Cleaning, polishing & dyeing		
27	Bleaches	10,088	6.68
73	Floor and furniture polish	806	2.30
276	Metal polishes	..	..
38	Scourers/detergents/dream cleaners	13,321	5.10
	DIY supplies		
152	Household adhesives	1,188	0.87
3	Decorating equipment	3,624	22.65
117	Paints	11,648	1.22
207	Wallpaper	1,489	0.26
96	Wood preserves	4,303	1.66
120	Power tools (non garden)	3,824	1.17
	Petcare		
153	Animal medicines & remedies	1,416	0.84
65	Cat food	16,909	2.76
93	Dog food	13,569	1.69
164	Other animal foods & accessories	1,137	0.70
	Household supplies		
208	Batteries	494	0.26
199	Food wrap, aluminium & plastic	474	0.32

Rank by A/S Ratio	Product category	Nielsen Media Research Expenditure[1] £'000s	Advertising/ Sales Ratio %
130	Fountain & ball pens	2,777	1.04
78	Household stationery & sundries	1,780	2.14
276	Insecticides & vermin killer	..	..
80	Kitchen towel	4,768	2.05
99	Toilet tissue	12,537	1.57
275	Cut flowers	..	..
Leisure equipment			
	Leisure equipment – audio		
255	Blank audio tapes	14	0.05
74	Compact disc players	2,032	2.28
47	Personal stereos	1,802	4.10
31	Pre-recorded records/CD	127,955	6.31
168	Radios	200	0.67
109	Stereo & hi-fi systems	8,195	1.36
198	Amplifiers	333	0.32
264	Tuners	3	0.03
204	Turntables	40	0.27
	Leisure equipment photographic		
119	SLR cameras	3,684	1.18
188	Compact cameras	1,640	0.42
9	Digital cameras	10,550	13.19
162	Photo films	1,413	0.71
176	Photo accessories	551	0.59
135	Camcorders	3,079	0.99
	Leisure equipment – video		
223	Blank video tapes	150	0.20
114	Pre-recorded videos	13,365	1.26
122	Pre recorded DVDs only	16,942	1.15
173	TV sets & satellite systems	13,804	0.64
241	Video cassette record/players	667	0.11
186	DVD video recorder/players	3,922	0.44
260	Satellite TV decoders	42	0.04
203	Satellite TV receivers	208	0.28
	Golf equipment		
125	Golf clubs/grips/shafts	2,243	1.12
97	Golf balls	1,229	1.64
	Leisure equipment games – recreation		
113	Musical instruments	2,965	1.28
214	Sports equipment	3,522	0.23
81	Toys & games	82,221	1.97
Entertainment & the media			
	Entertainment – sports		
140	Bookmakers	16,114	0.95
194	Football pools	1,151	0.35

Rank by A/S Ratio	Product category	Nielsen Media Research Expenditure[1] £'000s	Advertising/ Sales Ratio %
	Entertainment – museum & arts		
178	Cinemas	3,933	0.51
	Entertainment – other	94,518	
136	Lotteries/phone line/misc. activities	52,580	0.98
	Publishing – magazines		
133	Magazines (general consumer)	21,985	1.03
270	Business magazines/reports	148	0.01
	Publishing – newspapers		
77	British daily newspapers	62,259	2.17
	Publishing – books		
143	Books/prints	24,893	0.93
Gardening & agriculture			
	Gardening – products		
86	Fertilizers/compost/bark products	4,247	1.87
192	Fruit plants	40	0.37
205	Trees/shrubs/roses	202	0.27
233	Bulbs/miscellaneous plants	809	0.13
23	Weed killers	3,949	7.18
137	Pest/disease killers/repellant	421	0.98
	Gardening – equipment		
118	Garden furniture/ornaments	3,479	1.20
242	Garden tools	467	0.10
132	Lawnmowers	2,520	1.03
215	Hedge trimmer/cutter/strimmer	68	0.23
76	Greenhouses/summer houses	769	2.20
235	Sheds	153	0.13
190	Watering equipment	287	0.41
Motors			
	Motors – components & parts		
253	Automotive batteries	100	0.06
256	Brake & clutch linings & parts	346	0.05
263	Engines	102	0.03
240	Exhaust systems	358	0.11
247	Shock absorbers & springs	198	0.08
269	Spark plugs	51	0.01
268	Suspension	70	0.01
	Motors – fluids		
262	Motors – diesel & petrol	5,202	0.03
64	Motors – oil	3,601	2.95
	Motors – services		
57	Breakdown recovery	17,333	3.41
103	Vehicles	744,504	1.44
	In car entertainment (ICE)		

Rank by A/S Ratio	Product category	Nielsen Media Research Expenditure[1] £'000s	Advertising/ Sales Ratio %
111	Radio & in car entertainment	3,296	1.33
	Motors miscellaneous		
189	Driving schools	898	0.42
	Motors – other vehicles		
180	Other vehicles – caravans/motorhome	3,125	0.50
219	Other vehicles – motorcycles	1,367	0.22
139	Other vehicles – bicycles & accessories	4,185	0.96
Travel & transport			134
	Airlines	100,644	1.00
276	Airlines UK & international	12,616	
	Land		
196	Bus & coach transport	13,190	0.34
171	Railways	28,136	0.65
259	Taxis	1,098	0.04
	Sea – shipping		
126	Shipping – ferries	15,466	1.09
	Holidays UK		
184	Hotels/B&B UK general	21,100	0.45
	Holidays/overseas		
245	Overseas resorts	16,855	0.10
Finance			
	Insurance life		
238	Life assurance	18,348	0.12
150	Insurance – other	148,013	0.89
88	Insurance – private healthcare	17,784	1.80
206	Insurance – accident	913	0.26
52	Insurance – motor	62,677	3.53
154	Insurance – building & content	5,932	0.80
	Other financial services		
227	Stockbrokers/share dealing	3,023	0.16
Business & industrial			
	Utilities residential		
177	Land telecoms serv./networks	62,203	0.52
89	Post office services	18,451	1.78
257	Electricity suppliers	2,986	0.04
202	Gas suppliers	18,121	0.30
261	Water companies	859	0.03
Computers			
	Computer systems		
110	Comp – personal/desktop	22,924	1.34

Note(s): [1] TV and Press advertising at rate card rates.
Source(s): The Advertising Association's *Advertising Statistics Yearbook*, published by WARC. This publication also discusses the methods of data measurement and possible problems with the derivation of data.

INTERNATIONAL RETAILING

POPULATION AND PER CAPITA GNI, 2002[1]

Top 40 GNI per capita countries | **Bottom 40 GNI per capita countries**

Rank	Population (millions)	GNI[2] per capita (US$'000s)	Rank	Population (millions)	GNI[2] per capita (US$'000s)
1 Luxembourg	0.44	39.47	168 Zimbabwe[4]	13.00	0.48
2 Norway	4.54	38.73	169 India	1,048.64	0.47
3 Switzerland	7.29	36.17	170 Moldova	4.26	0.46
4 United States	288.37	35.40	171 Haiti	8.29	0.44
5 Japan	127.15	34.01	172 Vietnam	80.42	0.43
6 Denmark	5.37	30.26	173 Mongolia	2.45	0.43
7 Iceland	0.28	27.96	174 Pakistan	144.90	0.42
8 Sweden	8.92	25.97	175 Guinea	7.74	0.41
9 United Kingdom	59.23	25.51	176 Comoros	0.59	0.39
10 Hong Kong, China	6.79	24.69	177 Benin	6.55	0.38
11 Finland	5.20	23.89	178 Bangladesh	135.68	0.38
12 Austria	8.05	23.86	179 Sudan	32.79	0.37
13 Netherlands	16.14	23.39	180 Kenya	31.35	0.36
14 Ireland	3.92	23.03	181 Zambia	10.24	0.34
15 Belgium	10.33	22.94	182 Uzbekistan	25.27	0.31
16 Germany	82.50	22.74	183 Lao PDR	5.53	0.31
17 Canada	31.36	22.39	184 Nigeria	132.79	0.30
18 France[3]	59.49	22.24	185 São Tomé & Principe	0.15	0.30
19 Singapore	4.16	20.69	186 Cambodia	12.49	0.30
20 Australia	19.66	19.53	187 Kyrgyz Republic	5.00	0.29
21 Italy	57.69	19.08	188 Tanzania	35.18	0.29
22 Kuwait	2.33	16.34	189 Mauritania	2.79	0.28
23 Israel	6.57	16.02	190 Gambia, The	1.39	0.27
24 New Caledonia[4]	0.22	14.03	191 Ghana	20.27	0.27
25 Spain	40.92	14.58	192 Togo	4.76	0.27
26 The Bahamas[4]	0.31	14.86	193 Central African Rep.	3.82	0.25
27 Macao, China[4]	0.44	14.60	194 Burkina Faso	11.83	0.25
28 French Polynesia[4]	0.24	16.15	195 Uganda	24.60	0.24
29 New Zealand	3.94	13.26	196 Mali	11.37	0.24
30 Cyprus[4]	0.77	12.32	197 Madagascar	16.44	0.23
31 Greece	10.63	11.66	198 Nepal	24.13	0.23
32 Puerto Rico[4]	3.87	10.95	199 Rwanda	8.16	0.23
33 Portugal	10.18	10.72	200 Chad	8.34	0.21
34 Bahrain	0.70	10.50	201 Mozambique	18.44	0.20
35 Slovenia	1.96	10.37	202 Eritrea	4.30	0.19
36 Korea, Rep	47.64	9.93	203 Niger	11.43	0.18
37 Antigua & Barbuda	0.07	9.72	204 Tajikistan	6.27	0.18
38 Malta	0.40	9.26	205 Malawi	10.74	0.16
39 Barbados	0.27	8.79	206 Liberia	3.30	0.14
40 Saudi Arabia	21.89	8.53	207 Sierra Leone	5.24	0.14

Note(s): [1] Precise data are not available for: Bermuda (1), Cayman Islands (14), Channel Islands (8), Liechtenstein (5), Monaco (15), San Marino (11) estimated rankings given in brackets; or for: Afghanistan, Korea Dem. Rep., Myanmar and Somalia, which have an estimated average annual income of US$735 or below; or for: American Samoa, Libya, Mayotte, Northern Mariana Islands, which have an estimated income of US$2,936–9,075; or for: Andorra, Aruba, Brunei, Faroe Islands, Greenland, Guam, Isle of Man, Netherlands Antilles, Qatar, United Arab Emirates, The Virgin Islands (U.S.), which have an estimated income of US$9,076 or over; or for: Cuba and Iraq which have an estimated income of between US$736–2,935. [2] GNI is Gross National Income, previously GNP. [3] Data include the French overseas departments of French Guiana, Guadeloup, Martinique and Réunion. [4] 2002 data are not available, ranking is approximate.

Source(s): World Bank.

TOP 20 EUROPEAN RETAILERS, 2003

Ranked by turnover

Rank	Company	Home market	European turnover (€bn)[1,2]	No. of European countries	% sales in Europe	Ownership
1	Carrefour	France	61.2	13	87	Public
2	Metro	Germany	52.6	23	99	Public
3	Tesco	UK	40.7	8	92	Public
4	Rewe	Germany	39.2	13	100	Co-op
5	ITM	France	32.1	8	100	Co-op
6	Edeka	Germany	31.3	5	100	Co-op
7	Lidl & Schwarz	Germany	29.0	17	100	Private
8	Auchan	France	27.3	8	95	Private
9	Aldi	Germany	27.0	10	84	Private
10	Spar International	Netherlands	22.8	21	85	Symbol
11	Leclerc	France	22.4	6	100	Co-op
12	Wal-Mart	US	22.2	2	10	Public
13	Sainsbury	UK	20.8	1	100	Public
14	Casino	France	19.0	1	83	Public
15	Morrison/Safeway[3]	UK	18.6	3	100	Public
16	Tengelmann[4]	Germany	15.4	12	58	Private
17	Ahold[5]	Netherlands	13.8	6	25	Public
18	Migros	Switzerland	13.0	4	100	Co-op
19	El Corte Inglés[6]	Spain	12.0	2	100	Private
20	Système U	France	11.4	1	100	Co-op

Note(s): [1] Currency conversion: £1 = €1.4445. [2] Turnover excludes VAT. [3] Morrison/Safeway sales are estimated combined company sales for 2003. [4] Tengelmann results to April 2003 (short financial year). 2004 year-end 30/06/04. [5] Ahold data includes consolidated operations only. Ahold has operations in five markets and food service in one (Belgium). [6] El Corte Inglés sales include non-food operations. [7] Marks & Spencer operations in Europe (excluding Ireland) are franchises and have been excluded. [8] Karstadt Quelle turnover includes retail sales only.

Source(s): IGD Research.

TOP 25 FOOD AND DRINK MANUFACTURERS IN THE WORLD, 2003

Rank	Company	Currency	Total sales (US$m)	Food sales (US$m)	Year end
1	Altria Group Inc./Kraft Foods	$	81,832	31,010	12/03
2	Nestlé	SwF	65,368	61,615	12/03
3	Cargill	$	59,984	23,500	05/03
4	Unilever	€	53,950	29,938	12/03
5	Archer Daniels Midland Company	$	30,708	30,708	06/03
6	PepsiCo, Inc.	$	26,971	26,971	12/03
7	Tyson Foods	$	24,549	24,549	09/03
8	The Coca-Cola Company	$	21,044	21,044	12/03
9	Sara Lee Corporation	$	18,291	9,778	06/03
10	Mars	$	16,200	16,200	12/02
11	Diageo	£	15,425	14,642	06/03
12	Danone	€	14,850	14,850	12/03
13	ConAgra Foods Inc.	$	14,522	14,522	05/04
14	Anheuser-Busch	$	14,147	14,147	12/03
15	Kirin Brewery Co.	¥	12,724	11,452	12/03
16	Heineken	€	11,617	11,617	12/03
17	Asahi Breweries	¥	11,153	10,150	12/03
18	General Mills Inc.	$	11,070	11,070	05/04
19	Suntory	¥	11,023	9,925	12/02
20	Cadbury Schweppes	£	10,525	10,525	12/03
21	Dean Foods Company	$	9,185	8,940	12/03
22	Interbrew	€	8,842	8,842	12/03
23	Kellogg Company	$	8,812	8,812	12/03
24	HJ Heinz Company	$	8,415	8,415	04/04
25	SABMiller	$	8,295	8,295	03/03

Source(s): Leatherhead Food RA: Global Food Markets Database (*www.lfra.co.uk*).

GLOBAL MEGA BRAND FRANCHISES

The Global Mega Brand Franchises study looks at global brands that have evolved beyond their original product categories, launching sucessful product entries in both multiple categories and countries.

Global Mega Brand Franchises within Food, Beverages & Confectionery[1]

Brand owner	Brand Franchise	No. of regions (out of 5)	No. of countries (out of 50)	No. of categories[2]
Nestlé	Nestlé	5	50	17
Parmalat Finanziaria	Parmalat	5	32	12
Weight Watchers	Weight Watchers	4	18	12
H J Heinz	Heinz	5	48	11
Kraft Foods[3]	Kraft	5	44	8
McCain Foods	McCain	5	30	7
Unilever	Lipton	5	50	6
Unilever	Knorr	5	49	6
Cadbury Schweppes	Cadbury's	5	48	6
Kraft Foods[3]	Nabisco	5	37	6
Hershey Foods	Hershey	5	31	6
General Mills	Old El Paso	5	29	6
Mars	Mars	5	48	5
Nestle	Maggi	5	47	5
Mars	Milky Way	5	46	5
Barilla Alimentare	Barilla	5	41	5
Del Monte Foods	Del Monte	5	39	5
Mars	Uncle Ben's	5	37	5
Sara Lee	Sara Lee	5	24	5
Danone	Danone	5	46	4
Dole Foods	Dole	5	33	4
Kellogg	Kellogg's	5	47	3
Del Monte	S&W	5	16	3

Note(s): Research based on over 200 consumer packaged goods brands from more than 50 global manufacturers. [1] Personal care & cosmetics and homecare available on request. [2] Includes only those categories active in three or more countries. [3] Member of the Altria Group.

Source(s): 'Global Mega Brand Franchises', Report by ACNielsen.

PURCHASING PATTERNS BY COUNTRY AND CATEGORY

Household Penetration

	Sham-poo	Laundry detergents	Tooth-paste	Paper towels	Cat food	Potato chips	Carb. drinks	Coffee	Biscuits & Cookies	R cer
GB	75	94	84	80	27	92	94	86	99	9
Spain	80	99	88	97	17	90	98	97	98	65
Italy	87	93	88	98	26	58	89	94	95	57
France	79	96	85	94	–	63	90	–	92	64
Germany	77	91	89	81	29	61	85	95	95	20
Switzerland	63	89	80	71	34	72	83	84	94	68
Canada	79	89	86	84	39	90	95	81	93	93
USA	–	97	87	–	–	90	98	74	95	93
Chile	97	100	98	73	–	85	99	95	–	82
Australia	82	93	90	81	40	–	94	88	99	96
Hong Kong	92	82	96	43	–	79	87	40	98	76

Household Penetration, Spend per House

Euros

	Sham-poo	Laundry detergents	Tooth-paste	Paper towels	Cat food	Potato chips	Carb. drinks	Coffee	Biscuits & Cookies	RTE cereals
GB	12.94	44.19	12.67	14.27	132.88	39.60	65.81	36.06	74.10	58.65
Spain	11.83	35.55	7.98	17.06	27.93	10.46	41.58	20.12	18.23	12.87
Italy	17.80	40.70	16.20	31.60	92.20	7.50	36.10	47.10	38.40	21.45
France	17.30	45.90	12.30	25.30	–	7.50	44.30	–	27.50	29.70
Germany	8.83	24.11	9.42	8.85	94.85	9.92	51.34	59.94	21.96	15.32
Switzerland	14.10	50.71	15.95	11.01	173.32	22.45	57.13	57.46	52.93	33.59
Canada	11.72	26.63	7.49	11.24	60.23	24.63	63.68	29.03	30.42	49.97
USA	–	46.31	12.04	–	–	25.05	144.89	32.73	36.84	61.98
Chile	17.52	43.50	11.75	7.85	–	11.07	75.51	18.90	–	14.10
Australia	11.81	26.34	11.30	6.53	79.21	–	50.62	21.38	58.61	45.36
Hong Kong	19.92	13.65	10.56	5.66	–	14.27	24.74	13.87	28.03	10.77

Source(s): ACNielsen Global Consumer Panels (52 weeks ending December 2002).

KEY EUROPEAN SHOPPER STATISTICS

	GB	Spain	Italy	France	Germ.	Switz.	Can.	USA	Chile	Aust.	HK
Average spend per trip, €	22.96	13.20	16.92	37.56	14.35	32.33	12.59	19.75	18.93	14.78	7.71
Average spend per h'hold, €	3,249	1,756	4,180	4,871	3,288	4,640	1,772	2,777	1,028	1,397	2,301
Average shopping trips per year	142	130	247	130	229	125	150	140	72	98	300
Avg frequency of purchase (days)	2.8	2.8	1.5	2.8	1.6	2.9	2.4	2.6	5	3.7	1.2
% Spend in Supermarkets	89	89	55	82	72	87	73	67	88	96	46
Retailer share of top 5 stores, %	67	52	26	56	36	78	63	32	71	82	68
Share of top retailer, %	23	14	10	14	14	42	30	19	40	39	36
Loyalty to top retailer (%)	31	69	23	24	16	42	34	–	–	42	35

Source(s): ACNielsen Global Consumer Panels (52 weeks ending December 2002).

DEMOGRAPHIC DETAILS PER EUROPEAN COUNTRY, 2000

	No. of inhabitants (million)	No. of households (million)	Average size of household
Germany	82.5	36.9	2.2
Great Britain	59.3	23.6	2.5
France	59.0	23.1	2.5
Italy	57.3	20.3	2.8
Spain	39.4	11.9	3.3
Netherlands	16.2	6.9	2.3
Greece	10.6	3.8	2.8
Belgium[1]	10.2	4.1	2.5
Portugal	10.0	3.2	3.2
Sweden	8.9	4.0	2.2
Austria	8.1	3.2	2.6
Denmark	5.3	2.4	2.2
Finland	5.2	2.2	2.4
Ireland	3.7	1.1	3.3
Luxembourg	0.4	0.2	2.7

Note(s): [1] Figure including Luxembourg = 10.6 million.
Source(s): ACNielsen Global Consumer Panels.

FOOD RETAIL TURNOVER, 2001

	Turnover billion (€)	Trend (%) 2000–2001	Trend (%) 1996–2001
France	132.99	3	13
Great Britain[1]	110.11	1	16
Germany	99.16	2	1
Spain	39.08	5	22
Italy	38.78	6	–
Netherlands	21.60	5	20
Switzerland	17.05	3	9
Belgium	16.71	5	17
Sweden	15.93	3	13
Norway[1]	12.21	4	18
Austria	11.42	4	10
Ireland[2]	10.18	–	–
Denmark	9.77	7	22
Finland	9.63	0	11
Portugal	8.98	6	38
Greece[2]	7.57	4	22

Note(s): [1] Figures relate to 1999; trends to 1995–2000.   [2] Figures relate to 2000.
Source(s): ACNielsen Global Consumer Panels.

EUROPEAN PARALLEL RETAIL, 2000

	Outlets	Market share (%)
Hypermarkets (>2,500 m²)	5,249	35
Large supermarkets (1,200–2,500 m²)	14,850	24
Small supermarkets (400–1,200 m²)	41,300	23
Superettes (100–400 m²)	99,300	13
Traditionals (<100 m²)	272,600	5
Total	**433,299**	**100**

Source(s): ACNielsen.

EUROPEAN RETAIL LANDSCAPES, 2000

Austria: 8.1 million inhabitants

	Outlets	Market share (%)
Hypermarkets (>2,500 m²)	72	12
Large supermarkets (1,200–2,500 m²)	239	17
Small supermarkets (400–1,200 m²)	2,059	44
Superettes & Traditionals (<400 m²)	4,047	27
Total	**6,417**	**100**

Belgium: 10.2 million inhabitants (including Luxembourg: 10.6 million)

	Outlets	Market share (%)
Hypermarkets (>2,500 m²)	78	14
Large supermarkets (1,200–2,500 m²)	1,919	46
Small supermarkets (400–1,200 m²)	–	29
Superettes (100–400 m²)	2,642	8
Traditionals (<100 m²)	5,252	3
Total	**9,891**	**100**

Denmark: 5.3 million inhabitants

	Outlets	Market share (%)
Hypermarkets (>2,500 m²)	92	19
Large supermarkets (1,200–2,500 m²)	315	25
Small supermarkets (400–1,200 m²)	1,165	37
Superettes (100–400 m²)	1,256	17
Traditionals (<100 m²)	198	1
Total	**3,026**	**100**

EUROPEAN RETAIL LANDSCAPES 2000 (Cont.)

Finland: 5.2 million inhabitants

	Outlets	Market share (%)
Hypermarkets (>2,500 m²)	145	30
Large supermarkets (1,200–2,500 m²)	358	28
Small supermarkets (400–1,200 m²)	624	20
Superettes (100–400 m²)	1,716	22
Total	**2,843**	**100**

France: 59.0 million inhabitants

	Outlets	Market share (%)
Hypermarkets (>2,500 m²)	1,164	52
Large supermarkets (1,200–2,500 m²)	2,939	25
Small supermarkets (400–1,200 m²)	3,009	11
Superettes & Traditionals (<400 m²)	27,589	4
Hard discounters	2,858	8
Total	**37,559**	**100**

Germany: 82.5 million inhabitants

	Outlets	Market share (%)
Hypermarkets (>2,500 m²)	1,598	25
Large supermarkets (1,200–2,500 m²)	3,505	17
Small supermarkets (400–1,200 m²)	14,496	39
Superettes (100–400 m²)	16,094	14
Traditionals (<100 m²)	26,537	4
Total	**64,230**	**100**

Great Britain: 59.3 million inhabitants

	Outlets	Market share (%)
Hypermarkets (>2,500 m²)	1,026	53
Large supermarkets (1,200–1,500 m²)	1,423	24
Small supermarkets (400–1,200 m²)	2,425	12
Superettes & Traditionals (<400 m²)	28,474	11
Total	**33,348**	**100**

EUROPEAN RETAIL LANDSCAPES 2000 (Cont.)

Greece: 10.6 million inhabitants

	Outlets	Market share (%)
Hypermarkets (>2,500 m²)	57	19
Large supermarkets (1,200–2,500 m²)	301	19
Small supermarkets (400–1,200 m²)	885	30
Superettes (100–400 m²)	2,757	21
Traditionals	13,359	11
Total	**17,359**	**100**

Ireland: 3.7 million inhabitants

	Outlets	Market share (%)
Hypermarkets (>2,500 m²)	44	19
Large supermarkets (1,200–2,500 m²)	152	35
Small supermarkets (400–1,200 m²)	198	11
Superettes (100–400 m²)	6,100	34
Total	**9,118**	**100**

Italy: 57.3 million inhabitants

	Outlets	Market share (%)
Hypermarkets (>2,500 m²)	457	18
Large supermarkets (1,200–2,500 m²)	1,661	18
Small supermarkets (400–1,200 m²)	4,990	21
Superettes (100–400 m²)	13,112	19
Traditionals (<100 m²)	84,933	18
Hard discounters	2,516	6
Total	**107,669**	**100**

Netherlands: 16.2 million inhabitants

	Outlets[1]	Market share[2] (%)
Hypermarkets (>2,500 m²)	50	5
Large supermarkets (1,000–2,500 m²)	855	39
Supermarkets (700–1,000 m²)	1,025	28
Small supermarkets (400–700 m²)	1,014	19
Small shops (<400 m²)	1,719	9
Total	**4,663**	**100**

EUROPEAN RETAIL LANDSCAPES 2000 (Cont.)

Norway: 4.4 million inhabitants

	Outlets	Market share (%)
Hypermarkets (>2,500 m²)	26	4
Large supermarkets (1,200–2,500 m²)	237	18
Small supermarkets (400–1,200 m²)	1,366	47
Superettes (100–400 m²)	2,350	28
Traditionals (<100 m²)	585	2
Total	**4,564**	**100**

Portugal: 10.0 million inhabitants

	Outlets	Market share (%)
Hypermarkets (>2,500 m²)	53	36
Large supermarkets (1,200–2,500 m²)	262	25
Small supermarkets (400–1,200 m²)	601	17
Superettes (100–400 m²)	1,512	10
Traditionals (<100 m²)	22,566	13
Total	**24,994**	**100**

Spain: 39.4 million inhabitants

	Outlets	Market share (%)
Hypermarkets (>2,500 m²)	332	33
Large supermarkets (1,200–2,500 m²)	1,342	17
Small supermarkets (400–1,200 m²)	3,801	18
Superettes (100–400 m²)	8,645	18
Traditionals (<100 m²)	45,569	13
Total	**59,689**	**100**

Sweden: 8.9 million inhabitants

	Outlets	Market share (%)
Hypermarkets (>2,500 m²)	116	18
Large supermarkets (1,200–2,500 m²)	611	38
Small supermarkets (400–1,200 m²)	1,224	29
Superettes (100–400 m²)	1,911	13
Traditionals (<100 m²)	972	2
Total	**4,834**	**100**

EUROPEAN RETAIL LANDSCAPES 2000 (Cont.)

Switzerland: 7.0 million inhabitants

	Outlets	Market share (%)
Hypermarkets (>2,500 m²)	117	19
Large supermarkets (1,200–2,500 m²)	370	32
Small supermarkets (400–1,200 m²)	808	25
Superettes (100–400 m²)	2,345	19
Traditionals (<100 m²)	2,583	5
Total	**6,223**	**100**

United States: 265 million inhabitants

	Outlets	Market share (%)
Supermarkets (annual turnover > US$2 million)	30,700	78.4
Convenience stores	94,550	16.8
Wholesale clubs	750	5.0
Total	**126,000**	**100.0**
Supermarkets > $30 million	1,345	10.4
Supermarkets $12–30 million	10,840	43.7
Supermarkets < $12 million	18,515	24.3
Total	**30,700**	**78.4**

Note(s): [1] Figures are for 2003. [2] Figures are for 2002.
Source(s): ACNielsen.

RETAILING IN IRELAND

OUTLET TYPES BY GEOGRAPHICAL AREA, 2002

	Dublin City & Co.	Rest of Leinster	Munster	Connaught/ part of Ulster	Total
Grocers	652	1,095	1,916	1,413	5,076
TSNs/Kiosks	416	444	336	416	1,612
Garages with shop	196	465	585	401	1,647
Public houses	774	2,144	3,680	2,694	9,292
Off-licences	136	118	139	95	488
Licenced clubs	215	217	173	142	747
Licenced hotels	154	198	241	321	914
Restaurants	948	824	1,099	1,054	3,925
Chemists	269	294	406	289	1,258
Butchers/fishmongers/deli's	260	386	611	566	1,823
Greengrocers	103	107	88	77	375
Bakers/confectioners	61	74	153	86	374
Footwear	127	128	196	126	577
Drapery/boutique	777	931	1,174	812	3,694
Hardware/DIY	340	502	682	531	2,055
Electrical/TV	183	231	364	182	960
Booksellers/stationers	182	175	169	78	604
Furniture/furnishings	461	550	592	295	1,898
Jewellers	182	137	186	113	618
Video shops	144	172	208	116	640
Cinemas	15	16	21	12	64
Theatres	25	8	11	10	54
Hairdressers/beauty salons	834	1,025	1,386	840	4,085
Others	2,754	3,248	4,773	2,378	13,153
Total Retail Outlets	**10,208**	**13,489**	**19,189**	**13,047**	**55,933**

Source(s): ACNielsen Ireland.

GROCERY OUTLETS[1] AND POPULATION[2] BY AREA

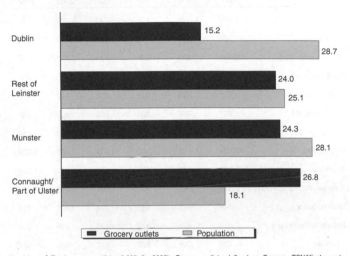

Dublin
- Grocery outlets: 15.2
- Population: 28.7

Rest of Leinster
- Grocery outlets: 24.0
- Population: 25.1

Munster
- Grocery outlets: 24.3
- Population: 28.1

Connaught/Part of Ulster
- Grocery outlets: 26.8
- Population: 18.1

■ Grocery outlets　▥ Population

Note(s): [1] Total grocery outlets: 8,335 (in 2002). Grocery outlets defined as Grocers, TSN/Kiosks and Garages with a shop. [2] Total population estimated at 3.917 million (in 2002).
Source(s): ACNielsen Ireland; Irish Central Statistics Office.

POPULATION OF IRELAND, 1986–2002 (%)

Age	1986 3.450m	1991 3.526m	1997 3.640m	2000 3.787m	2002 3.917m
0–14	28.9	26.7	23.1	21.8	21.1
15–24	17.4	17.1	17.4	17.4	17.1
25–34	14.2	14.1	14.6	15.0	15.8
35–49	16.5	18.5	20.0	20.2	20.2
50–64	12.1	12.3	13.5	14.4	14.7
65+	10.9	11.4	11.4	11.2	11.2

Source(s): ACNielsen Ireland Central Statistics Office.

TRENDS IN THE NUMBER OF SELECTED SHOPS BY TYPE

	1991	1993	1996	1998	2000	2002
Grocers	7,087	6,827	6,231	5,747	5,280	5,076
TSNs/kiosks	1,864	1,863	1,942	1,812	1,717	1,612
Garages with shop	1,186	979	1,282	1,449	2,121	1,647
Public houses	7,561	8,041	8,268	8,300	8,350	9,292
Off-licences	142	232	322	342	425	488
Licensed clubs	617	766	839	850	888	747
Licensed hotels	712	638	724	750	920	914
Restaurants	2,534	2,603	2,906	3,102	3,595	3,925
Chemists	1,151	1,172	1,163	1,180	1,203	1,258
Butchers/fishmongers/deli's	2,077	2,017	1,987	1,867	1,893	1,823
Greengrocers	544	505	481	496	425	375
Bakers/confectioners	419	424	479	494	446	374
Footwear	727	706	638	611	585	577
Drapery/boutiques	4,039	3,780	3,798	3,648	3,747	3,694
Hardware/DIY	1,823	2,048	2,176	2,110	2,299	2,055
Electrical/TV	1,144	1,216	1,201	1,143	1,107	960
Booksellers/stationers	677	713	781	760	844	604
Furniture/furnishings	1,365	1,678	1,855	1,865	1,925	1,898
Jewellers	513	551	628	606	657	618
Video shops	620	716	732	741	702	640
Cinemas	95	77	68	66	92	64
Theatres	28	39	43	46	58	54
Hairdressers/beauty salons	2,778	3,365	3,634	3,721	4,144	4,085
All others	7,756	10,314	10,175	10,885	12,160	13,153
Total Retail Outlets	**47,459**	**51,270**	**52,353**	**52,591**	**55,583**	**55,933**

Source(s): ACNielsen Ireland.

FOOD AND CONFECTIONERY OUTLETS

Trend in Shop Numbers, 1991–2002

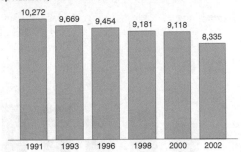

1991	1993	1996	1998	2000	2002
10,272	9,669	9,454	9,181	9,118	8,335

Source(s): ACNielsen Ireland.

Food and Confectionery Shop Numbers by Area, 2002

Percent of total

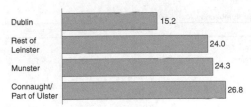

Dublin	15.2
Rest of Leinster	24.0
Munster	24.3
Connaught/ Part of Ulster	26.8

Source(s): ACNielsen Ireland.

Shop Numbers by Trade Sector, 1996–2002

	1996	1998	2000	2002
Multiples	149	157	155	161
Symbol groups	1,084	959	975	955
Independent grocers	4,997	4,631	4,150	3,970
TSNs	1,942	1,812	1,717	1,602
Garages with shops	1,282	1,256	1,872	1,426
Garages with symbol groups	–	193	249	221
Total	**9,454**	**9,008**	**9,118**	**8,335**

Detailed Outlet Breakdown, 2002

Outlet	No. of stores	Outlet	No. of stores
Tesco	78	Centra	307
Dunnes	64	Mace	225
Superquinn	19	Londis	114
Super Valu	164	Spar	365

Source(s): ACNielsen Ireland.

LIQUOR OUTLETS

Trend in Shop Numbers[1], 1994–2002

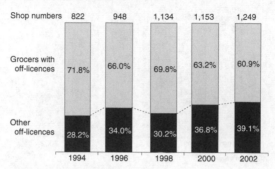

Note(s): [1] Exludes wine only outlets.
Source(s): ACNielsen Ireland.

Liquor Shop Numbers by Area, 2002

	Pubs	Clubs	Hotels	Total
Dublin	774	215	154	1,143
Rest of Leinster	2,144	217	198	2,559
Munster	3,680	173	241	4,094
Connaught/part Ulster	2,694	142	321	3,157
Total	**9,292**	**747**	**914**	**10,953**

Source(s): ACNielsen Ireland.

OFF-LICENCE OUTLETS

Trend in Shop Numbers by Area, 2002

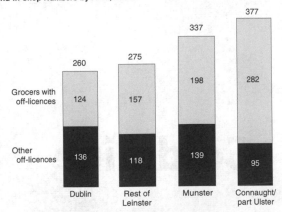

	Dublin	Rest of Leinster	Munster	Connaught/part Ulster
Total	260	275	337	377
Grocers with off-licences	124	157	198	282
Other off-licences	136	118	139	95

Source(s): ACNielsen Ireland.

INDEPENDENT OUTLETS

Trend in Shop Numbers, 1996–2002

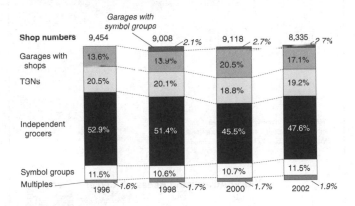

Garages with symbol groups

Shop numbers	1996	1998	2000	2002
	9,454	9,008	9,118	8,335
		2.1%	2.7%	2.7%
Garages with shops	13.6%	13.9%	20.5%	17.1%
TSNs	20.5%	20.1%	18.8%	19.2%
Independent grocers	52.9%	51.4%	45.5%	47.6%
Symbol groups	11.5%	10.6%	10.7%	11.5%
Multiples	1.6%	1.7%	1.7%	1.9%

Source(s): ACNielsen Ireland.

Goldmine

Rich veins of thinking waiting to be discovered. **FREE** 7-day excavation at warc.com/gold

WARC.com – knowledge and inspiration for marketing, advertising and media professionals. Visit www.warc.com/gold now for your free trial.

World Advertising Research Center

SOME USEFUL ADDRESSES

RETAIL ORGANISATIONS

Alliance of Independent Retailers Limited
Adam House, 73 Waterworks Road, Worcester
WR1 3EZ
Tel: 01905 612733   Fax: 01905 21501
www.indretailer.co.uk
Publishes the monthly journal Independent Retailer.

Association of Convenience Stores Ltd.
Federation House, 17 Farnborough Street,
Farnbourough, Hampshire GU14 8AG
Tel: 01252 515001   Fax: 01252 515002
www.thelocalshop.com
An association for private grocers and off-licences.

British Council of Shopping Centres
1 Queen Anne's Gate, London SW1H 9BT
Tel: 020 7222 1122   Fax: 020 7222 4440
www.bcsc.org.uk

British Hardware Federation
225 Bristol Road, Edgbaston, Birmingham B5 7UB
Tel: 0121 446 6688   Fax: 0121 446 5215
www.bhfgroup.co.uk

British Retail Consortium
2nd Floor, 21 Dartmouth Street, London SW1H 9BP
Tel: 020 7854 8900   Fax: 020 7854 8901
www.brc.org.uk
*A consortium of retail associations which publishes
statistics on the retail trade.*

British Shops and Stores Association
Middleton House, 2 Main Road, Middleton Cheney,
Banbury, Oxfordshire OX17 2TN
Tel: 01295 712277   Fax: 01295 711665
www.british-shops.co.uk
An association for the retail furnishing industry.

Independent Food Retailers Confederation
21 Baldock Street, Ware, Hertfordshire
SG12 9DH
Tel: 01920 468061   Fax: 01920 461632

Institute of Grocery Distribution
Grange Lane, Letchmore Heath, Watford,
Hertfordshire WD25 8GD
Tel: 01923 857141   Fax: 01923 852531
www.igd.com

The Mail Order Traders Association
P.O. Box 51909, London, SW99 OWZ
Tel: 020 7735 3410

National Federation of Meat and Food Traders
1 Belgrove, Royal Tunbridge Wells, Kent TN1 1YW
Tel: 01892 541412   Fax: 01892 535462

National Federation of Retail Newsagents
Yeoman House, Sekforde Street, London EC1R 0HF
Tel: 020 7253 4225   Fax: 020 7250 0927
www.nfrn.org.uk

RETAIL PRESS

Co-operative News
c/o The Co-operative Union, Holyoake House,
Hanover Street, Manchester M60 0AS
Tel: 0161 214 0874   Fax: 0161 214 0878
Weekly.

Convenience Store
William Reed Publishing, Broadfield Park, Crawley,
West Sussex RH11 9RT
Tel: 01293 613400   Fax: 01293 610330
Fortnightly.

Drapers Record
EMAP, Angel House, 338–346 Goswell Road,
London, EC1V 7QP
Tel: 020 7520 1509
www.drapersrecord.com
Weekly.

The Franchise Magazine
Franchise Development Services Ltd, Franchise
House, 56 Surrey Street, Norwich NR1 3FD
Tel: 01603 620301   Fax: 01603 630174
www.thefranchisemagazine.net
10 issues per year.

The Grocer
William Reed Publishing, Broadfield Park, Crawley,
West Sussex RH11 9RT
Tel: 01293 613400   Fax: 01293 610330
Weekly.

Independent Retail News
Cumulus Business Media, Anne Boleyn House, 9–13
Ewell Road, Cheam, Surrey, SM3 8BZ.
Tel: 020 8722 6207   Fax: 020 8722 6098
Fortnightly.

Institute of Grocery Distribution
Grange Lane, Letchmore Heath, Watford,
Hertfordshire WD25 8GD
Tel: 01923 857141   Fax: 01923 852531
www.igd.com
*Publishes both the monthly Grocery Market Bulletin
and the monthly Food Industry Statistics Update.*

Pricecheck
William Reed Publishing, Broadfield Park, Crawley,
West Sussex RH11 9RT
Tel: 01293 613400   Fax: 01293 610330
Monthly.

Retail Grocer
Ulster Magazines Ltd, Crescent House, 58 Rugby
Road, Belfast BT7 1PT
Tel: 02890 230425
Monthly.

Retail Newsagent
Newtrade Publishing Ltd, Unit 11, Angel Gate, City
Road, London EC1V 2SD
Tel: 020 7689 0600   Fax: 020 7689 0500
www.newtrade.co.uk
Weekly.

Retail Week
3rd Floor, 33–39 Bowling Green Lane, London
EC1R 0DA
Tel: 020 7505 8000   Fax: 020 7520 3529
www.retail-week.com
Weekly.

Scottish Grocer
Peebles Media Group, Begius House, 20 Clifton
Street, Glasgow G3 7LA
Tel: 0141 567 6050   Fax: 0141 331 395
Monthly.

RETAIL DIRECTORIES

Co-operative Directory
Holyoake House, Hanover Street, Manchester
M60 0AS
Tel: 0161 832 4300   Fax: 0161 831 7684

**Directory of European Retailers & International
Buying Agents**
Newman Books, 32 Vauxhall Bridge Road, London
SW1V 2SS
Tel: 020 7973 6402   Fax: 020 7233 5057

European Directory of Retailers & Wholesalers
Euromonitor Publications, 60–61 Britton Street,
London EC1X 5UX
Tel: 020 7251 8024   Fax: 020 7608 3149
www.euromonitor.com

Franchise World – Directory
Franchise World, Highlands House, 165 The
Broadway, London SW19 1NE
Tel: 020 8605 2555   Fax: 020 8605 2556
www.franchiseworld.co.uk

Grocer Food & Drink Directory
William Reed Directories, Broadfield Park, Crawley,
West Sussex RH11 9RT
Tel: 01293 613400   Fax: 01293 610322
www.foodanddrink.co.uk
Profile of 5,000 product suppliers.

Grocer Non-Food Directory
William Reed Directories, Broadfield Park, Crawley,
West Sussex RH11 9RT
Tel: 01293 613400   Fax: 01293 610322
www.william-reed.co.uk

Grocery Stores Directory
Institution of Grocery Distribution, Grange Lane,
Letchmore Heath, Watford WD25 8GD
Tel: 01923 857141   Fax: 01923 852531
www.igd.com

**National Federation of Retail Newsagents Annual
Yearbook**
National Federation of Retail Newsagents, Yeoman
House, Sekforde, London EC1R 0HS
Tel: 020 7253 4225   Fax: 020 7250 0927
www.nfrn.org.uk

**Official Yearbook of the Association of
Convenience Stores**
Reed Business Publishing, Quadrant House, The
Quadrant, Sutton, Surrey SM2 5AS
Tel: 020 8652 3500   Fax: 020 8652 8932
*Incorporates Independent Grocer's Marketing
Directory.*

Retail Directory
Hemming Information Services, 32 Vauxhall Bridge
Road, London, SW1V 2SS
Tel: 020 7973 6694   Fax: 020 7233 5052
www.retaildirectory.co.uk

Retail Grocer Yearbook and Marketing Guide
Ulster Magazines Ltd, Crescent House, 58 Rugby
Road, Belfast, BT1 1PT
Tel: 02890 230425

The UK Franchise Directory
Franchise Development Services Ltd, Franchise
House, 56 Surrey Street, Norwich NR1 3FD
Tel: 01603 620301   Fax: 01603 630174

World Retail Directory
Euromonitor Publications Ltd, 60–61 Britton Street,
London EC1M 5UX
Tel: 020 7251 8024   Fax: 020 7608 3149
www.euromonitor.com

RETAIL MARKET RESEARCH

ACNielsen
ACNielsen House, Headington, Oxford OX3 9RX
Tel: 01865 742742   Fax: 01865 732461
www.acnielsen.com

CACI Ltd
CACI House, Kensington Village, Avonmore Road,
London W14 8TS
Tel: 020 7602 6000   Fax: 020 7603 5862
www.caci.co.uk

Claritas UK
Park House, Station Road, Teddington, Middlesex
TW11 9AD
Tel: 020 8213 5500   Fax: 020 8213 5588
*Conduct the National Shopping Survey into people's
shopping behaviour.*
www.claritas.co.uk

Experian
Talbot House, Talbot Street, Nottingham NG1 5HF
Tel: 0115 941 0888   Fax: 0115 934 4905
www.experian.com

Institute of Grocery Distribution
Grange Lane, Letchmore Heath, Watford,
Hertfordshire WD25 8GD
Tel: 01923 857141   Fax: 01923 852531
www.igd.com

IRI Infoscan Ltd
Eagle House, The Ring, Bracknell RG12 1HS
Tel: 01344 746000   Fax: 01344 746001

Management Horizons Europe
Europa House, Church Street, Isleworth, Middlesex,
TN7 6DA
Tel: 020 8560 9393   Fax: 020 8580 8310
www.mheurope.co.uk

Marketing Sciences Ltd
8 St. Clement Street, Winchester, Hampshire
SO23 9DR
Tel: 01962 842211   Fax: 01962 840486
www.marketing-sciences.com

Retail Knowledge Bank
3rd Floor, 33–39 Bowling Green Lane, London
EC1R 0DA
Tel: 020 7520 3538   Fax: 020 7520 3529
www.retailknowledgebank.com

Retail Locations
30 The Broadway, Woodford Green, Essex IG8 0HQ
Tel: 020 8559 1944   Fax: 020 8559 1930
www.retaillocations.co.uk

Taylor Nelson Sofres
Westgate, London W5 1UA
Tel: 020 8967 0007   Fax: 020 8967 4060
www.tnsofres.com

The Outlook for Western European Retail
FT Retail & Consumer Publishing, Maple House, 149
Tottenham Court Road, London W1P 9LL
Tel: 020 7896 2325   Fax: 020 7896 2333

Verdict Research
Newlands House, 40 Berners Street, London
W1T 3DU
Tel: 020 7255 6400   Fax: 020 7637 5951
www.verdict.co.uk

Other titles in WARC's prestigious Pocket Book Series include:

The Marketing Pocket Book

The Drink Pocket Book

The European Marketing Pocket Book

Asia Pacific Marketing Pocket Book

The Americas Marketing Pocket Book

The Financial Marketing Pocket Book

The UK Consumer Marketplace

Insurance Pocket Book

The Pensions Pocket Book

The Retail Pocket Book

World Drinks Trends

To order any of the titles featured or for further information on these and other WARC publications, please contact:

WARC

Farm Road   Henley-on-Thames
~~shire~~   RG9 1GB   United Kingdom

139695